Living English Structure

Books by the same author include
Living English Structure for Schools
and *Living English Speech*

Living English Structure

A practice book for foreign students by

W. Stannard Allen

Longman

LONGMAN GROUP LIMITED
Longman House, Burnt Mill, Harlow,
Essex CM20 2JE, England
and Associated Companies throughout the world.

Fifth edition © Longman Group Limited
1959, 1974

First published 1947
Second Edition with key 1950
Third Edition 1955
(with complete key)
Fourth Edition 1959
(with key as a separate book)
Fifth edition 1974
Ninth impression 1984

ISBN 0 582 52506 3

Printed in Hong Kong by
Sheck Wah Tong Printing Press Ltd

Contents

Introduction

The common problems of English language structure have to be overcome by all students, and the difficulties they find are similar in all parts of the world. Regional differences can always be dealt with by the teacher, who should be aware of the particular problems of his students. The following general principles are self-evident:

1 All students want to speak, write and read the normal accepted English of today.

2 This can only be achieved by constant practice of existing forms, with some rational explanation of the grammatical devices employed, wherever this is possible.

The exercises in this book have been devised and revised over a period of many years, and are the results of practical experience with classes of foreign adults, including students of Latin, Teutonic, Slavonic, and Arabic mother tongues. All the exercises have been tried out and found practicable, and I hope they will prove useful and valuable to many other teachers of English.

HOW THE BOOK SHOULD BE USED

This book is an attempt to answer the foreign student's grammatical problems empirically, and to give him a large number of appropriate exercises to practise the acceptable forms. An English schoolboy does 'grammar' as an analytical exercise, but the foreign student needs to learn the mechanics of the language. Many existing grammar books were designed originally for the English schoolboy, and even a large number of those that are intended for foreigners have not managed to free themselves entirely from the purely analytical point of view.

Teachers will find in this book a great deal that is unconventional, perhaps even revolutionary, for it does not pretend to tell the student what he OUGHT TO SAY in English, but tries to show him what IS ACTUALLY SAID. Many of the exercises are based on the results of personal 'structure-counts' – in imitation of 'word-counts' – carried out while listening to the speech of educated English people over considerable periods. A great deal of thought has been given to the use of tenses and auxiliary verbs, and a proportionately large amount of space devoted to them. The division of the exercises into Elementary, Intermediate, and Advanced is a rough guide to their suitability for various classes. The approximate grading is as follows:

Elementary: Up to 1½ or 2 years of English.
Intermediate: Up to about the standard demanded for the University of Cambridge Lower Certificate in English.*
Advanced: Up to and beyond the University of Cambridge Proficiency in English examination.

People may ask why the book has not been divided accordingly into three parts. But the only advantage of this would be an apparent tidiness, for experience has shown that grouping the exercises by subject is far more practical. An immediate advantage of this is that most cross-references in the notes will be found within a page or two of the exercise being done; whereas with a 'tidy' division of the book into three graded sections such important references would send the teacher and students flying from one end of the book to the other; or in order to avoid this, the notes would have to be duplicated wastefully in each section. A less apparent advantage is a psychological one for the student. Any teacher of foreign adults knows that their standard can only be very roughly graded. An 'intermediate' students' class, for instance, finds it very comforting if the 'elementary' exercise on a point they are not very familiar with is found only a page or so back; and it is very encouraging to be told that one has done an exercise very well, and instead of leaving out the next exercise, marked 'advanced', to be allowed to have a shot at that also.

The vocabulary is graded as well as the structures used, but advanced exercises do not necessarily contain difficult words. Emphasis is on form throughout, and as much variety as possible has been introduced without concealing the structure to be practised among a welter of unnecessarily complicated words. The material is arranged in rough structural groups, the subject-matter and grading of the exercises being linked together within each group. The index at the back is very full, and for the sake of simplicity references are all to exercise numbers instead of pages.

The purpose of this book is to provide ample material for
* From 1975 the First Certificate in English.

teaching classes of adult students. As the exercises are designed primarily for oral practice, teachers may make whatever changes they think necessary if they wish to use some of them for written work. Much of the material in the notes will be familiar, and so no space has been wasted in needless elaboration. Many ideas appear for the first time in a form that can be practised, e.g. *fairly* and *rather*, the unreal past, certain response devices, etc., etc. Some ideas are new, or frankly unorthodox, and here the teacher's notes are more fully set out. For example, in order to help promote a clearer and less clumsy spoken style, *which* and *whom* have been rigorously excluded from the Defining Relative, and end-prepositions insisted on; but end-prepositions do not appear in the Non-defining Relatives. The bias towards speech structure has made me banish *whom* altogether from Interrogatives. Teachers who still have a liking for 'To whom do you think you are talking?' or 'For whom do you take me?' may reinstate the word where they think fit! The future tense is approached from a new angle, notionally instead of formally, bringing several familiar speech devices into a rational form for the first time.

Since ninety per cent of this book consists of practice for the student, the notes should be developed where necessary into appropriate blackboard work prior to working through the exercise.

Cyril and Maisie of the Intermediate exercises are, needless to say, quite fictitious. I hope no zealous teacher ever asks for a character sketch of Cyril or Maisie from his students – I shudder to think of the consequences.

Grateful acknowledgements are due to several people. Firstly, to my wife, who did invaluable work copying, adding to, compiling from and checking the original manuscript, and without whose help this book would probably never have been completed. Ideas and advice were freely given by some of my colleagues in the British Council, notably Mr A. C. Cawley, Mr David Hicks, Mr Norman Whitworth, and Mr Rylands. Nor should I forget the very thankless task of Miss Porteous, of the Egypt office of the British Council, who typed out the hundreds of manuscript pages of the first draft. My sincere thanks are due to all of them.

W Stannard Allen

Note to the Fifth Edition

This edition has been completely reset and designed to make the book easier for students and teachers to use. Many points in the exercises and notes have been brought up to date. I am particularly indebted to Mr D K Swan for suggesting many valuable improvements.

W Stannard Allen
Guildford 1973

1 Countables and Uncountables

1.1
Elementary

Nouns naming things that we cannot count (UNCOUNTABLE or MASS nouns) have no indefinite article, and usually no plural.

> ink, water, wood.

* * *

● Put into the plural:

1   A dog is an animal.
2   A potato is a vegetable.
3   A student is not always good.
4   A chair is made of wood.
5   A husband is a man.
6   A pencil is like a pen.
7   An eye is blue or brown.
8   A fish can swim.
9   A cow gives milk.
10 An airport is a busy place.
11 A motorway is a fast road for a motor-car.
12 A garden has a tree.
13 We drink tea out of a cup.
14 An apple grows on a tree.
15 A mother is kind to a little child.
16 A girl likes a sweet.
17 A teacher is a man or a woman.
18 A fly is an insect.
19 A dog hates a cat.
20 A box has a lid.
21 A chicken is a bird.
22 A cat eats meat.
23 We can make a cake with flour, milk and an egg.
24 We fill our pen with ink.
25 A writer writes a book.

1.2
Elementary

● Put into the singular:
1   Horses are animals.
2   Balls are toys.

3   Novels are books.
4   Boots are kinds of shoes.
5   Watches are small clocks.
6   Tables are pieces of furniture.
7   Roses are beautiful flowers.
8   Frenchmen are Europeans.
9   Girls wear dresses.
10   Children are not always good.
11   There are always tables in dining-rooms.
12   Exercises are not always easy for beginners.
13   Hungry boys eat large dinners.
14   Stockings are long socks.
15   Soldiers are brave men.
16   Coats have collars.
17   Nouns are words.
18   Houses have roofs.
19   Postmen wear caps.
20   Oranges are good to eat.
21   Classrooms have blackboards.
22   Dogs are good friends to men.
23   Big men eat more than small boys.
24   Cities are big towns.
25   Schools are large buildings.

**1.3
Elementary**

Remember that only COUNTABLE (or UNIT) nouns take *a* or *an*.

*   *   *

● Add *a* or *an* where necessary:
1   — cigarette is made of — tobacco and — paper.
2   — milk comes from — cow.
3   We make — butter and — cheese from — milk.
4   — window is made of — glass.
5   — handkerchief is made of — piece of cloth.
6   — grass always grows in — English field.
7   — chair is made of — wood.
8   — cat has — tail.
9   — man eats — meat.
10   — ring is made of — gold or — silver.
11   — coffee is — drink.
12   — coat is made of — wool.
13   — fish swims in — water.

14 We can write — letter on — paper.
15 — piano makes — music.
16 — iron is — metal.
17 — bread is made from — flour, and — flour is made from — wheat.
18 — orange grows on — tree.
19 — child must have — food.
20 — sugar is nice in — cup of tea.
21 We use — spoon for — soup.
22 — knife is made of — metal.
23 — cow eats — grass in — summer.
24 I like — jam on — piece of — bread.
25 I can write — letter in — ink or with — pencil.

1.4
Elementary

UNCOUNTABLE nouns, and COUNTABLE nouns in the plural, are preceded by *some* when 'a certain quantity, or number' is implied.

> Bread is good for us.   (All bread, in general.)
> Give me some bread.   (A certain quantity.)

*   *   *

● Add *a*, *an*, or *some* where necessary:

1 — table has four legs.
2 We can write on — paper or on — blackboard.
3 — apple has — sweet taste.
4 — fruit is very good to eat.
5 Please give me — milk.
6 There is — dirt on this plate and — dirty mark on the tablecloth.
7 — man gave me — books this morning.
8 — good pupil is never late for — lesson.
9 — book about — philosophy is not good for — child.
10 Put — lemon in your soup instead of — salt.
11 I want — glass of — lemonade with — sugar in it.
12 — bed made of — iron is better than one made of wood.
13 — Australian sheep give us — very good wool.
14 You must write in — ink; here is — pen.
15 Give me — ink to write — letter.
16 Do you take — sugar in — tea?
17 — garden usually has — flowers in it.

18 I like — music very much.
19 — house made of — stone can be very pretty.
20 There is — pencil and — writing-paper.

1.5
Intermediate
Some nouns are COUNTABLE or UNCOUNTABLE according to context.

*   *   *

● Say which of the following words take the indefinite article; notice which words can be either countable or uncountable; make sentences with these.

air	darkness	breath	literature
soup	bacon	class	artist
marmalade	sunshine	book	foreigner
friendship	camel	sleep	beef
daytime	pin	music	tennis
shop	dirt	hair	mutton
smoke	butter	mountain	help
news	truth	apple	dress
corner	poetry	television	step
fish	vacuum	poem	rain
cheese	drink	ice	sand
glass	clothing	grass	ink
sea	onion	coffee	stupidity
storm	sky	garlic	

Can you suggest why *garlic* is an apparent exception. Why is it so rarely a countable? Consider other words like it; *mint, celery, rhubarb*, etc. What have they in common?

1.6
Intermediate
Exclamations with *What a — !* (countables singular)
                    What — ! (plural, and uncountables)

*   *   *

● Complete the following exclamations:
1 — good idea!
2 — grand ideas you have!
3 — horrible song!
4 — awful news!
5 — charming girl!
6 — lovely eyes she has!
7 — silly mistake to make!
8 — hard sentences these are!
9 — clever student you are!

10 — beautiful music they are playing!
11 — fun your friend Maisie is!
12 — strange name to give a dog!
13 — funny thing to say!
14 — good meat this is!
15 — pity Cyril couldn't come!

1.7
Elementary

A(n) is used for any one example of a COUNTABLE noun. The plural of this is *some*. It means 'an unknown number of' the things named by that noun. We prefer to use *There is (are, was,* etc.) to introduce this idea instead of the simple verb *to be*. (See also Exercise 50.1.)

> *There is a* broken chair in the corner of the room.
> *There were some* books on this table yesterday.
> *There'll be a* picnic in the forest next Friday.

The DEFINITE ARTICLE *the* is used whenever the noun is identified for us as 'one special, known example' (or 'certain known examples' in the plural).

> *A* man and *a* boy were going along *a* dusty road. *The* man was pushing *the* boy along *the* road on *a* toy bicycle. *The* bicycle belonged to *the* boy's sister . . .

*   *   *

● Supply *a(n)*, *the* or *some* where necessary:
1 — children love — fruit.
2 — child ran across — street.
3 It is pleasant to read — book in — afternoon.
4 There is — garden behind — house.
5 I have — pen and — pencil.
6 — tea is very hot, I must put — milk in it.
7 — postman has just put — letter under — door.
8 Give me — knife and — small spoon.
9 — cat loves — milk.
10 Mary wants — doll with — blue eyes.
11 You must give him — food and — cup of coffee.
12 — car made — loud noise.
13 — vegetables are good for — health.
14 — girls do not often wear — hats.
15 — door of — garage is broken.
16 There are — beautiful flowers in — park.
17 I want — glass of — milk.

18 — student at — back of — class is reading — newspaper.
19 It is not good to smoke — cigarette before — meal.
20 — page of — book is torn.

1.8
Intermediate

See Exercise 1.7.
Where there can be only 'one certain' example that is meant, we normally use *the*. (*The* sun, sky, ceiling, station, etc.) An important group of common nouns (mostly names of places) are used WITHOUT an article in phrases closely associated with their special purpose or function, but WITH an article in a more general sense.

He went to bed (to sleep).	He went to the bed (approached it).
He's at school (learning).	I'll meet you at the school.
The ship's in (dry) dock.	We walked round the dock(s).
Put it on paper (=write it).	There's a mark on the paper.

And similarly with: *prison, college, hospital, market, church, harbour (port), barracks, deck, (under) canvas, (at) sea, by train*, and a few others.
Compare the following:

There's *a horse* in the garden. (any single horse)
Horses are animals. (all)
Perhaps we'll see *some horses* there. (a certain number)
The horses are ready. (definite horses we know about)

*   *   *

● Supply *a(n)*, *some*, or *the* where necessary:
1 There is — fly in — lemonade.
2 — youngest brother is at — school now. If you go to — school by — bus, you will be just in — time to meet him.
3 — birds can fly very high in — sky.
4 — book on that shelf is — interesting one about — history.
5 — ship you were speaking about has just come into — port. She has been at — sea for — long time. Look!   — captain has just come on — deck!

6 It is pleasant to play — game of — tennis on — summer afternoon.

7 He makes — toys in — evening.

8 — butcher opposite — library always sells — good meat.

9 They have sent Cyril to — prison for hitting — policeman on — head. I'll go to — prison tomorrow to take him — books.

10 — donkeys are — stupid animals.

11 Put — butter on — potatoes.

12 I am fond of — apples with — cheese.

13 — honesty is — best of all — virtues.

14 He took up — swimming as — sport — last year.

15 He always smokes — cigarette with — cup of — coffee.

16 I should like — house in — country.

17 We had — dinner at — new restaurant — last night.

18 Let's get — strawberries for — tea.

19 Take — umbrella with you to — office. It may rain.

20 — car is ready now.

21 Jack and Jill went up — hill to fetch — pail of — water.

22 Do you prefer — book of — poetry or — stories of adventure?

23 I want — tin of — peaches, — sugar, and — pound of — raspberry jam.

24 — clouds over — sea are lovely today.

25 Maisie travelled in — second-class carriage with — Americans.

2 Elementary Negatives and Questions

**2.1
Elementary**

Questions by simple inversion; negative with *not*. Use short form of negative for oral exercise. (See also Exercise 2.2.)

*   *   *

(2.1) ● Make the following statements (a) negative, (b) questions:

1 He can read English.
2 She has a brother.
3 I must do it now.
4 He is very late.
5 They have time to do it.
6 You can wait here.
7 I am right.
8 We can see from here.
9 He must eat it.
10 They are French.
11 You must tell him everything.
12 He can leave now.
13 You have a penny.
14 She can put it on the table.
15 I must keep it.
16 I am early.
17 They can go now.
18 You must write to her.
19 He has a good one.
20 I can come tomorrow.

2.2   Use of *do* in questions and negatives.
Elementary

*   *   *

● Make the following statements (a) negative, (b) questions:

1 John likes tea.
2 He sells good cakes.
3 You speak softly.
4 It tastes good.
5 I read well.
6 He takes English lessons.
7 They often go to the pictures.
8 It costs five pence.
9 She swims well.
10 They try to understand.
11 He walks to work.
12 I do it well.
13 You sleep well.
14 They play football.
15 He loves his wife.
16 We believe him.

17 I keep it in my pocket.
18 You write to them every day.
19 He lives in this house.
20 She feels well.

3 Possessives

**3.1
Elementary**

Explain *my – mine, your – yours,* etc., if necessary.

*   *   *

● ALL BOOKS SHUT.

1   Is this my, your, her, our, etc. — paper, book, girl, etc.?
2   Is this book, paper, hat, parcel, girl, coat, etc. — mine, yours, his, theirs, etc.?
3   Whose is this?
4   Mix the three above types.

**3.2
Intermediate**

● Add the missing possessives:

1   This doesn't look like — book; it must be —.
2   Tell him not to forget — ticket; she mustn't forget —, either.
3   'Tell me, isn't that — old car over there?'
    'Oh no. It was — last week, but I sold it to — friend Maisie.'
4   It was very good chocolate, but I've eaten all —; can you give me a little piece of — ?
5   They have two of — houses in this street, and the house on the corner is also —.
6   I see that he has lost — pencil; perhaps you can lend him —.
7   — is a very bad one, what's — like? (all persons)
8   You can take — and give me —.
9   John has come to see me; — father and — were school friends.
10 We've taken — share; has she taken — ?

3.3
Intermediate
The type *He's a friend of mine* (=one of my friends).

* * *

● Add the possessives:
1 I saw a cousin of — in the street this morning.
2 You said you would introduce me to a friend of —
who had a car to sell.
3 He wants you to return a book of — you
borrowed last week.
4 They told me to call on a friend of — in Paris.
5 An uncle of — has just crashed his car on the
motorway.
6 They suggested my friend Maisie should try
massage; I think it was a good idea of —.
7 Let's collect some friends of — and some of —,
and have a big party.
8 My friend Cyril met a friend of — at the party.
9 She wants to know if you've seen a book of —
lying about somewhere.
10 A great friend of — has just told us that she's
going to marry a millionaire.

4 *—self*

4.1
Intermediate
Uses of *self* as reflexive or emphatic. The idiomatic (*all*) *by*
—self meaning 'quite alone' or 'without any help'.

* * *

● Fill in the blank spaces with possessives or *self*-forms:
1 That's not — , it's — ; I bought it — .
2 It was given to me by the queen — .
3 She makes all — own clothes — .
4 I cut — with a knife the other day.
5 It's — ; they bought it — (and all other persons).
6 We enjoyed — very much at the air show.
7 She has made — very unpopular.
8 I don't think he'll be able to manage by — .
9 Why is Maisie sitting here all by — in the dark?
10 You must all look after — on — trip to England.
(Reflexive)

11 Cyril says the hat is not —, although it's just like the one he bought — last week.

12 One must remember to behave — in — own house just as well as in other people's.

13 I always have to remind — that this grammar book is — and not —; one day I'll take it away with — own books by mistake.

14 Have we got to do it all by —?

15 This book is —; I wrote — name in it —. (Do No. 15 with all persons.)

5 Adverb Order

**5.1
Intermediate**

Order of adverbials is very elastic in English, and many shades of emphasis, etc., can be expressed by a change of position. The following represents the normal order of adverbials.

1 Except for FREQUENCY ADVERBS, see Section 25, and SPECIAL ADVERBS (*only*, *just*, etc.) the normal position of adverbials is at the end of a sentence, in the order MANNER, PLACE and TIME.

He spoke *well   at the debate   this morning*.

2 WARNING – Students, especially those speaking Latin and Slavonic languages, are prone to the mistake of separating verb and object by an adverb ('I speak well English', 'I write quickly my homework', etc.).

3 With verbs of movement, the adverbial of PLACE acts as a kind of object notionally, and comes immediately after the verb.

He went   *to the station*   by taxi.

4 The adverbial of TIME is often placed at the very beginning of a sentence; this is particularly useful when there are many adverbials in the sentence. This is a more emphatic position for time adverbials, but the emphasis is only slight. A useful rough-and-ready rule is that time adverbials may come at either end of the sentence, but not in the middle.

The more particular expressions of time come before the more general.

He was born *at six o'clock   on Christmas morning in the year 1822.*

* * *

(5.1)   ● Use the adverbials in their correct place:
1   She went (**to school, at 10 o'clock**).
2   He was born (**in the year 1923, at 10 a.m., on June 14th**).
3   She drinks coffee (**every morning, at home**).
4   Our teacher spoke to us (**in class, very rudely, this morning**).
5   I saw my friend off (**at 7 o'clock, at the station, this morning**).
6   He loved her (**all his life, passionately**).
7   Cyril was working (**at his office, very hard, all day yesterday**).
8   Maisie speaks English (**very well**); but she writes French (**badly**).
9   They stayed (**all day, quietly, there**).
10 I like coffee (**in the morning, very much**).
11 The train arrived (**this morning, late**).
12 He played (**at the Town Hall, last night, beautifully, in the concert**).
13 I shall meet you (**outside your office, tomorrow, at 2 o'clock**).
14 We are going (**for a week, to Switzerland, on Saturday**).
15 Let's go (**tonight, to the pictures**).

6 Pronouns

6.1
Elementary

A number of verbs have a DIRECT OBJECT (naming a thing) and an INDIRECT OBJECT (*to* or *for* a person). The usual pattern is VERB + PERSON + THING, without a preposition:

Show Mary the book.

If we wish to give more emphasis to the person, we can put it after the direct object, WITH the preposition:

Show the book to Mary. (That is, not to anyone else.)

The verbs *explain* and *say* always have this second pattern.

* * *

● Replace the expressions in bold type by pronouns, using the word-order pattern without *to* or *for*:

1 John gave the book to **Henry.**
2 Jane bought some sweets for **her mother.**
3 Tell the answer to **the student.**
4 **My sister and I** told a story to **my little brother.**
5 **Alec and Mary** gave some chocolates to **my sister and me.**
6 **You and I** must give a present to **John.**
7 John will find her coat for **Mary.**
8 **Henry and Alec** gave a cake to **me and my wife.**
9 Give this one to **the baby.**
10 **My friend and I** told **John** about **our journey** last week.

6.2
Elementary

● Choose the correct word:

1 We/Us all went with themselves/them.
2 They knew all about my friend and I/me.
3 Mr Jones and he/him/himself came last night.
4 I came here with John and her/she.
5 Basil gave Harry and I/me an ice-cream, and then we went to the pictures with he/him and his friend.
6 He told Mary and me/I to go with he/him and his mother.
7 An old man asked my friend and I/me what the time was.
8 Go and see he/him and his friend.
9 There are some letters for you and me/I.
10 Go with John and her/she to visit they/them.

6.3
Intermediate
CASE

1 When a pronoun is not felt to be the active subject of a sentence, it is normally found in the objective form. This is sometimes called the DISJUNCTIVE or SEPARATED pronoun. (Compare the French *C'est moi*, etc.)

> Who's there? It's only me!
> That's him over there!
> If I were her, I wouldn't listen to him.
> (*Showing a photo*) ... and this is me (standing) in front of the Louvre.

2 *Between* and *let* require the objective case after them.

> Let him have something to eat.
> There was an argument between him and me.

* * *

(6.3)   ● Choose the right words:
1 This island belongs to **we/us** who were here first.
2 'Who's there?' 'It's only **me/I** and my friend Maisie.'
3 That's **she/her**. It's **she/her** that we saw at the scene of the murder.
4 Let Cyril and **I/me** play a duet.
5 There's a friendly agreement between Mr Tumbrill and **me/I**.
6 What would you do if you were **he/him**?
7 Let you and **me/I** be friends!
8 'Who did that?' 'Please, sir, it wasn't **I/me**!'
9 She rang me up this morning and asked my friend and **I/me** to tea.
10 Well, let's pretend for a moment! I'll be **her/she** and you be **I/me**. Now imagine there's a quarrel between **her/she** and **I/me**. How would you settle it?

6.4
Advanced

Notice the following two points from Exercise 6.3:
1 Objective case preferred in predicatives.
2 Pronoun controlled by its own clause, and not affected by a relative clause following.

Give it to them that (or who) understand such things.

But relatives sometimes influence the case of the preceding pronoun. Note the effect of RELATIVE ATTRACTION in such sentences as the following:

It was *she that* went out just now, wasn't it?
It was *her* you meant, wasn't it?

Than and *As*.   These are really conjunctions, and the case after them varies accordingly.

I like you more than she (does).
I like you more than her (= than I like her).

But in spoken English, sentence stress prevents confusion, the objective case is frequently heard, as if both these words were prepositions.

You're much cleverer than her.

The objective case is invariably used, even in writing, if the pronoun is further qualified by *both* or *all*.

He is cleverer than us all.

A stone is heavy and the sand weighty; but a fool's
wrath is heavier than them both (*Bible*).

Such as is usually followed by the subjective case, as
the verb *be* can easily be supplied. There is some doubt
when a preposition is present.

I wouldn't give it to a man such as he? him?
or, I wouldn't give it to such a man as him.

But, Except. The reverse process has taken place with
these two words. They were originally prepositions taking
the objective case, just as the very similar *apart from* still
does; but nowadays, especially in written English, there is
a very strong tendency to use them as conjunctions.

There was no one there except me.
(Historically correct; normal spoken form.)
Whence all but he had fled.
(Historically incorrect; normal literary form.)

SUMMING UP. It seems that the general practice in English,
especially spoken English, is to use a pronoun in the subjective case only when there is a strong feeling that it is the
real active subject of the sentence. All isolated, predicative
and exclamatory uses of pronouns prefer the objective.

What! Me fight a big chap like him? Not me!
Fancy him dying so young; and him only fifty!

The following quotation from Shakespeare is of interest:
Think what is best; that best I wish for thee;
This wish I have, then ten times happy me.

* * *

● Choose the right pronoun:
1 We're much stronger than **they/them** at football.
2 Just between you and **me/I**, it's **him/he** I'm afraid
of, not **she/her**.
3 Let **we/us** all go for a walk except **she/her**, since
she/her is so tired.
4 I know you're bigger than **I/me**, in fact you're
bigger than **we/us** both, but we're not afraid of you.
5 You're as tall as **I/me**, so you can easily ride my
bike, but you're much fatter than either **I/me** or
my brother, so we can't lend you a sports jacket.
6 Do you think **he/him** is stronger than **I/me**?
7 How can you talk to a woman such as **she/her**?
8 It's only **we/us** : **I/me** and my friend Maisie!

9   Which is your friend Cyril? What **he/him**! I
    thought he was a big chap like **I/me**.
10 Help **I/me** carry **she/her**; **she/her** has fainted.
11 Nobody could answer except **I/me**.
12 I think you're prettier than **they/them** all. Let's
    go for a walk, just you and **I/me**.
13 What! **I/me** accept a present from **they/them**?
    I/me never even speak to **they/them**.
14 It was **he/him** I was talking about.
15 Damned be **he/him** that first cries 'Hold,
    enough!' (Shakespeare.)
16 I thought it was **they/them** who went with **she/her**.
17 Was it **we/us** they were talking about? I expect so,
    since it was **we/us** who pushed the old man in the
    river. Still, he began the quarrel, not **we/us**.
18 It is **she/her** that likes sugar in her tea, not **I/me**.
19 **I/me** learn shorthand! Not **I/me**! **I/me** should hate
    it.
20 What! **I/me** angry! Surely it's **he/him** with the red
    nose you mean, not **I/me**.

7 Possessive Case

**7.1
Elementary**

Proper names in —*s* normally have *'s* [iz], unless they are
classical.

> Charles's, St James's, Archimedes' Law, Phoebus'
> chariot

But less usual names in —*s* often follow the classical model:

> Pears' soap, Keats' (or Keats's) poetry

Compounds denoting one idea are treated as single words:

> Jacob and Esau's quarrel; Gilbert and Sullivan's
> operas; but Henry's and Herbert's books, or Henry's
> books and Herbert's

* * *

● Put into the possessive:
1   The father of James
2   The clothes of the boys

3 The coat of the boy
4 The club of the women
5 The fur of the fox
6 The shop of Jones Brothers
7 The orders of the Commander-in-Chief
8 The glass of someone else[1]
9 The name of my sister-in-law
10 The poems of Keats
11 The Park of St James
12 The countries of Caesar and Cleopatra
13 The wedding of William and Mary
14 The hats of ladies
15 The toys of my children

7.2
Intermediate

Read notes to Exercise 7.1.

Words in apposition: here the last word in the group usually takes the *'s*.

> Hicks the plumber's daughter
> (Compare: Betty, the plumber's daughter)

Of may replace almost any possessive case. It is useful for avoiding a complicated series of —*'s*.

> 'I am my friend's sister's second child's godmother'

although it is a fantastic example hardly likely to occur, is better expressed

> I'm godmother to the second child of my friend's sister.

Of is the normal possessive for inanimate objects. Exceptions are certain accepted idioms, mostly of time or measure: *I live a stone's throw from here*; *out of harm's way*; *three days' holiday*; *I'm at my wits' end*.

* * *

● Put into the possessive:
1 The typist of Mr Sims
2 The new tie of my friend Cyril
3 The War of a Hundred Years
4 She's done the work of a whole day.
5 In the time of a week or two
6 The crown of the King of England
7 The birthday of the President of Chile

[1] For *else*, see also Section 37.

8   The parents of all the other boys
9   The famous shop of Fortnum and Mason
10 The houses of Henry and Mr Jones
11 During the holiday of two weeks of my friend
    Maisie
12 A wrist-watch of a lady or gentleman
13 At (the shop of) Murdoch, the bookseller
14 The army of Cyrus
15 He's the favourite of the boss.

Here is an old puzzle:
'The son of Pharaoh's daughter was the daughter of
Pharaoh's son.'
It makes sense only if we read *daughter-of-Pharaoh* as one
unit having the same meaning as *Pharaoh's daughter*.
Pharaoh (ruler of Ancient Egypt) is pronounced ['feərəu].

8   Introduction to Interrogatives
who? what? and *which?*

8.1
Elementary

Interrogatives and relatives are dealt with as a group
(Sections 44, 45), but a preliminary exercise or two, merely
to practise the question-words, should come quite early.
This exercise is restricted to the present tense and interrogatives in the subjective case. The uses of *who? what?*
and *which?* should be clearly demonstrated on the blackboard.

* * *

● Add a question-word to the following questions:
1   — is your name?
2   — is that pretty girl?
3   — is your telephone number?
4   Here are the books!   — is yours?
5   — is coming to tea?
6   — trees grow in Egypt?
7   — is yours, the orange or the banana?
8   — colour is it?
9   — makes your shoes?

10 — makes tea sweet?
11 — wants a piece of bread?
12 — piece of bread is yours?
13 — is the name of your baker?
14 — is his shop, the one at the end of the road, or the one near the post office?
15 — understands this exercise?
16 — of you understand this exercise?
17 — is the answer to my question?
18 — knows the answer?
19 — teaches you English?
20 — are you learning now?

9 Telling the Time

9.1
Elementary

Half past; (*a*) *quarter to*; *ten* (*minutes*) *past*. The word *minutes* is usually omitted if a multiple of five is used.

* * *

● Say the following times:
11.09 – 9.30 – 10.15 – 3.45 – 6.10 – 7.25 – 11.35 – 12.45 – 1.05 – 2.50 – 6.45 – 6.40 – 4.56 – 12.00.

10 *too* and *enough*

10.1
Elementary

Too. An adverb of excess; with *to* + infinitive and/or *for* + (pro)noun.

This soup is very hot; I can't drink it.
This soup is too hot (for me) to drink.*

That's a lot of money; a book like that shouldn't cost so much.
That's too much money for a book like that.

(* Expect the mistake: 'This soup is too hot for me to drink it.' The infinitive, even of a transitive verb, has no

object if this would represent the same person or thing as the subject of the main verb, *be*, *seem*, etc.)
(See also Exercises 38.3, 38.4.)

*   *   *

(10.1) ● Remake these sentences, using *too*:

1   It's very cold; we can't go out.
2   This book is very difficult; I can't read it.
3   She came very late; the lesson was over.
4   This hat is very big; he's only a little boy.
5   It's very far; we can't walk.
6   He's very stupid; he can't understand.
7   It's very small; this is a big room.
8   This mountain is very high; we can't climb it.
9   It's very good; it can't be true.
10 It's very dark; I can't see anything.
11 This dress is very old; I can't wear it any more.
12 It is very wet; you mustn't go out.
13 This grammar is very difficult; a child can't understand it.
14 The music is very soft; we can't hear it.
15 It is very hot; I can't go out.

10.2
Elementary

Enough.   Whereas *too* (Exercise 10.1) has a negative sense, *enough*, also with infinitive, has positive sense. Compare:

He is too ill to need a doctor.
= He is so ill that it's useless to send for a doctor.
He is ill enough to need a doctor.
= He is so ill that we must send for a doctor at once.

Enough comes in front of a noun and after an adjective or adverb.
(See also Exercises 38.3, 38.4.)

*   *   *

● Reword the following, using *enough to*:

1   You are quite clever; you understand perfectly.
2   You are quite old now; you ought to know better.
3   I am very tired; I can sleep all night.
4   Are you very tall?   Can you reach that picture?
5   The fruit is ripe; we can pick it.

6   The story is short; we can read it in one lesson.
7   The moon is very bright; I can read a book by it.
8   The wind is very strong; it will blow the roof off.
9   That man is quite stupid; he believes me.
10   I have enough money; I can pay the bill.

11   *some* and *any*

11.1
Elementary

The rough-and-ready rule of *some* in affirmative statements, and *any* in negatives and questions makes a useful
preliminary exercise.

* * *

● Make the following sentences (*a*) negative, (*b*) interrogative:
1   I have some books.
2   He bought some ties.
3   There is some news.
4   They want some paper.
5   You ate some apples.
6   You asked some questions.
7   We shall have some rain.
8   The boy has some more cake.
9   I have seen you somewhere before.
10   He knows something.
11   They found it somewhere.
12   You have some.
13   You saw someone there.
14   He has sent me some letters.
15   He gave you some ink.
16   He put some more sugar in his tea.
17   There are some pictures in this book.
18   He told someone else.
19   I saw somebody at the window.
20   She wants some more like that.

11.2
Elementary

● Add *some* or *any* as required:
1   There isn't — boot-polish in this tin.
2   'Please give me — more pudding.' 'I'm sorry
     but there isn't —.'

3 You have — fine flowers in your garden.
4 Go and ask him for — more paper. I haven't
   — in my desk.
5 I have — more letters for you to write.
6 I like those roses; please give me —.   What a pity
   there aren't — red ones!
7 I can't eat — more potatoes, but I should
   like — more beans.
8 I don't think there is —one here who can speak
   French.
9 I must have — ink and — paper, or I can't write
   —thing.
10 We had — tea, but there wasn't — sugar to
    put in it.
11 You must tell us — more of your adventures.
12 There aren't — matches left; we must buy —
    more
13 Put — salt on your meat, the cook hasn't put
    — in.
14 You can have — of my chocolate when you
    haven't — more of your own left.
15 You can't have — more dates because I want
    — for myself.
16 There is — tea in the kitchen, but there isn't —
    milk.
17 I want to buy — flowers; we haven't — in the
    garden now.
18 He wants — more pudding.   Give him —.
19 She asked me for — ice, but I can't find —.
20 Put — bread on the table; we shall need — more.

11.3
Intermediate

One cannot be used with uncountables. It has a plural
form, *ones*.
Any is natural in all doubtful statements and is usually
found with *scarcely*, *hardly*, *barely*, etc., and clauses of
doubt, condition, etc.

*   *   *

● Add *some*, *any*, *one*, or *ones*, as required:
1 I want — new potatoes; have you —?
2 You have a lot of apples; please give me —.
3 I asked him for — soap, but he hadn't —.

4 These loaves are stale; please give me — new —.
5 I'll have a cigarette. Will you have — too?
6 I want — flour, but the grocer hasn't —.
7 You have — lovely gramophone records; will
   you play me just — before I go?
8 I asked him for — ink, and he gave me —.
9 I've lost my pencil. Have you — to lend me?
10 So this is your house. It's a very pretty —.
11 I doubt if there are — sweets left. You'd better
   give — chocolate to the children that haven't
   had —.
12 I want — oranges. Give me these big —.
13 You can take these eggs if you want —, but I've
   got — better — inside.
14 If you need — more money, you must get — out
   of the bank; there is hardly — in the house.
15 They say the blue — are best. I'll buy — if you
   have — left.
16 We have — new shirts in today. Do you want to
   buy —? This green — is very nice.
17 Don't make — noise. He wants to get — sleep.
18 Have you had — tea? I can give you —.
19 Do you want — bananas? Here are — nice
   ripe —.
20 Are there — more books? I've read all these
   old —.

11.4
Intermediate
and
Advanced

The root meaning of *some* is 'particular' or 'known'; of *any*
is 'general', 'whatever you like'. Consider the sentence:

> You may come to see me any day, but you must come
> some day.

From this has developed the use of *some* for affirmative
statements, and *any* for the vague and unknown.
But in questions the use of *some* or *any* depends on the
expected or implied reply. Apropos of nothing at all, somebody may suddenly ask me,

> I say, is there anything on in the street?
> (= I'm just curious about the state of affairs
> outside)

But if a loud noise disturbs the people in the room, that
question would naturally take the form:

I say, is there something on in the street?
(= I hear a noise that suggests something particular)

NOTE: (a) Didn't you do some work *yes*terday? (= I feel certain you did)
(b) Didn't you do any *work* yesterday? (= I thought you did, but apparently I was wrong)
Intonation in (a) has low tone on '*yes*terday', in (b) has low tone on '*work*'.
Naturally, most questions may be with either *some* or *any* unless we are sure of the exact setting.

*   *   *

(11.4)   ● Use *some* or *any* where required:

1   Will you have — more tea?
2   Won't you have — more cake?   (What are the implications of *some* or *any* here?)
3   Did you go —where last night?
4   You're expecting —one to call, aren't you?
5   Haven't I given you — money this week?   I must have forgotten you!
6   Didn't I give you — money yesterday?   I feel certain I did!
7   Can you give me — more information?
8   If you haven't — money, you can get — from the bank.
9   Why don't you ask the bank for — money?
10   Can you get — more money from the bank?
11   You look as if you were expecting —one.   Is — friend of yours coming?
12   Are you expecting —one else?   If not, we'll go —where for a drink.
13   I haven't — time to do — more now; you can do — yourself.
14   Have you — cigarettes?   Would you give me — for my case, if you have?
15   What is the use of practising — more verbs?
16   Did you have — trouble with your car today?   I heard you had — yesterday.
17   These aren't *my* books.   Did I take — of yours by mistake?
18   Wouldn't you like —thing to drink?   Have — cherry brandy?

19   Have you read — good books lately?
20   Are there — lemons in the cupboard? We could
     make — lemonade.

12⁻ *no = not . . . any*

Compare:
>   Come nowhere near me!
>   Don't come anywhere near me!

Both are grammatically correct, but the *not . . . any* form is
the normal one for ordinary statements. In fact several of
the sentences below sound unusual in speech.

*   *   *

● Reword the following *no*-sentences in the *not . . . any* form.
  Use the contracted *-n't* forms:

1   I have no time to help you.
2   There is no more sugar.
3   I can see my hat nowhere.
4   He likes no girls with red hair.
5   We have seen nobody we know yet.
6   They want nothing to eat.
7   I have no more money.
8   There are no apples on the tree.
9   There was nobody in the garden.
10 The poor little boy has no shoes to wear.
11 There is nowhere for you to sleep.
12 The cook has put no salt in the cabbage.
13 They will do no more work.
14 There was nothing left.
15 The chicken has laid no eggs today.
16 I want no more, thank you.
17 He gave me nothing to drink.
18 I'll give it to nobody else.
19 He gave me no ink, so I could write no more.
20 My uncle can see nothing without his glasses.

**12.2
Elementary**

The *no*-forms are chiefly used as short negative answers to questions.

Where are you going? – Nowhere.

Remember: *neither* of two; *none* of many.

*   *   *

● Answer the following questions in the negative; respond quickly:

1   Where are you going?
2   How many exercises have you done today?
3   Who were you talking to?
4   How much did these flowers cost?
5   What are you doing?
6   Where has she been?
7   Who did you meet?
8   Who phoned this morning?
9   How many will you give me?
10   What did you say?
11   Who told you to put it under the table?
12   What do they want?
13   Who do they want to see?
14   Which of these two books have you read?
15   How many have I given you already?
16   Who told you to do that?
17   What are you thinking about?
18   How many of these are mine?
19   Where did you go last night?
20   Which foot have you hurt?

**12.3
Intermediate**

Read notes on Exercise 12.1.
Notice that *neither* = 'not either'.
Students should be reminded that several of the sentences below sound unusual in speech.

*   *   *

● Reword the following *no*-sentences in the *not . . . any* form:

1   We had eaten no meat for four days.
2   They found nobody at home.
3   He gave his wife no money for her clothes.
4   They went nowhere after supper.
5   How odd! This door has no hinges.
6   I hope you've said nothing to Maisie.

7 They're dirty; I want neither of them.
8 I spoke to no one except you.
9 My friend Cyril would talk to nobody like her.
10 We had no money for our fare.
11 Why do you think an Englishman speaks no language but his own?
12 I've read no poetry since I was at school.
13 I've been nowhere this summer. I've had no time.
14 I'll speak neither to him nor to his wife.
15 We met nobody on the way, and we saw nothing unusual.
16 My car needs no new tyres.
17 I've been nowhere else.
18 He could remember neither the words nor the music.
19 I wonder why he told me nothing else.
20 I have no more money, so I can buy nothing else.

12.4
Intermediate

Read note to Exercise 12.2. Short negative answers in *no*-form.

What are you doing? – Nothing.
Which of the two do you want? – Neither.

* * *

● Answer the following questions in the negative; respond quickly:

1 Which of these two books have you read?
2 Who did you meet in the park last night?
3 Where have you been?
4 What have you done with it?
5 What are you whispering to Maisie about?
6 How many glasses did you break at the party?
7 What were you doing in the garden just now?
8 Who made that dirty mark on the ceiling?
9 What did you see when you opened the door?
10 Which shoe of this pair is too tight?
11 How many exercises have you done for me this week?
12 Where did Cyril take you?
13 What are you doing next weekend?
14 Which of these two umbrellas is mine?
15 How many letters did you get this morning?

16   Where did you two go last night?
17   How many five-letter words are there in sentence 11?
18   Which of the two girls is your sister?
19   What were you doing at the station?
20   Who brings you to your English lesson?

13   Comparisons

**13.1
Elementary**

The idea

> He is less stupid than I thought he was.

is better expressed by

> EITHER He is not so stupid as I thought he was.
> OR He is cleverer than I thought he was.

*   *   *

● The following sentences are not good ones as they stand. Reword them in the two ways suggested above.

1   Your house is less near than I thought.
2   This book is less big than yours.
3   This exercise is less good than your last one.
4   My mother is less old than you think she is.
5   These grapes are less expensive than those.
6   Kenneth is less short than his brother.
7   A donkey is less beautiful than a horse.
8   We're less bad than you think we are.
9   This hill is less low than I thought it was.
10   She is less ugly than you said she was.
11   I am less light than you.
12   The grass is less short here than in our garden.
13   A cigarette is less strong than a cigar. (mild)
14   Apples are less cheap than oranges.
15   The garden is less big than we hoped.
16   A tram is less quick than a bus.
17   My brother is less hard-working than me.
18   Our house is less low than yours.
19   This street is less wide than the next one.
20   My bag is less heavy than my friend's.

13.2

Intermediate ●

Read note on Exercise 13.1.

The following sentences are not good ones as they stand. Reword them in the ways suggested in Exercise 13.1.

1   The sea was less smooth than I had hoped. (rough)
2   The river is less deep near the ford. (shallow)
3   It is less dangerous to tease a lion than scorn a woman. (safe)
4   Maisie is much less young than she looks.
5   She is less proud than her sister. (humble)
6   The film was less interesting than the play. (dull)
7   Richard Burton is much less ugly than Cyril. (handsome)
8   He is less obstinate than his brothers. (co-operative)
9   She's less sophisticated than she makes herself out to be. (naïve, simple)
10   You'd be less well off if you were married. (badly off)
11   My cigarettes are less good than yours.
12   A well-dressed woman is much less humble than a peacock.   (Do in the affirmative form only.)
13   The river was less shallow than he expected.
14   John is much less intelligent than his sister. (dull)
15   My wife is much less economical than yours. (extravagant)

14   Negatives and Questions of Auxiliary Verbs

When these exercises are done orally, short forms should be used throughout.

AUXILIARY VERBS are sometimes called ANOMALOUS FINITES, SPECIAL FINITES, or MODAL AUXILIARIES.

In the first year students should be acquainted with the following:

> *be, have, do, did, can, could, must, shall, will.*

In the second year the others should be known:

> *should, would, may, might, ought to, used to, daren't, needn't, had better, would rather.*

Students should be well drilled in the natural use of weak (unemphatic) forms in speech.

Example: *can* = [kn] in *I can do it.*

Complete list of Auxiliary Verbs:

be am is are was were	*may* might
have has had	*must* have to, am to
do does did	*ought to*
shall should	*used to*
will would	*need*
can could	*dare*

For contracted negatives add *-n't*. Exceptions are *I'm not, can't, shan't, won't.*

Need and *dare* are used as true auxiliaries in QUESTIONS and NEGATIVES only.

Except for certain uses of *have, need* and *used to,* all question and negative constructions are made without *do.*

SHORT-FORM NEGATIVE

14.1　● Make the following sentences negative:
Elementary

1 He must do it again.
2 She could understand everything.
3 They had time to tell her.
4 It was very late.
5 We're coming tomorrow morning.
6 He can speak French.
7 He'll come if you can. (Note the stress.)
8 You must come this morning.
9 He comes here every day.
10 We like her very much.
11 They arrived at six o'clock.
12 There were many people at the concert.
13 Why did you come with him?
14 We could see as far as the mountains.
15 You shall have another one tomorrow.
16 Our teacher wants the homework now.
17 You must look out of the window.
18 Eric can understand what you say.
19 There are some more cakes.
20 He has enough to eat.

14.2
Elementary

Have takes the form *haven't* or *have you?* only if used as PERFECT TENSE auxiliary, or with its fundamental meaning of 'possess' or 'own'. (See also Exercise 33.1.)

* * *

● Answer the following questions in the negative:

1 Can you drink tea?
2 Mustn't you eat fish?
3 Ought you to have any coffee?
4 Can you stay up late?
5 Will you have another cigarette?
6 Couldn't he telephone?
7 Mustn't you go out so late at night?
8 Have you any brothers or sisters?
9 Do you have lunch at one o'clock?
10 Can you speak Czech?
11 Did you read last night's paper?
12 Have you seen my hat anywhere?
13 Do stupid people always have stupid faces?
14 Ought he to work so hard?
15 Were there many people at the party?

14.3
Intermediate

Have WITHOUT *do*
(In American English *have* normally takes *do* for all its uses except PERFECT TENSES. This usage is becoming common in British English.)

1 When meaning to 'possess' or 'own' an object or a characteristic.

Maisie hasn't any handkerchiefs.
A circle hasn't any corners.

2 As auxiliary for PERFECT TENSES.

Have WITH *do*.

1 Meaning occasional (not permanent) possession.

Maisie doesn't have a clean handkerchief every day.
We don't have lunch before midday.
(Similarly with all meals.)

2 Causative. See Exercise 15.1.

You didn't have it mended.

3 Meaning to 'experience'.

Did you have a good time last night?

Similarly *have trouble, bother, difficulty, a good (bad) trip* or *journey, a lesson, the opportunity of, occasion to.*

Have WITH or WITHOUT *do*; as *have to*, replacing *must*.

> Have you to work hard?
> Do you have to work hard?

For *have got* see Exercises 33.1, 2.

Dare.   Question and negative form WITHOUT *do*. In the affirmative it is followed by infinitive WITH *to*.

> Dare he go alone?
> He dared to call me a fool.

But note the expression *I dare say* . . .

Need.   Questions and negatives are usually made WITHOUT *do* and WITHOUT the infinitive particle *to*. In the affirmative *need* is followed by the infinitive WITH *to*.

> *Q.* Need he run so fast?
> *A.* Yes, he must.   (Yes, he needs to.)
>   He needs to speak more slowly.   (= must)

See Exercises 16.1–5.

Used to.   Should logically be used WITHOUT *do*, but forms WITH *do* are undoubtedly the most widespread, especially as responses and question-tags.

> (*a*) Used you[1] to live here? Did you use to[2] live here?
> (*b*) You used to[2] live here, use(d)n't[3] you? didn't you?
> (*c*) You used to[2] pay me every week. Used[4] I? Did I?

The most usual negative form seems to be with *never*, which conveniently avoids the difficulty.

> You never used to treat me like this.

TENTATIVE ADVICE: In (*b*) and (*c*) above (responses, §19, and question-tags, §32), we prefer forms WITH *do*; in (*a*) we prefer forms WITH *do* in spoken English, WITHOUT *do* in written English. *Never* is a useful device for negatives.

*   *   *

(14.3)   ● Answer these questions in the negative:

1 You never used to smoke so much, did you?
2 Have you any more like this?

[1] ['ju:stju]
[2] ['ju:stə]
[3] ['ju:snt]
[4] [ju:st]

3   Did you have a comfortable journey?

4   Who used to take you out for walks when you
    were little?   (Answer in affirmative, of course.)

5   'Need I do it at once?' 'No, you —.'

6   'Ought you to make so much noise?'   'No, I
    suppose I —.'

7   Do I have to come at nine?

8   Did you have to write in ink?

9   Did you have sausages for breakfast?

10 Have we any sausages in the house?

11 Need she put on a clean dress?

12 'Who wrote that rude remark on the blackboard?'
    'I —.'

13 Did you use to live here?   (Used you to live here?)

14 Dare he come without our invitation?

15 Did you have your shoes cleaned this morning?

16 Need it be finished by Saturday?

17 Do you want any more rice pudding?

18 Dare they do it again?

19 Did he dare to call you a thief to your face?
    (Answer in affirmative.)

20 Didn't you use to go to school with him?
    (Usedn't you to go to school with him?)

15   Causative use of *have*

15.1
Intermediate
and
Advanced

Causing something to be done by someone else is expressed by *have* or *get* with a past participle.

> He must have (get) his pen mended. (= Someone
> must mend it for him.)
> I had (got) my shoes cleaned. (= I asked someone
> to clean them for me.)

Questions and negatives are made with *do*.

*   *   *

● Reword the following sentences, using *have* or *get* with a
  past participle:

1   Someone washed my car for me yesterday.

2   Someone doesn't clean them for us every day.

3   I asked someone to paint the gate last week.
4   Someone tuned her piano for her yesterday.
5   Somebody will have to see to it for you.
6   I asked a man to mend my shoes.
7   Somebody sends Maisie her dresses from Paris.
8   Your hair wants cutting. You must —.
9   Tell someone to translate it into English.
10   Our season tickets need renewing. We must —.
11   I'll ask someone to make a new one.
12   We ordered somebody to whitewash the ceiling.
13   Order someone to send it round to the house.
14   The knives want sharpening. We must —.
15   We must find somebody to chop all this wood up.
16   Tell him to take another photograph.
17   I'm going to tell someone to add an extra room.
18   Your car wants servicing. You must —.
19   He asked his tailor to lengthen the trousers.
20   Tell someone to bring it to you on a tray.

16   *must, have to, need*

16.1
Elementary
MUST AND
MUST NOT

Must and *have* (*got*) *to* are commands or obligations.
Must not and *am/is/are not to* are prohibitions (negative commands).
They are PRESENT and FUTURE in meaning; but future obligation can be made more precise with the form *shall have to*.

PAST TENSE:
Had (*got*) *to* is an obligation in the past.
Was/were not to is a prohibition in the past: it occurs mostly in reported speech.

*   *   *

● Read each sentence as it stands, then make it refer to the past:

1   You must do it at once.
2   He mustn't tell me.
3   She has to wash the glasses.
4   He is not to come before seven.
5   You'll have to read it again.

6 He says I'm not to be trusted.
7 They must sell it at once.
8 We shall have to leave in the morning.
9 I'm not to repeat it.
10 I shall have to come again.
11 He says you are not to listen to them.
12 They must change their shoes.
13 He is surprised that he is not to bring one with him.
14 You are not to choose a green one.
15 We have to begin before five o'clock.
16 I must work as hard as I can.
17 We shall have to do it again.
18 He says you're not to drink it all.
19 I have to light a fire.
20 He has to go home early.
21 He mustn't read the whole book.
22 She says I'm not to lay the table before twelve o'clock.
23 I shall have to give you a new one.
24 She mustn't go home alone.
25 They'll have to do what they're told.

16.2
Elementary
MUST AND *NEEDN'T*

To express the absence of obligation or necessity to do something (that is, the opposite of *must*), the form *need not* is used.

> You must go now. — No, you needn't go just yet, you can stay a little longer.

Alternative forms are *haven't got to, don't have to, don't need to*.

FUTURE is the same as the above, but we use *shan't (won't) have to* and *shan't (won't) need to* if we wish to be more precise.

PAST forms are *hadn't got to, didn't have to*, and *didn't need to*.

For the form *needn't have done* see Exercise 16.5.

* * *

● Read each sentence as it stands, then make it refer to the past:

1 You needn't spend it all.
2 She won't have to come again.
3 I needn't do my homework again.

4 My sister doesn't have to go to work.
5 The children won't need to get up so early.
6 They haven't got to go back alone, have they?
7 She needn't cook them all.
8 I must go at once, but you needn't.
9 They must pay twice, but we shan't have to.
10 You haven't got to answer all the questions.
11 You don't need to carry so much.
12 So I shan't have to go out after all.
13 He won't have to come on foot, will he?
14 We needn't listen to them.
15 The students don't have to write in ink.
16 They won't have to read the whole book, will they?
17 She doesn't have to come every week.
18 I shan't have to buy another one.
19 We don't need to call him 'Sir'.
20 She won't have to walk the whole way, will she?

**16.3
Elementary
and
Intermediate**
MUST AND
HAVE TO

See Exercises 16.1 and 16.2.
There is usually a difference of meaning between the
present tense forms *must* and *have to* in affirmative statements:

> *Must* expresses obligation or compulsion FROM THE
> SPEAKER'S VIEWPOINT.
> *Have to* expresses EXTERNAL obligation.

Compare the following pairs of situations, where these two
forms are used in their natural context.

> You must go now. (I want to go to bed.)
> What a pity you have to go now. (It's time for you
> to catch your train.)
> We must begin before five (or we shan't finish in time
> for our supper).
> We have to begin before five. (That's the time ar-
> ranged.)
> They must take it away. (I won't have it here any
> longer.)
> They have to take it away. (They've been told to do so.)
> He must stay the night. (I (we) press him to do so.)
> He has to stay the night. (He can't get back tonight.)
> He must move the furniture himself (for all I care; I
> shan't help him).
> He has to move the furniture himself (poor chap; he's
> got no one to help him).

You must call me 'Sir'. (I like it that way.)
You have to call me 'Sir'. (That's the regulation address.)
You must change your shoes. (I won't have you in here with muddy feet.)
You have to change your shoes. (... such is the custom on entering a mosque.)

*Am/is/*etc. *to* is used for definite commands or prohibitions. This form, or *must*, is used for instructions on notices or orders (*have to* is never used here).

Passengers must cross the lines by the footbridge. (The railway company instructs them to.)
Porters often have to walk across the lines. (The nature of their work compels them to.)
All junior officers are to report to the colonel at once. (Military order)
Soldiers have to salute their officers. (Such is the custom.)

* * *

● Read each of the following sentences as it stands, then in the negative (i.e. remove the idea of obligation):

1 I must get there before eight.
2 You will have to come again.
3 They must leave before dinner.
4 She must wash up all the glasses.
5 We had to change our shoes.
6 You'll have to pay him in advance.
7 He had to give it back.
8 The workmen have to take it away again.
9 Our teacher must write it on the blackboard.
10 We had to finish it by today.
11 We shall have to leave earlier than usual.
12 You must answer at once.
13 We had to begin very early.
14 You'll have to bring your own ink with you.
15 You must eat them all.
16 I shall have to buy a new one.
17 They must learn the whole poem.
18 She has to make some new ones. (*N.B.* some–any)
19 I had to read it aloud.
20 She must wear a hat.
21 You'll have to stand outside.

22   I had to show my passport.
23   You must lock the box up again.
24   We shall have to tell them our address.
25   You must do the whole exercise again.

16.4
Intermediate
HAVE TO
AND *NEED*
(WITH AND
WITHOUT
DO)

See Exercises 16.2 and 16.3.
In questions and negatives the present tense forms:

Do I have to ... ?   I don't have to ...
Do I need to ... ?   I don't need to ...

are mostly used for HABITUAL ACTIONS; whereas the forms

Have I got to ... ?   I haven't got to ...
Need I ... ?[1]   I needn't ...
Must I ... ?[1]

are mostly used for ONE PARTICULAR OCCASION.

This is a preference, not a rule, and except where one of the above aspects requires emphasis, all four forms are interchangeable. For some speakers there is a difference of meaning between *Need you go shopping this afternoon?* (which may sound like a protest) and *Do you need to go shopping this afternoon?* (a simple enquiry).

The forms of *have to* and *need* (with and without the auxiliary *do*) can be compared in the following examples, where the idea of one special occasion or of habit is strongly present.

Must you get up early tomorrow morning? (Have you got to ...)
Do you have to get up early (every morning)?
Must I show it to him now? (Have I got to ...)
Do I have to show my pass every time I go in?
OR   Do I need to show my pass every time ... ? (I hope it isn't necessary.)
You needn't do it just now.
You don't have to do it every time you see him. (You don't need to.)

*   *   *

[1] *Need* is used wherever there is a strong element of negation or doubt, or when the speaker seeks or expects a negative answer. Cf. the following examples:

Must she come tomorrow? (open question)
Need she come tomorrow? (hoping for negative answer)
Must I be present? (Do you want me?)
I wonder if I need be present. (statement of doubt)

● Read each of the following sentences as it stands, then in the negative (i.e. remove the idea of compulsion):

1 You must answer in English.
2 He will have to pay me back before Christmas.
3 We had to bend it to get it into the box.
4 They must brush their own shoes.
5 They have to brush their own shoes every day.
6 You'll have to buy us some more.
7 You must ring him up before tomorrow.
8 She'll have to carry both of them.
9 We must change our clothes for dinner.
10 We had to cook them first.
11 You must cut it in three equal pieces.
12 You must write yours now, and she'll have to write hers when she comes in.
13 She had to drink it without sugar.
14 We had to pay them for it, and we shall have to pay them some more next week.
15 You must put all the eggs in one basket.
16 Grandfather had to finish reading it in bed.
17 You must give it back to me before you go.
18 She'll have to go back before nightfall.
19 They had to light a fire to cook their supper.
20 You must listen to this talk on potato-planting.
21 We shall have to wait (a) long (time) for our holidays.[1]
22 Last year we even had to book accommodation.
23 In any case we have to get train tickets, because we are taking our bicycles.
24 We shall have to take a lot of food with us.[2]
25 We must even take a cooking stove.

16.5
Intermediate and Advanced
DIDN'T NEED TO GO AND *NEEDN'T HAVE GONE*

See Exercises 16.3 and 16.4.
didn't need to: It wasn't necessary, so probably not done.
needn't have: It wasn't necessary. but done nevertheless.
Both are opposites of *I had to*, with the above difference of meaning.

> My tea was already sweetened, so I *needn't have put* any sugar in.
> But I did, and made it too sweet.

[1] See Exercise 53.2 (*a long time*).
[2] See Exercise 53.1 (*a lot of*).

My tea was already sweetened, so I *didn't need to put* any sugar in.
I drank it as it was.
I didn't need to change my suit (= didn't have to).
So I went in the clothes I had on.
I needn't have changed my suit.
But I did! I see *now* that it wasn't necessary.

*   *   *

(16.5) ● Insert *didn't need to* or *needn't have* according to the sense:

1   I — (answer) the questions, but I'm glad I did.
2   I — (answer) the questions, so I turned to the next page.
3   I — (buy) a new one, so I've brought the old one back.
4   You — (spend) all that money; now we've got nothing left.
5   They — (push) it into the corner, because it was there already.
6   I — (go) by sea, but flying would have cost more.
7   We — (open) the drawer, seeing that it was already open.
8   She — (open) the drawer, seeing that she found it empty when she did.
9   You — (pay) him a penny; he gets more than enough from me.
10   I — (pay) for it, because it was put on my father's account.
11   We — (say) anything at all, which was a great comfort.
12   You — (say) anything; then he would never have known.
13   I know I — (lock) the door after me, but how was I to know you wanted to come out, too?
14   He — (lock) the door, because somebody else had already done so.
15   We — (wait) long; he was back before you could say 'Jack Robinson'.
16   We — (wait) for her, because she never came at all.
17   You — (stay) if you hadn't wanted to.
18   I — (take) my ink because I knew I should find some there.

19 I — (tell) him personally; I wrote him a letter.
20 You — (bring) any food, but since you have,
    let's eat it now.
21 You — (wake) me up; there's another hour
    before the train leaves.
22 I — (wake) him up, because he was already
    sitting on the bed, putting his socks on.
23 You — (write) such a long composition,
    because I shan't have time to mark it.
24 I — (ring) the bell, because the door opened before
    I got to it.
25 You — (wait) for me; I could have found the way
    all right.

THE FOREGOING POINTS REVIEWED IN TABULAR FORM

The forms in square brackets do not occur very frequently
and need not be practised.

OBLIGATION (must)	PROHIBITION (mustn't)[1]	NO OBLIGATION (needn't)[2]
PRESENT		
he must go[3]	he mustn't go	he needn't go
he has (got) to go[3]	he isn't to go	he hasn't got to go[4]
[he needs to go]		he doesn't need to go[4]
		he doesn't have to go[4]
FUTURE		
As above, and	As above	As above, and
he'll have to go[5]		he won't have to go
[he'll need to go]		he won't need to go
PAST		
he had (got) to go	he wasn't to go	he hadn't got to go
[he needed to go]		he didn't have to go
		he didn't need to go[6]
		he needn't have gone

[1] Exercise 16.1.
[2] Exercises 16.2–4.
[3] See note to Exercise 16.3.
[4] See note to Exercise 16.4.
[5] See also Exercise 51.6.
[6] Exercise 16.5.

17 *can*

17.1
**Elementary
and
Intermediate**

Can has two main uses:

1 to express permission or possibility (= may).

You can go now.

2 to express ability or capacity (= know how to).

I can swim very well.

	1	2
FUTURE	can	shall (will) be able to
PAST	could	could OR
		was (were) able to

But see also next exercise.

* * *

● Say the following using the given time-expressions, first for the future and then for the past.

EXAMPLE

You can drive. *when you are* 17/*after you got your licence.*

ANSWER 1: You can drive when you are 17.

ANSWER 2: You could drive after you got your licence.

1 He can leave it here. **for an hour/whenever he wanted to.**

2 He can play chess. **this afternoon/when he was young.**

3 I can fly a plane. **after a few more lessons/when I was in the air force.**

4 We can do this exercise. **next week/last week.**

5 She can cook very well. **with more practice/when I knew her.**

6 I can go early. **if he lets me/every day last summer.**

7 She can make her own dresses. **in a few years' time/before she got married.**

8 She can read easily. **with her new glasses/before her eye trouble.**

9 He says I can have another one. **tomorrow/He said — yesterday.**

10 I can go swimming. **when it is warmer/whenever I liked**.

11 She can play the piano. **when her arm is better/a few years ago**.

12 We can't find it. **until tomorrow/when we looked for it**.

13 John can stay up late. **tonight/even when he was a small boy**.

14 I can meet you. **on Saturday/whenever I liked**.

15 My sister can sew very well. **soon/before she lost her eyesight**.

16 We can speak English. **soon/when we were in London**.

17 I can't have a car. **until I am older/until I was twenty-one**.

18 He can find a good answer. **if you ask him tonight/whenever I asked him a question**.

19 My father can help me. **when he comes home/when he had time**.

20 We can see the sea. **a little farther on/from the top of the hill**.

21 You can borrow the book. **tomorrow/whenever you wanted to**.

22 Jill can climb trees. **when she is a bit older/when she was younger**.

23 We can't understand. **until you explain it again/when he spoke so quickly**.

24 She can bring a friend. **with her this afternoon/any time she liked**.

25 They can build better houses. **in the year 2050/in 1850**.

(Notice that in some of these *can* may mean either 'may' or 'know how to'.)

17.2
Advanced

See Exercise 17.1.

Seeing in a grammar book that *could* can be past or conditional of *can*, students are always puzzled by having such sentences as:

'I could pass my examination ten years ago.'
'I could go to the country yesterday and had a good time, . . . ' etc.

corrected to *was able to*.

A careful analysis of all sentences where we CANNOT use *could* as simple past tense of *can* shows the following idea to be common to all of them. They deal with THE ATTAINMENT OF SOMETHING THROUGH SOME CAPACITY. Mere capacity may have *could* or *was able to*.

> He could (was able to) swim very well when he was young. (*Could* is more usual.)

But something attained through a capacity may not have *could*.

> He was able to swim half-way before he collapsed. (*Could* is impossible here.)

Managed to also expresses this idea.
The past of *can* meaning PERMISSION always has *could*.

> I could put it wherever I liked. (permission granted)
> I was able to put it on the top shelf. (capacity or ability to reach)

* * *

(17.2) ● Say the following using the given time-expressions, first for the future and then for the past. (See the example for Exercise 17.1.) Distinguish when *can* may have more than one meaning.

1 We can climb to the top of this mountain. **tomorrow/yesterday.**
2 She can come. **next week/whenever she wanted to.**
3 I can join the broken ends. **when I get some glue/with glue yesterday.**
4 I can cover at least half of it. **by the time you get back/before he got back.**
5 He can eat anything. **when the doctor gives him permission/before he was ill.**
6 Mother says I can go out with you. **tonight/ Mother said — tonight.**
7 She can write with her left hand. **if she practises for an hour/when she had to.**
8 You can do what you like. **this afternoon/always.**
9 I can reach London. **by the weekend/yesterday.**
10 My sister can make a very nice pudding. **for dinner, tomorrow/when she had her own kitchen.**
11 My wife can leave hospital. **in a week's time/a few days ago.**

12 I can help you with your homework.   **after tea/ when you were in difficulties yesterday.**

13 Our army can win a battle.   **when it has enough ammunition/a few days ago.**

14 We can sit in the garden.   **next weekend/when it stopped raining.**

15 You can have a look at the baby.   **when it has been fed/she said I —.**

16 Cyril can improve his position.   **after a year or two/when his employer died.**

17 We can catch the 2.30 (two-thirty) train. **tomorrow afternoon/in spite of the fog.**

18 Maisie says she can come out with me.   **on Saturday/Maisie said — on Saturday.**

19 We can finish it.   **by ten o'clock/before it was wanted.**

20 Simon can shoot well.   **in a few weeks/before his accident.**

21 They can put the fire out.   **when another engine comes/after two hours.**

22 She can pass her examination.   **next June/last June.**

23 You can pour out the tea.   **when it is ready/I thought they said (that) I —.**

24 No one can undo that bolt.   **until it is oiled/until it was oiled.**

25 I can pick a lot of fruit off that tree.   **next week/ last year.**

Go through this exercise again and see which sentences can make their past with *managed to*.

18   Short-form Negative, Revision

18.1
Advanced

Read note to Exercise 14.3.
Must.   Notice that the negative form *mustn't* is a negative obligation; the opposite of *must* is *needn't*. This is important for correct responses.

> He *needn't* do that, need he? – Yes, I'm afraid he *must*.
> *Must* I go? – No, you *needn't*.

Have to.   The above distinctions are also made in the *have to* forms.

OBLIGATION	NO OBLIGATION	PROHIBITION
He must go	He needn't go	He mustn't go
⌠He has to go	⌠He doesn't have to go	He isn't to go
⌊He has got to go	⌊He hasn't got to go	

Look at the following sentences and notice how the forms *don't have to* and *am not to* are used.

My doctor says I'm not to (= mustn't) eat meat, but I don't have to (or haven't got to) (= needn't) take his advice if I don't want to.

I've told my husband he isn't to (mustn't) smoke in the drawing-room.

I don't have to (haven't got to) tell *my* husband such things; he's a born gentleman. (= needn't, not necessary)

My mother says I mustn't (I'm not to) be out after eight o'clock, but I haven't got to (don't have to) do what she tells me!

The forms *He's not to, you're not to*, etc. are more usual than *he isn't to, you aren't to*, etc.

The form *he hasn't got to* is more usual in spoken British English than the form *he doesn't have to* (= he needn't).

See Exercises 16.1–5 for opposite and negative of *must*.

Need.   See Exercise 16.5 for the expression of NO OBLIGATION in the past.

*   *   *

(18.1)   ● Read the following in the negative:

1 He does his work by himself, doesn't he?
2 Need he go there after all?
3 That needs a lot of thinking about.
4 He used to come and see me every day.
5 Guy Fawkes used bombs to try and blow up Parliament.
6 I'm used to funny people like you.
7 He had to use a dictionary for his translation.   (2 answers: (*a*) opposite; (*b*) prohibition.)
8 They used to have two cows and a lame donkey.
9 I had it put in the dining-room.
10 He has a pair of new boots.
11 He has a new pair of boots every day.

12   He has to stay here all day.   (2 answers:
     (a) opposite; (b) prohibition.)
13   He has eaten his breakfast.
14   He had his breakfast before nine o'clock.
15   He had a very pleasant journey here.
16   The Victorians had influenza like the people of
     today.
17   A pyramid has five sides.
18   I had some trouble in finding where you lived.
19   I had to have someone to show me the way from
     the station.   (opposite here, not negative).
20   Dare he jump from a first-floor window like this?

     (For *have got = have*, see Exercises 33.1–3.)

19   Short-form Responses using Auxiliary Verbs

19.1
Elementary

The most important function of the auxiliaries, or special
finites, is their use in short answers and responses.

> Are you fond of fish? No, I'm not. Yes, I am.
> Do you like fish? No, I don't. Yes, I do.

Contracted forms are always used.

*   *   *

● Give short-form answers to the following questions:
1   Can you speak English?
2   Have you met my Uncle Jim?
3   Are you enjoying yourself?
4   Will you come again tomorrow?   Yes, ...
5   Is your friend here today?
6   Have you been to a football match this week?
7   Must I be there in time?   Yes, ...
8   Did you meet him yesterday?
9   Has your friend gone home?
10   Does he play chess?
11   Could you come a little later?
12   Will you forget what you have learnt today?
     No, ...

13 Did you drink it all?
14 Oughtn't he to pay you at once? Yes, he ...
15 Does your sister like chocolates?
16 Did you say anything?
17 May I go out? Yes, you ...
18 Will your brother be there?
19 Were you at the cinema last night?
20 Are you reading?

19.2
Intermediate

Remember that the affirmative response to *need* is usually *must*, and the negative response to *must* is usually *needn't*. See Exercises 16.1, 2.

> Need I get up so soon? Yes, I'm afraid you must.
> Must I go by train? Oh no, you needn't.

*   *   *

● Give short answers to the following questions:

1 Will the weather clear up this afternoon? No, I'm afraid ...
2 Do you think he would come if I asked him? No, I doubt whether ...
3 Must you always make so much noise? No, I ...
4 Dare you pull Cyril's beard? No, I ...
5 Need you leave your papers lying all over the floor? Yes, ...
6 Do you really think he used to live here? (a) Yes, I ...; (b) I'm sure he ...
7 Did you have any difficulty in finding my house?
8 Must you drive at 120 kilometres an hour?
9 Oughtn't you to be more careful?
10 Will you have enough money to buy it? No, ...
11 Do they all speak as well as you?
12 Need you bring Maisie with you? Yes, I'm afraid ...
13 Usedn't he to work at Brighton?
14 Must you always wear that old coat? No, I suppose I ...
15 Does he want me to give him an interview?
16 Must I take an umbrella? No, you ...
17 Were you able to finish your work?
18 Should the baby be playing with a box of matches?

19   Need we change for dinner?   Yes, you . . .

20   Oughtn't you to answer that letter now?

19.3
Elementary

The auxiliaries are great time-savers when answering 'question-word questions' (where *yes* or *no* cannot be used).

> Who told you that I was coming at five o'clock? – John did.

*   *   *

●   Give short-form answers to the following questions:

1   Who wrote *Hamlet*?

2   How many of you can speak English fluently?

3   Which of you must clean the blackboard?

4   How many of you play tennis?   Most of us . . .

5   How many of you can play chess?   None of us . . .

6   Who teaches you English?

7   What fell on the floor just now?

8   Which is better, this one or that one?

9   Which cost more, these or those?

10   How many of you ought to know the answer?   All of us . . .

11   Who made that noise?

12   Which of you likes ice-cream?   We all . . .

13   What fruit tastes nice? All . . .

14   How many of you must answer this question? We all . . .

15   Who shut the door?

16   Which gives more light, the sun or the moon?

17   What makes people fat?   Eating . . .

18   Which of you finished your homework yesterday? None . . .

19   Who broke my pencil?

20   Who wants to go for a walk?

19.4
Intermediate

●   Give short-form answers to the following questions:

1   How many of you need new books?

2   Who's the present ruler of England?

3   Who's taken my books?   (No one . . .)

4   Who discovered America?

5   What was the world's biggest island before Australia was discovered?   (Answer, if you need it, can be found after Exercise 57.3.)

6   Which of the two weighs more, Cyril or Maisie?
    Probably ...
7   Who'll come with me to the Zoo? (We all ...)
8   Who used to live in this old house?
9   Who dares to jump over this stream? Nobody ...
10 What's the capital of France?
11 Who saw Maisie in the town yesterday?
12 Which of you knows the shortest way to the
    station?
13 How many of you ought to be in bed by now?
14 How many of you have breakfast before seven in
    the morning?
15 Who likes chocolate?
16 Who came late today?
17 Who taught you to swim?
18 How many of you ought to do more homework?
    We all ...
19 Who can answer my questions? (Most of us ...)
20 Which takes longer to say: Ightham or Llanfair-
    pwllgwyngyllgogerwchwyndrobbwllllandyrilio-
    gogogoch?

19.5
Elementary
AGREEMENT

See also Exercise 19.20.
The auxiliaries are commonly used when we agree with
someone:
using *yes* for simple agreement.

> It's very hot today. – Yes, it is.

using *so* for surprise.

> Your glass is empty. – So it is.

using *of course*, etc., for something obvious.

> They say we shall win. – Of course we shall.

The teacher reads the statement and the student responds.

*   *   *

● Agree with the following remarks:
1   The door is shut. So ...
2   Mr Smith is sitting down. Yes ...
3   That music sounds pleasant. Yes ...
4   You've got some ink on your sleeve. So ...
5   You are all learning English very quickly. Of
    course ...

6 I am already smoking a cigarette. So ...
7 His brother has gone to Paris. Yes ...
8 Perhaps you are right. Of course ...
9 She swims better than I do. Yes ...
10 They must return the money. Of course ...
11 We shall soon see what happens. Yes ...
12 He ought to go home. Yes ...
13 Miners always expect high wages. Yes ...
14 There's a hole in your coat. So ...
15 I can speak English very well. Of course ...

19.6
Intermediate
AGREEMENT

Read Note to Exercise 19.5.
The teacher reads the statement; the student responds.

*   *   *

● Agree with the following remarks:
1 Your uncle would like to meet him.
2 The flies are a nuisance.
3 He'll probably be arrested.
4 The book has fallen on the floor.
5 They say we'll win the match.
6 I believe your friend Cyril works in an insurance office.
7 He told me you were going to see the director today.
8 They are showing *South Pacific* here next week.
9 You must do what he tells you.
10 Maisie only likes me for my money.
11 Probably anybody could speak English if they tried.
12 I expect you can give me a match, can't you?
13 You've spilt some coffee down your dress.
14 If you threw a book out of the window, I dare say it would fall.
15 I can't leave without paying.

Other suitable introductory phrases for 'obvious' types are: *obviously, indeed, I'm sure, you can see, it's quite clear,* etc.

19.7
Elementary
DISAGREEMENT

When we disagree with someone we respond with *no* or *oh, no* followed by the appropriate auxiliary. *But* may be used for disagreeing with a question or an assumption.

> The box is open. – No, it isn't.
> Why didn't you write to me? – But I did.

The teacher reads the statement; the student responds.

* * *

● Disagree with the following remarks:

1 He will have to see a doctor.
2 English grammar is too difficult for you.
3 Why are you so angry?
4 Bucharest is of course the capital of Hungary.
5 Don't hurry, we have plenty of time.
6 Why are you working so hard in these summer days?
7 The bank will certainly lend you some money.
8 You've done this exercise before.
9 He has plenty of money.
10 He likes me better than you.
11 I feel sure this dog will bite me.
12 You have made a mistake.
13 I think this is a ripe one.
14 How did you go to town yesterday?
15 The door is locked.
16 She wants to talk to you.
17 They can come again tomorrow.
18 Why did you break my pencil?
19 You bought one like this yesterday.
20 We've been here before.

19.8
Intermediate

See Exercise 19.7. Remember that the OPPOSITE of *must* is *needn't*.
The teacher reads the statement; the student responds.

* * *

● Disagree with the following remarks:

1 You ought to do at least five exercises a week.
2 Why did you come so late today?
3 You have used up all the money I gave you, I suppose.
4 A compositor is a man who writes music.

5 Six and five makes ten.
6 Maisie is very pretty, but she uses too much make-up.
7 Cyril spends too much time sitting about in cafés.
8 Of course you will be late, as usual!
9 The characteristic cry of a cat is a loud roar.
10 I'm sure you would like to meet her.
11 You'll have forgotten this exercise by next week.
12 He's forgotten to pay you for his ticket.
13 Why have you forgotten to buy me a ticket?
14 Of course your sister will forget to call for us.
15 A loafer is a man who bakes bread.
16 I suppose I must put on my other shoes for the party.
17 You used to wear a yellow shirt and a green tie.
18 I'll forget to get off the bus at the right stop.
19 I suppose you must be home early tonight.
20 I was here long before you.

19.9
Elementary
DISAGREEMENT
WITH
NEGATIVE

Here we commonly use the auxiliaries, generally with stress, preceded by (*oh*) *but*, or (*oh*) *yes*.

     You can't eat all that! – (Oh) yes, I can.
                        (Oh) but I can!

Notice that *but* is a weak form – [bət].
The teacher reads the statement; the student responds.

           *   *   *

● Disagree with the following remarks:
1 You can't read this.
2 I haven't time to do it!
3 They don't have lunch before one o'clock.
4 You didn't buy any sugar!
5 He won't give it to me.
6 I know you don't like chocolate.
7 I haven't been here before.
8 You couldn't understand a word!
9 You won't see me again!
10 I didn't see you.
11 They're not afraid of you!
12 It wasn't me!
13 I'm not late today.

14   You didn't catch any fish.
15   They weren't all Americans.
16   You can't see from there.
17   He doesn't like dogs.
18   You won't know how to do it.
19   She hasn't given you a clean plate!
20   You didn't pay him for it!

19.10
Intermediate
DISAGREEMENT
WITH
NEGATIVE

See Exercise 19.9.
Remember the opposite of *needn't* is *must*.
The teacher reads the statement; the student responds.

*   *   *

● Disagree with the following remarks:

1   He didn't say a word about it!
2   I'm not a half-wit, you know.
3   He couldn't have seen me!
4   She needn't come tomorrow.
5   You didn't have a very good trip.
6   There used not to be a house here.   (There never used to be . . .)
7   The trams don't run after midnight.
8   Cyril doesn't like you any more.
9   Maisie won't have anything to do with you.
10   You can't eat it all at once.
11   The situation couldn't be much worse.
12   You needn't have given it back to him!   (See Exercise 16.5 for *needn't have*.)
13   I'm not going to bed yet!
14   It can't possibly happen to me.
15   You needn't pay for it.
16   The train never used to stop here!
17   Why have you thrown the best one away?
18   Surely he didn't forget you!
19   I'm sure she won't listen to me now.
20   But really, I can't possibly go any further.

19.11
Elementary
ADDITIONS
TO REMARKS

Affirmative addition is made by using the appropriate auxiliary, introduced by *so*; INVERSION takes place.

John likes fish. – *So do I.*
He must go. – *So must the others.*

● Read the following remarks and add to them, either freely or using the suggestion in brackets:

1   He came early. (I)
2   I like you very much. (she)
3   You can come whenever you like. (your friend)
4   Apples were very dear. (bananas)
5   She knows you quite well. (her husband)
6   He ought to listen more carefully. (you)
7   My friend lives in Chicago. (his sister)
8   A stone sinks. (iron)
9   Watt was an inventor. (Edison)
10 We arrived yesterday. (our wives)
11 Mary could do it. (her teacher)
12 Dogs like meat. (cats)
13 They must do as they are told. (you)
14 The No. 7 bus goes to the Opera House. (the No. 24)
15 Browning wrote poetry. (Tennyson)
16 She must go home. (I)
17 They were late for the concert. (you)
18 Dick wrote me a letter. (his mother)
19 I like sweets. (we all)
20 The potatoes are too salt. (the beans)

19.12
Elementary
ADDITIONS
TO REMARKS

Negative addition is made by using the appropriate auxiliary, introduced by *nor* or *neither*; INVERSION takes place.

He can't read this. – Nor *can I.*
Potatoes won't grow here. – Neither *will roses.*

*   *   *

● Read the following remarks and add to them, either freely or using the suggestion in brackets:

1   Dogs don't fly. (pigs)
2   Dogs can't fly. (cats)
3   He wasn't late. (you)
4   He hasn't any time. (I)
5   These books don't belong to me. (those)
6   These aren't my books. (those)
7   A chair can't stand on three legs. (a table)
8   He oughtn't to make such a mistake. (you)
9   We couldn't remember his name. (they)

10 Water hasn't any taste. (this soup)
11 I haven't any more money. (my wife)
12 Fruit wasn't cheap. (meat)
13 That young man couldn't come. (his sister)
14 John didn't stay to supper. (Henry)
15 I don't believe it. (my friend)
16 Your brother oughtn't to be so rude. (your sister)
17 I have never been to Berlin. (he)
18 This clock doesn't show the right time. (my watch)
19 Animals don't like the hot weather. (I)
20 Joan can't eat fish. (my cousin Tom)

19.13   See Exercises 19.11, 12.
Intermediate
                          *   *   *

● Read the following remarks and make additions to them, either freely, or using the added suggestions:

1   My little brother wants me to help him with his homework. (my little sister)
2   You may want to leave before the concert is over. (we all)
3   Mr White gets up late on holidays. (the rest of his family)
4   The bride didn't turn up at the wedding. (the bridegroom)
5   My friend Maisie drops her h's. (lots of other people)
6   The stupid fellow couldn't answer a single question. (you)
7   She ought to come home before midnight. (her little sister)
8   The first bomb didn't explode. (the second)
9   Moths fly about at night. (bats)
10 You four needn't arrive till five o'clock. (the other two)
11 I haven't seen the new film at the Metro. (any of my friends)
12 This chair needs repairing. (the one I'm sitting on)
13 Fish isn't so dear this week. (poultry)
14 They had none of their meals at the proper time. (any of their friends)

15 Cyril didn't understand any of your jokes. (I)
16 I can't eat any more. (my small brother)
17 The ant works very hard. (I)
18 Jean gave them a beautiful wedding present.
     (James)
19 Alexander was a famous general. (Hannibal)
20 The maid never finishes her work properly. (the
     cook)

19.14
Elementary
CONTRARY
ADDITIONS
TO REMARKS

Here the appropriate auxiliary is introduced by *but*.
        He can read French. – But I can't.

The stress is generally on the SUBJECT of the addition.
Notice that in all these additions to remarks, the added
section may be spoken by the original speaker or by a
second person.

*   *   *

● Read the following remarks and add a contrary statement,
either freely or using the suggestion in brackets:

1   She wants to go to the pictures. (I)
2   We can come tomorrow. (they)
3   I have a lot of time. (he)
4   My wife likes playing bridge. (I)
5   My knife cuts very well. (my friend's)
6   Her dress looked lovely. (she)
7   You were very late. (your mother)
8   The others went for a swim. (I)
9   The king spoke to us. (the queen)
10 Your room is quite large. (mine)
11 I know her very well. (he)
12 He was pleased to see me. (you)
13 I can write with my left hand. (you)
14 Trees grow very well here. (grass)
15 He's a very good student. (you)
16 The door is open. (window)
17 I left early. (my brother)
18 The buses were full. (trams)
19 He always makes mistakes. (you)
20 A cat can climb trees. (a dog)

19.15
Elementary
CONTRARY
ADDITIONS

See Exercise 19.14.

Exercise on contrary additions to negative remarks.

> He can't read French. – But *I* can.

Stress is generally on the SUBJECT of the addition, with strong form of auxiliary.

*   *   *

● Read the following remarks and add a contrary statement, either freely or using the suggestion in brackets:

1 He doesn't understand you. (I)
2 I haven't any time. (he)
3 He won't give you one. (she)
4 Grapes aren't cheap now. (figs)
5 I don't like films. (my sister)
6 He didn't listen to the lecture. (I)
7 You haven't paid me yet. (your friend)
8 A cat can't swim very well. (a dog)
9 She doesn't want to come. (her sister)
10 He didn't thank me. (you)
11 My wife couldn't explain. (I)
12 I haven't seen them. (Henry)
13 You can't play the piano. (I)
14 I haven't done my homework. (they)
15 He won't tell you anything. (I)
16 You didn't hear me. (your friend)
17 He won't leave tomorrow. (we)
18 The forks weren't clean. (knives)
19 I don't speak French. (John)
20 They couldn't see well. (we)

19.16
Intermediate
CONTRARY
ADDITIONS

See Exercises 19.14 and 19.15.

Remember the contrary of *must* is *needn't*; and that *can* (= ability) has *can't* for its opposite, but *can* (= permission) has *mustn't* or less commonly *mayn't*.

> He can swim – but I can't (= ability).
> He can go now – but I mustn't (= may).
> You needn't do it – but I must.
> I must be home before seven – but you needn't.

Stress on SUBJECT of addition; strong form of auxiliary.

*   *   *

● Read the following remarks and make contrary additions to them, either freely or using the suggestions in brackets:

1 Pears are very expensive now. (apples)
2 Dogs can't climb trees. (cats)
3 She always used to get up before seven. (her husband)
4 He can smoke if he wants to. (his sister)
5 You needn't get there very early. (I)
6 They couldn't understand a single word. (I)
7 A small boat won't be safe enough. (a big one)
8 You needn't pay any attention to Maisie. (I)
9 They used to think Cyril was intelligent. (I)
10 The others had a lot of trouble finding your house. (we)
11 The fish must be fried. (the potatoes)
12 The captain could go ashore when he liked. (the sailors)
13 His shoes didn't fit him at all well. (his suit)
14 The student mustn't write in pencil. (the teacher)
15 He hasn't got to leave just yet. (his brother)
16 You're not to stay up so late. (your father)
17 My friends never used to object. (my mother)
18 My husband needn't stay at home. (I)
19 Cabbage ought to be boiled. (tomatoes)
20 The ladies didn't need to go on foot. (the gentlemen)

19.17
Elementary

Introduction to QUESTION-TAGS.

This device is treated fully in Section 32, and the following exercises are merely to acquaint the student with the form, so that it can be used for certain responses.

To turn statements into rhetorical questions (cf. French *n'est-ce pas*, German *nicht wahr*, etc.), in English, the appropriate auxiliary is used as a tag at the end of the remark.

An AFFIRMATIVE remark has a NEGATIVE tag.

> You are coming tomorrow, aren't you?
> He has seen it, hasn't he?
> You know her, don't you?

A NEGATIVE remark has a POSITIVE tag.

> You don't know, do you?
> They won't find it, will they?

*   *   *

(19.17)   ●   Read the following, and add a question-tag:

1 He is French.
2 We are late.
3 They weren't angry.
4 They have two children.
5 You understand it.
6 You'll tell us.
7 He isn't our teacher.
8 I mustn't be late.
9 He can explain.
10 We shall see you tomorrow.
11 You've torn your dress.
12 You came by air.
13 I wasn't long.
14 She has just come.
15 They couldn't do it.
16 Dinner's ready.
17 You've taken it.
18 You needn't go yet.
19 He can have another one.
20 They must come again.

19.18
Elementary
AGREEMENT
WITH
NEGATIVE

A form of question-tag, preceded by *no*, is used frequently here. Notice that the negative auxiliary and its tag both have a falling stress, never a rising one.

    'He wasn't late last time.' 'No, he wasn't, was he.'

A question mark could perhaps be added, but the sense doesn't really demand one.
The teacher reads the statement; the student responds.

       *   *   *

●   Agree with the following negative remarks, using a question-tag:

1 He doesn't understand you.
2 They won't like it.
3 We can't cross the street here.
4 You mustn't spend it all.
5 They couldn't answer any of the questions.
6 You didn't come early enough.
7 We aren't clever enough.
8 He wasn't at the party.
9 It hasn't rained for weeks.

10   We haven't come very far.
11   There isn't enough for us all.
12   We shan't see you till next week.
13   It's not a very big house.
14   The horses didn't run very well.
15   You mustn't put your feet on the chair.
16   They didn't give us very good cakes.
17   Your shoes aren't very clean.
18   She can't sing so well as her sister.
19   This chair wasn't broken yesterday.
20   I'm not very good at English.

19.19
Intermediate

See Exercise 19.18.
The teacher reads the statement; the student responds.

*   *   *

● Agree with the following remarks:
1   He doesn't understand what we're saying.
2   You aren't late today.
3   She hasn't come yet.
4   They weren't all Americans.
5   Such a person shouldn't drive a car.
6   He didn't say anything about it.
7   You mustn't suck your fingers.
8   Maisie usedn't to be so pretty.
9   They didn't have any dinner.
10   John Bull wasn't a real person.
11   Cyril doesn't know you.
12   There was never any talk of such a thing.
13   We can't invite them all.
14   They couldn't possibly have got here before us.
15   Reading a lot of books won't help you to speak better.

19.20
Elementary
AGREEMENT
WITH AN
AFFIRMATIVE

See Exercises 19.5 and 19.6.
A question-tag is also used here instead of *so*, etc.
    'You're rather late.'   'Yes, I am, aren't I.'
Double-falling stress, as in Exercise 19.18.

*   *   *

● Agree with the following remarks, using a question-tag:
1   I'm rather sleepy today.

2   She's very fond of her mother.
3   We shall have to go at once.
4   We've come a long way.
5   That man was at the party.
6   It rained hard last night.
7   There'll be enough for him, too.
8   It's a very large school.
9   They swam very well.
10 You must leave earlier today.
11 They gave us a lovely tea.
12 Your new suit is very nice.
13 This chair has been mended.
14 You can buy some at the tobacconist's.
15 I'm very good at English.
16 You're getting fat.
17 It was very hot yesterday.
18 The apples will soon be ripe.
19 Your mother seemed very cheerful.
20 You'll have to do it all again.

20 Imperative

**20.1
Elementary**

The following is a simple drill, and should be carried out
with BOOKS SHUT. The student should in all cases do as his
colleague bids him. Teach the use of *please* before or after
the imperative.

Imperative drills might well be divided and scattered over
many periods; also combined with PRESENT CONTINUOUS
tense drills. (See Exercises 21.1, 2.)

DRILL. BOOKS SHUT. Students to make the imperatives.

*　　*　　*

● Tell X to:

1   open his (her) book, mouth, eyes, bag.
2   shut ditto.
3   stand in the corner, by me, on a chair, on his head.
4   go to sleep, wake up.
5   take — off his desk, a book from me.

6   push the door, Mr Y, a book off the desk, me into
     the corner.
7   hold a book, Miss Z's hand, up his hand.
8   make a mark on the board, a noise, a noise like a
     cat, pig, fish.
9   talk loudly (softly) to Miss Y.
10   break his pencil, a piece of chalk, a match.
11   tell you the time, the date, the name of the class,
     the teacher's name, his name.
12   meet you at five, at the corner of the street.
13   fall off his chair.
14   fight Mr P.

          etc., WITH OTHER KNOWN VERBS.

20.2   Answer in imperative. BOOKS SHUT.
Intermediate
                              *   *   *

●   Tell me how to:
1   write with a ball-point pen, a fibre-tip pen.
2   light a cigarette.
3   make tea, coffee.
4   fry an egg.
5   take a photo.
6   light a fire.
7   sew on a button.
8   annoy X.
9   bath a baby, a dog.
10   frighten Y.
11   keep well, make myself ill, cure a cold.
12   grow flowers, cabbages.
13   send a telegram, make a trunk call.
14   start a car, a sewing-machine.
15   get to the station, cinema, post office, etc.

20.3   *Don't* + verb stem; introduced by *please* for polite
Elementary   requests.
and   BOOKS SHUT. Students to make the imperatives.
Intermediate
NEGATIVE   *   *   *
IMPERATIVE

●   Tell X NOT to:
1   talk so loudly.
2   put his feet on the desk.

3   copy from the next person.
4   bite his pencil, lips, nails.
5   fold the paper.
6   kick Y.
7   leave the room.
8   talk, whisper, write notes to, annoy Miss Z.
9   point at the teacher.
10 shout, laugh loudly, look out of the window.
11 throw things at me.
12 lend anything to P.
13 think so hard.
14 forget homework.
15 smoke in class.
16 play with pencil.
17 listen to what Z says.
18 look at you like that.
19 look at Miss Q like that.
20 eat in class.

etc., WITH OTHER KNOWN VERBS.

**20.4
Intermediate**

When the verb has some particle with it, this is normally heard at the end of a spoken imperative. For example,

Take your ugly face away!

is more usual than 'Take away your ugly face!' (Though, of course, neither is very polite, even with the addition of *please*.)

* * *

● Say the following imperatives, putting the particle after the object:

1   Put on your coat.
2   Take off your shoes.
3   Do up your buttons.
4   Clear up this mess!
5   Take away these books.
6   Write down these sentences in pencil.
7   Drink up your tea.
8   Cover up your legs.
9   Eat up your dinner.
10 Take out my friend Maisie to lunch.
11 Put back the clock one hour.
12 Read out the message aloud.

13   Pull up all the weeds.
14   Switch on the light.
15   Turn off the radio.
16   Pick up that piece of paper.
17   Wake up my friend Cyril.
18   Put out your tongue.
19   Pour out the tea.
20   Put down your pens.

20.5
Advanced

Emphatic commands with *go* and *come* and adverbs of direction are given added force by inversion.

> Up you come! Off you go!

Notice also the forms

> Off with you! Off with her head! Out with it!

*   *   *

● Make similar emphatic commands with *go*, *come* and *get* combined with the following adverbial particles:

in, out, away, up, down, back, over, off, round, under.

21   The Present Tense

THE REAL PRESENT – INTRODUCTORY DRILLS

21.1
Elementary

The PRESENT CONTINUOUS tense (REAL PRESENT), is a better introduction to the verb than the simple present. The verb *be* is already known, the *-ing* form of the verb is regular, and statements and questions in this tense have immediate practical value. It is obvious that the form *Do you write? Do you catch the chalk? Do you go to the door?* etc. cannot be easily practised, whereas the form *Are you writing, going to the door, speaking?* etc., can.

The elementary drill might well be combined with Exercise 20.1 on the imperative, by practising imperatives and asking about them in the present continuous tense.

ALL BOOKS SHUT.

*   *   *

(21.1)   ● Is X, are you, am I, are we
              writing, reading, standing, sitting, smoking,
              singing, walking to the door, shutting the window,
              opening a book, talking, folding or cutting paper,
              taking or putting something, touching the wall,
              holding something? (and so on with any other
              verbs known to the students).

21.2   BOOKS SHUT:
Elementary
                                          *   *   *

            ● Stand up X. What are you (is he) doing? The same
              with:
              Walk to the door, take Miss Y out of the room,
              eat a sweet, count the students, leave the room,
              stand on a chair, read from a book, write on the
              board, fetch a piece of chalk, bring me a pencil,
              go into the corner, cut some paper (and so on with
              any other verbs known).

              For difference between PRESENT SIMPLE and PRESENT CON-
              TINUOUS see Exercises 21.7–9.

21.3   PRESENT SIMPLE. This tense occurs in speech far less
Elementary frequently than the Present Continuous. It doesn't really
              describe PRESENT action, but something permanent or
              habitual.
              Question-word *when?* cannot be used with PRESENT CON-
              TINUOUS tense, except when this tense is used to express
              immediate future.
              DRILL. BOOKS SHUT.

                                          *   *   *

            ● When do we (I, you, etc.)
              shut books; open books; go to sleep; wake up;
              eat; drink; come to the lesson; go to the pictures;
              feel ill (happy, unhappy); get some homework;
              have lunch; hear the news on the radio; help our
              friends; laugh; learn English; like to eat ice-cream;
              listen to the teacher; lie down; look at the
              blackboard; look out of the window; make a
              special cake; play games; put on our clothes;
              ring a bell; run; say 'Hallo'; see snow; sit down;

walk in the park; want a cup of tea; take our
clothes off; thank a person; think; try to be good;
wash our hands; sing; talk softly; cry

PLUS ANY OTHER VERBS KNOWN.

**21.4
Elementary**

The only inflexion in the PRESENT SIMPLE is the -*s* of the
third person singular, but students of English seem to have
great difficulty in remembering it.

* * *

● Read quickly in the singular:
1 They often **go** fishing and **catch** nothing.
2 My friends **work** in London; they **buy** and **sell** cars.
3 They **sit** at the window and **watch** the traffic.
4 Their little girls **thank** them when they **give** them a
present.
5 Animals **find** shelter when it rains.
6 They **wash** their hands and **dry** them on a towel.
7 They **hit** their dog with a stick when they **are**
angry with it.
8 **Do** these ladies generally go to the theatre on
Saturday evenings, or **do** they stay at home?
9 Birds **build** their nests in the summer and **fly** to the
south in the winter.
10 They never **find** the money they **lose**.
11 The children **play** all the morning and **sleep** in the
afternoon.
12 These apples **are** very green.
13 My friends **like** meat, but **do** not like fish.
14 They **live** in small houses which **have** only three
rooms.
15 His brothers **work** hard all day, and **want** to rest in
the evening.
16 They **get** new books from the library every week.
17 They **have** breakfast at eight o'clock and **eat** their
lunch at half past one.
18 The postmen **bring** the letters three times a day.
19 These chairs **are** very comfortable but they **are** too
expensive.
20 They **want** to buy some toys, because their sons
have a birthday tomorrow.

**21.5
Intermediate**

See Exercise 21.4.   *   *   *

● Read quickly in the singular:

1   They **tell** me that when they **get** home every
afternoon they **have** some food and then **change**
their clothes; they never **eat** or **drink** anything
while they **are** at the office, unless the hot weather
makes them very thirsty.

2   These boys **say** that they always **listen** carefully,
but **do** not always understand their teachers
because they **speak** too quickly and **choose** very
difficult words.

3   Careful students always **put** back the books they
have read before they **take** out others. These girls
come to our library every Thursday and **read** a
book every week; they **like** English and **want** to
learn quickly.

4   Their children **walk** to school every morning and
look for their friends on the way; when they **see**
them they **run** to them and **laugh** and **play** and
enjoy themselves until they **hear** the school bell.

5   Our friends **leave** for Torquay at three today and
arrive there about seven; they **spend** their holidays
there every year and **swim** in the sea or **sleep**
nearly all the time. They **forget** their work, **enjoy**
the sea air and **live** as free as birds. Their
holidays **finish** in August, they **catch** an early train
back to London and **feel** well and happy when
they **return** to work.

6   The boys **wake** up at seven o'clock, **wash, dress**
quickly and **run** into the dining-room for
breakfast. They **wait** until they **hear** the bell and
then **go** to school.

7   These men **go** to work by train every day. They
stay in the train for half an hour and **sit** or **stand**
there and **read** their newspapers. They **try** to read
all the news during the journey and in that way
know a lot about the topics of the day.

8   Two of my friends **hate** reading but **love** to go to

the pictures; such people **lose** a lot of pleasure in
life and generally **get** bored very quickly.

9   These boys **play** in the garden every morning and
usually **break** something or **tear** their clothes or
cut themselves when they **fall**. Small boys **cry** when
they **hurt** themselves, but as they **grow** older they
hide their feelings and **become** less noisy.

10   My friends **tell** me that professors **are** people who
think a lot, but **say** little, and that school-
teachers **are** people who **say** a lot but **think** little.

11   Housewives **have** to work very hard. They **cook**
the meals, **lay** the table and **wash** up, **clean** the
house and **mend** the clothes. Sometimes they also
do the washing and ironing and **look** after the
garden.

12   My friends **go** to the office every day, and **play**
cards every evening. On Saturdays they **go** to the
cinema, and Sundays they **spend** by the river.

13   Dogs **make** better pets than cats because they **are**
more friendly. They **understand** and **obey** their
masters, but cats **like** to live their own life.

14   They **go** to France on business several times a
year. They **take** a train to Dover and **cross** the
Channel by hovercraft. At Calais they **hire** a car,
drive to the place they **want** to reach, and **find** a
good hotel there.

15   Babies **are** a great nuisance; they **need** attention
all the time. If they **do** not disturb you by crying,
they **have** to be fed, bathed or looked after.
They **do** not even thank the people who **take** care
of them.

21.6
Intermediate

The auxiliary verbs (except *do*, *be*, and *have*) take no -*s* in
the third person singular.

*   *   *

● Read quickly in the singular:

1   They **know** English well and **can** answer all my
questions.

2   My friends **do** not understand when they **speak**
quickly.

3 **Must** they leave before supper or **have** they time to stay until my friends **come**?

4 They **may** go to London but they **are** not certain yet.

5 These books **cost** more than my friends **want** to pay.

6 Those ladies **play** tennis well, but they **cannot** swim.

7 Where **have** they been today and where **do** they go tomorrow?

8 When **will** these girls finish the exercises they **were** doing last week?

9 My children **get** up very early and **must** walk to school every day.

10 Little boys sometimes **push** little girls and **pull** their hair.

11 Our fathers **work** in an office and **do** not come home for lunch.

12 They **cannot** speak French and **have** never learnt English.

13 If your friends **are** tired, they **ought** to spend a holiday by the sea.

14 Why **do** they open all the windows and let the flies come in?

15 They **think** that their friends **may** come later.

16 Their teachers **tell** them that they **make** too many mistakes in their homework.

17 If students **read** their homework when they **have** finished it, they **will** generally find many mistakes themselves.

18 They **go** to work by car and **come** home on foot.

19 They **do** not believe her stories because they **know** they **are** not true.

20 **Can** the police find the books they **have** lost?

PRESENT TENSE

**21.7
Elementary**

Make sure the fundamental distinction between the PRESENT SIMPLE and CONTINUOUS is well understood.
PRESENT SIMPLE. Habitual actions and general truths; not necessarily NOW.
PRESENT CONTINUOUS, the REAL PRESENT = NOW at this moment.

*   *   *

● Supply a suitable present tense of the given verb:

1 She (go) to school every day.
2 We now (learn) English.
3 The sun always (shine) in Egypt.
4 I (sit) on a chair and (eat) a banana.
5 Bad students never (work) hard.
6 It (rain) in winter. It (rain) now.
7 I (wake up) at seven and (have) breakfast at half past.
8 He generally (sing) in English but today he (sing) in French.
9 The teacher (point) at the blackboard when he (want) to explain something.
10 Mother (cook) some food in the kitchen at present; she always (cook) in the mornings.
11 The sun (rise) in the east; now it (set) and night (fall).
12 That man in the white hat who (walk) past the window (live) next door.
13 Architects (make) the plans of buildings.
14 I (wear) a coat because the sun (not shine).
15 I always (meet) you on the corner of this street.
16 The baby (cry) because it is hungry now.
17 I (spend) this weekend in Eastbourne. I (go) there nearly every week.
18 'Where are you?' 'I (sit) in the kitchen.' 'What you (do) there?' 'I (help) my mother.'
19 'Why you (wash) those clothes this morning?' 'Because the sun (shine); I never (wash) clothes when there are clouds in the sky.'
20 'Where you (go) now?' 'I (go) to the theatre.' 'I (go) tonight also, but I (not go) very often.' 'I (go) every week, but tonight I (go) for the second time in three days.'

21.8
Intermediate

Remember that *when* is not used with PRESENT CONTINU-OUS, unless it has the sense of immediate future. The answer always echoes the tense of the question.

* * *

● Answer the following questions:

1 Are you eating anything? When do you eat?

2 What are you doing? What am I doing? Do I do this every lesson?

3 Do you dance? Is X dancing?

4 Does Miss Y sing? Is Miss Y singing?

5 Why do you look so sad? Are you falling in love? When did you fall in love?

6 Is that a personal question? Do you answer personal questions? Why not? Am I being rude to ask such questions? What do you think?

7 What are you thinking of? Do you think hard when you do your homework?

8 Where do you live? Do you come here by tram? Do you sleep at home every night?

9 Are you sleeping now? Do you ever sleep in class?

10 Why do I teach you English? Am I teaching you today? Do you teach English? Are you learning any English?

11 What are you doing here? Mr X is learning English too, isn't he? Do you think he learns very much? Perhaps he works harder than (not so hard as) you.

12 Why are you laughing (smiling), Miss P?

13 Do I like correcting your homework? Why not?

14 Are you listening carefully, Mr Z? Do you listen to the questions I ask the other students? Ought we to do that?

15 Do you understand the use of the two present tenses quite well? Are you making notes about them? Do you ever make language notes?

**21.9
Intermediate**

Certain verbs are practically never used in the PRESENT CONTINUOUS, even when describing the real present. These are mainly verbs of condition or behaviour not strictly under human control; consequently they go on whether we like it or not. Take an obvious example:

I *see* a man outside; he *is looking* at me.

Although these are both 'real' present, the verb *see* is not used in the continuous form. I have no control over what I see; I see all the time my eyes are open; but I can decide what to look at, and can change the direction of my gaze from one NOW to the next. Cf. *hear* and *listen to*. (For list of such verbs, see Exercise 21.10.)

Also point out *I am coming soon*, etc., as an immediate future.

*   *   *

● Supply a suitable present tense:

1   Ships (travel) from Southampton to New York in four or five days.
2   John (travel) to England tomorrow.
3   On my way to work I generally (meet) many children who (go) to school.
4   Look, a man (run) after the bus.   He (want) to catch it.
5   It (be) very cold now.   You (think) it (freeze)?
6   The sun (warm) the air and (give) us light.
7   'What you (read) when you are on holiday?'   'I (read) detective stories. Now I (read) *The Shut Door* by Ivor Lock.'
8   'You (hear) anything?'   'I (listen) hard but I can't hear anything.'
9   'I (see) that you (wear) your best clothes. You (go) to a party?'   'No, I (go) to a wedding.'   'And who is the unhappy man who (throw) away his freedom?   You must tell him I (feel) sorry for him.'   'He (speak) to you now!'
10   'You (speak) French?'   'I only (use) a foreign language when I (travel) abroad.'
11   My children (work) very hard.   John (study) for an examination now.
12   Joan (swim) very well, but she (not dive).
13   'What music you (play) next?'   'Sheila (sing) a song by Schubert; she (sing) it very well.'
14   Wood (float) on water, but iron (not float).
15   'You (understand) the present tense now?'   'I (do) an exercise on it at this moment and I (think) that I (know) how to use it now.'

21.10
Advanced
The following list contains the more important verbs that are not usually found in CONTINUOUS tense forms.

> *have* (=possess, own)
> *be* (except in PASSIVE VOICE)
>
> *see, hear, notice, recognize*
> *smell* and *taste* (when intransitive)

> *believe, feel (that), think (that)*
> *know, understand*
> *remember, recollect, forget*
> *suppose, mean, gather (that)*
>
> *want, wish*
> *forgive, refuse*
>
> *love, hate, (dis)like, care*
>
> *seem, appear* (=seem), *belong to, contain,*
>   *consist of, possess, own, matter*

In general these verbs are found in the continuous form only when we wish to give special emphasis to their particular application to this very moment; more rarely as an immediate future. Most of these exceptional uses are more frequent in spoken English; notice in particular the present continuous with *always* or *for ever*, meaning 'at all times, but especially now at this moment'.

> You're always seeing something strange.
> Your mother is for ever refusing to do something or other.

Here are a few more exceptional continuous forms:

> I'm seeing him tomorrow.
> We are certainly not recognizing such a fantastic claim.
> I was just thinking it might be a good idea . . .
> Are you forgetting your manners?
> Are you supposing I'm going to take you out?
> How are you liking it (= enjoy)?
> We are thinking of going out.
> Now you're just being silly.

*   *   *

(21.10)   ● Make sentences using some of the verbs in the list given above in the Present or Past Continuous tense.

22 Notes on English Tenses

FOR THE TEACHER OR ADVANCED STUDENTS
Before proceeding with the tenses, a few notes on the presentation of the English verb system might be appropriate. Students who have been learning English for

eighteen months or more are presumably already acquainted with the English tenses. It is however unlikely that they have any conception of the tense-scheme as a whole, and such students should be shown its general mechanism as a kind of bird's-eye-view revision. More elementary students should gradually be made aware of this scheme as the various new tenses offer points of comparison with those already learnt. Advanced students might also find this very enlightening before they attempt any of the later advanced exercises on the use of tenses.

ASPECT OF GENERAL TIME

English has three main time divisions, PAST, PRESENT, and FUTURE, expressed by the simple tenses. They should be shown as forming three main blocks of tenses, each being subdivided so as to express other aspects within its general time. The PRESENT SIMPLE tense is also used to express eternal truths; it has the least definite TIME ASPECT, as it frequently includes PAST, PRESENT, and FUTURE.

> Man is mortal.
> The sun rises in the east.

ASPECT OF ACTION

Here we are concerned with an act AT THE TIME OF ITS OCCURRENCE. The SIMPLE tenses are used to express such an action, completed in the past, present, or future. The time may be more or less precise according to the time adverb. *I bought a new hat last Thursday*, is clearly more precise than *I bought a new hat last week*. The CONTINUOUS forms also describe the very act, and do so while it is in progress; we are not interested in its beginning or end. So by using the continuous form as a time background, we can make our simple tense actions even more precise. For example, in *I was buying a hat when I first met my wife*, the background of hat-buying (we are not interested in its beginning or end, only in its taking place) marks the exact time of this momentous meeting, an act that was completed within the framework of hat-buying. Compare the following sentences:

> He took my photo while I was having dinner.
> I had my dinner while he was taking my photo.

The first one is the normal arrangement, but the second

suggests either that the photographer is exceptionally slow or that I am a very quick eater.

ASPECT OF FACT

Here we are not interested in the action but in the completed fact and its relationship to a given general time aspect. The PERFECT tenses express this idea. When we say, for example, *I've bought a new hat*, we are calling attention to the present possession of the article and not the previous act of buying. But if I add *yesterday*, I must say *I bought*, because the mention of a past time automatically throws our mind back into the time when the action took place.

The same idea is similarly expressed in the other general time aspects. In the past, *I had bought* + a past moment to bring it into proper perspective; and in the future *I shall have bought* ... by some stipulated point in the future. The form *I have bought* is naturally considered in relation to NOW. This relation to NOW may be real, e.g. *I've read three books since I last saw you* (where the past moment is actually connected to NOW by *since*); or the present interest in a past action may be emphasized by *already, just, not yet*, or *ever*; or we may use this tense when we do not imply any definite time in the past and are merely interested in the completed fact as we know it now. This is probably the commonest form; e.g.

> I've read that book. (= I know what it's all about)
> I read it years ago. (interest in the past action)
>
> Have you done your homework? (= Is it here now?)
> Did you do your homework last night? (= interest in last night's activities)
>
> She has eaten all the cream cakes. (= and now there aren't any left for me)
> She ate all the cream cakes. (Extract from someone's description of a party. He is relating a sequence of events during this well-defined past period of the party; he is interested in the young lady's gluttonous act as it took place and not in the lack of cakes caused by it.)
>
> I've never seen one. (So I don't know what it looks like)
> I saw a pink one in a shop window. (The definite place implies a definite past time)

I've already asked you three times for a glass of
water. (and this is the fourth time)

Perhaps the names Before-past, Before-present and Before-
future might be more reasonable names than PERFECT,
because this name is given to a tense made in the same way
as the English PRESENT PERFECT in many other European
languages. But with most of these languages the distinction
between PAST SIMPLE (Preterite) and PRESENT PERFECT has
been lost, so that we have a confusion that is not possible
in English. The form of the English PRESENT PERFECT is
now commonly used in other languages as a sort of colloquial past, and it is very difficult to stamp out the foreign
student's desire to use the English tense in the same way.
Compare the following random examples, where the
presence or omission of the time-adverb seems immaterial;
in English the tense must change too.

> Je l'ai vu (hier).
> L'ho visto (ieri).
> Am văzut-o (eri).
> Ich habe ihn (gestern) gesehen.
> Viděl jsem ho (včera).

The greatest care must be taken to impress on students
that the PRESENT PERFECT tense belongs to PRESENT TIME
and may not under any circumstances be used on an
occasion notionally defined or implied as PAST.

23 Present Perfect Tense

**23.1
Elementary**

See appropriate remarks in preceding note on English
verb system.

The PRESENT PERFECT is probably the commonest tense in
the English language, but it is the one the student of
English usually finds the most difficult to learn.

Characteristics that a student must eventually grasp:

The three PERFECT tenses (present, past and future)
express the completion or 'perfection' of an action BY a
given time; NOT an act done AT a given time.

The PRESENT PERFECT therefore expresses the completion
or 'perfection' of an action by NOW.

Therefore it is, strictly speaking, a kind of present tense,
because

we are NOT interested in WHEN the action took place, we are only interested in the PRESENT state of completion; i.e. its effect NOW.

So this tense must never be used if we state or suggest a definite time in the past. This is perhaps the commonest misuse of the tense.

Having learnt how to form the tense, the students can practise it in a drill similar to that for the present continuous tense, answering by simple imitation of the question in a natural setting.

*   *   *

(23.1)   ●   DRILL. BOOKS SHUT.

1   John, open your book at page 3.   What have you done?

2   Mary, go to the door.   (To Bill.) Where has she gone?

3   Peter, say to Mary, 'Go back to your place.'   What have you just said?   What have you done, Mary?

4   Mr X, shut the window.   What have you done?

5   (Teacher drops chalk.)   What have I done, Miss Y?

6   (Teacher picks up chalk.)   What have I put on my desk, Mr A?

7   Peter, write your name on the board.   What is he doing, Mr S?   What have you done, Peter?

8   Helen, walk slowly to the window.   What is she doing, Miss Y?   What have you done, Helen?

9   Mr Q, say to Helen, 'Stay at the window.'   What has he just said to Helen?

10   Teacher throws chalk at Mr Z and asks Miss Y, 'What have I just done?'

11   Mr B, read the first three sentences on page 8.   What is he doing?   What have you done, Mr B?

12   Mr P, give Miss T your exercise book. What have you given her?   What has he written on page 1, Miss T?

13   Have you done any homework for me today?

14   Joan, rub out Peter's name.   What is she doing, George?   What have you done, Joan?

15   What are you doing at the window, Helen?   Have you been to the pictures this week, Helen?

16   Mr Z, say to Helen, 'Walk slowly back to your

place.'   What has he just said, Mr X?   What are
you doing, Helen? What has Helen done, Mr Z?

17   Have you seen . . . (name of current film)?
18   Have you read a drama by Shakespeare?
19   Have you ever eaten mangoes?   fish-soup?
     apple-pie?
20   Have we read anything today?   Has Mr Z given
     the chalk back to me yet?   Where is it now?
     Have you learnt anything in this lesson?   What
     have you learnt?

23.2   Short-form answers omit the past participle.
Elementary   'Have you seen him?'   'No, I haven't.'

* * *

● Answer the following questions; short-form answers:
1   Have you been to the Zoo?
2   Have you lived here all your life?
3   Has Miss X read to me today?
4   Have you had your dinner?
5   Have you learnt the Perfect tenses before?
6   Has anyone cleaned the blackboard?
7   Have you done any homework this week?
8   Have you seen a good film recently?
9   Have you been up in a helicopter?
10 What good books have you read during the last
    few months?
11 Have you ever seen a hippopotamus?
12 Where have you put your pencil?
13 Who has just gone out of (come into) the room?
14 Have you bought a new hat (suit, dress)?
15 Have you done any work today?
16 Who has taken my pencil?
17 Have you left any books at home?
18 Why have you brought an exercise book?
19 Has Mr X (Miss Y) understood everything?
20 Have you written down all these questions?

23.3   *Since* and *For*.   *Since* is always associated with a PER-
Elementary   FECT tense. *For* is also used with the PRESENT PERFECT tense
                when it means 'length of time up to NOW'.
                Since denotes 'from some definite POINT or PERIOD in the

past till NOW'. (Time other than NOW need not concern us
for the moment.)
For denotes 'a LENGTH of time till NOW'.

    I haven't seen you *since Monday.*
    I haven't seen you *for a week.*

The difference between *since* and *for* is not made in all
languages (cf. French *depuis*, German *seit*), and the tense
in other languages is usually simple present.

    Je suis ici depuis une heure, depuis six heures et
    demie.
    Ich bin hier seit einer Stunde ... seit halb sieben.

Since and *for* must be constantly practised.

       *   *   *

(23.3)   ●   Complete the following sentences with the given alternatives:

1   I haven't seen you.   **Christmas/three days.**
2   We've been here.   **an hour and a half/January.**
3   She hasn't spoken to me.   **more than two years/last
week.**
4   They have lived in this street.   **1919/the last ten
years/a long time.**
5   I haven't had time to do it.   **I was ill/last Monday.**
6   We haven't bought any new ones.   **a week/ages/
then.**
7   There hasn't been a famine here.   **centuries/the
Middle Ages.**
8   I haven't eaten any meat.   **over a year/I was a
boy.**
9   Nobody has written to me.   **many weeks/my
birthday.**
10   You've asked the same question every day.   **the
beginning of the year/the last fortnight.**
11   You haven't sent me any money.   **last Saturday/
fifteen days.**
12   She has worn the same old dress.   **at least a
month/the beginning of the month.**
13   I haven't spoken Spanish.   **1925/ten years.**
14   I haven't ridden a bicycle.   **longer than I can
remember/my childhood.**
15   It hasn't rained here.   **more than a month/March.**
See also Exercise 23.7.

23.4
Elementary
PRESENT
PERFECT
CONTINUOUS

Sometimes an action, beginning indefinitely in the past, is still continuing at the present moment. This frequently happens with verbs of a static nature, such as *stay*, *wait*, *sit*, *stand*, *lie*, *study*, *learn*, *live*, *rest*, etc. Such verbs are rarely found in the simple PRESENT PERFECT, because by their very nature they continue into the present. So *has lain*, etc. is rare; *has been lying*, etc., common.

If we do not suggest duration from the past, the PRESENT CONTINUOUS is used; but as soon as we imply a relationship between the past and NOW, the PERFECT CONTINUOUS must be used.

> He is lying on the floor. (NOW)
> He has been lying there for three hours. (= and there he is still)
> I'm writing a letter to my friend. (NOW)
> I've written three letters since breakfast. (= completed up to NOW)
> I've been writing letters all the morning. (= and I'm still writing NOW)

*   *   *

● Read the following, putting the verbs into the PRESENT PERFECT CONTINUOUS form:

1 I (live) here since 1928.
2 The cat (sit) in front of the fire since tea-time.
3 I (look) at this picture for five minutes, but I can't see you in it.
4 I'm afraid you (look) at the wrong one.
5 I know you (talk) about grammar for the last half-hour, but I'm afraid I (not listen).
6 You (wait) long for me?
7 Yes! I (stand) here in the rain for half an hour.
8 He (learn) English for three years, but he can't even read a newspaper yet.
9 Nobody has come to see us since we (live) in our new house.
10 What you (do) while I have been out? We (sit) here writing our homework, but it's not quite finished yet.
11 He (work) in the Post Office for twenty years.
12 Lunch is not quite ready yet, although I (cook) all the morning.
13 She ought to stop work; she has a headache because she (read) too long.

14   They are tired because they (work) in the garden since nine o'clock.

15   Look! that light (burn) all night.

We sometimes use the PRESENT PERFECT CONTINUOUS merely to emphasize the fact that an action has been uninterrupted, even though it is not continuing now.

I'm cold because I've been swimming for an hour.
I'm very tired; I've been running round the town all day.

23.5
Elementary
and
Intermediate ●

See Exercise 23.4

*   *   *

Read the following with the verbs in the correct form, PRESENT PERFECT SIMPLE and CONTINUOUS:

1   I (not see) you for a long time.

2   You must tell me what you (do) since I last saw you.

3   He (not be) here since Christmas; I wonder where he (live) since then.

4   I (try) to learn English for years, but I (not succeed) yet.

5   We (live) here for the last six months, and just (decide) to move.

6   You already (drink) three cups of tea since I (sit) here.

7   That book (lie) on the table for weeks.   You (not read) it yet?

8   I (wait) here for her since seven o'clock and she (not come) yet.

9   He (not have) a holiday for nine years because he (be) too busy.

10   Since you gave me your number I (phone) you four times and (not find) you at home.

11   You (be) asleep all the morning?   I (ring) the bell for the last twenty minutes.

12   She (work) so hard this week that she (not have) time to go to the hairdresser's.

13   He (write) a novel for the last two years, but he (not finish) it yet.

14   I (not find) a wife, though I (look) for one ever
since I was twenty.

15   Mary (rest) in the garden all day because she (be)
ill.

23.6
Intermediate   See Exercise 23.4.
and   Notice:
Advanced

He has *gone to* London.
He has *been to* London.

Students are often puzzled by this apparent misuse of the
preposition *to* after the verb *be*. Actually *I have been* must
be considered as part of the verb *go*, an extension of *I have
gone* with the meaning 'I have gone and come back again.'
So

He has gone to London
– and that's where you can find him now
He has been to London
– and so he can tell you what he did there; he
knows London now.

*   *   *

● Read the following, putting the verb in the correct form,
PRESENT PERFECT SIMPLE and CONTINUOUS:

1   John isn't in.   He (go) to the pictures again
although he (be = go) twice already this week.

2   They (not speak) to each other since they
quarrelled.

3   That grandfather clock (stand) there for as long as
I can remember.

4   Cyril (try) to take me out to dinner for the last
three weeks.

5   How long you (learn) English?

6   I (wait) here nearly half an hour for Maisie; do
you think she (forget) to come?

7   My clothes (hang) in the wardrobe all the time I
was away, and now I see the moths (eat) great
holes in them.

8   My watch (go) for three days and it (not run down)
yet.

9   He (lose) his books.   He (look) for them all the
afternoon, but they (not turn up) yet.

10   You ever (see) a live rhinoceros?   You just (look)

at the picture of one I shot in Africa last year.
11 Jack (go) to Switzerland for a holiday; I never
    (be = go) there.
12 He only (write) to me once since he went away; I
    (send) him four letters.
13 She (read) all the works of Dickens and Scott.
    How many you (read)?
14 I (sit) for my portrait for the last six months,
    but the artist (not finish) it yet.
15 You must wake her! She (sleep) soundly for ten
    hours!

23.7
Elementary

Since and *For* with PRESENT PERFECT SIMPLE and CON-
TINUOUS.
Remember: *Since* = from a POINT in past till NOW.
For = LENGTH of time till NOW.

Fuller notes in Exercise 23.3.

*   *   *

● Add *since* or *for*:
1   He has been selling cars — ten years.
2   He has been living here — 1934.
3   I've been waiting — five o'clock.
4   I've been mending your socks — the last two hours.
5   We've been reading this book — last January.
6   We've been studying English — three months.
7   He has been sleeping — seven hours.
8   He has been working — seven o'clock this
    morning.
9   They've been very busy — the last week.
10 They've been living here — last week.
11 I haven't worn this dress — two years.
12 We have been climbing — an hour and a half.
13 She has been teaching in that school — 1968.
14 My friend has been ill — a long time.
15 It has been raining — yesterday morning.
16 I haven't done any work — a month.
17 What have you been doing — yesterday?
18 That church has been standing here — centuries.
19 He hasn't been here — three weeks.
20 She hasn't bought any new clothes — the beginning
    of the year.

23.8   *Since* and *for*. See Exercise 23.3.
Intermediate
                              *   *   *

● Put the verb in a suitable tense and add *since* or *for*:

1   — the last two years clothes (be) very dear.
2   Coal (become) dearer — the end of last year.
3   I (write) ten letters — breakfast.
4   — last year the streets (become) more crowded.
5   'You (see) Cyril lately?' 'Not — three or four days.'
6   'You (take) Maisie out to tea recently?' 'Not — last Wednesday.'
7   I (not see) him — more than a week.
8   'How long you (wait)?' '— half an hour.'
9   'How long that fire (burn)?' '— last night.'
10 'You (wait) long?' 'No, not — long.'[1]
11 That boy (not wash) his face — some time.
12 She (not buy) a new hat — six months.
13 They (stay) at the same hotel every year — five years.
14 They (build) that bridge — several months, but they (not finish) it yet.
15 Poor old Henry (not have) a holiday — the year before last.
16 I (wait) — two hours, but she (not come) yet.
17 She (practise) the piano — six o'clock; I hope she'll soon finish.
18 Although Walter (study) at the University — five years, he (not get) his degree yet.
19 I (not have) a good night's sleep — last week.
20 He (learn) to drive — seven years now, but he still (not pass) his driving test.

FINAL NOTE ON PRESENT PERFECT TENSE

Certain uses of the PRESENT PERFECT, quite natural to an English-speaking person, strike a foreign student as being very odd. One has already been mentioned (see Exercise 23.6). Another oddity rises out of the use of the PRESENT PERFECT for a period of time that is not yet over. We use this tense with *this year*, *this month*, *this week*, etc., because

[1] For *long* = 'a long time', etc., see Exercise 53.2.

the action referred to is automatically brought up to NOW, since the time passes on into the future.

> I've been to the pictures twice this week.
> You haven't done me a single exercise this month.
> Have you had a holiday this year?
> What have you been doing today?

But notice that we unconsciously change the tense with *this morning* or *this afternoon*, according to the time of the day when we are speaking.

> (11.0 a.m.) We've done a lot of work this morning, haven't we?
> (8.0 p.m.) We did a lot of work this morning, didn't we?

A very strong, though unconscious, sense of time is present in English speech, and one of its most important manifestations is in this clear-cut division between PRESENT PERFECT and PAST tenses.

It is, of course, possible to say *I saw him this week* (*some time*), where the speaker is fixing his mind on a definite moment of past time and considering the act at that particular moment; the speaker just couldn't remember the exact day. Also, as a short cut: *I went to the pictures twice last week and once this week*, where *I've been* should be inserted after *and*.

24 Past Tense

**24.1
Elementary
FORM OF
PAST TENSE**

The great majority of English verbs form the PAST SIMPLE TENSE and PAST PARTICIPLE by adding the sound [d], [t], or [id] to the stem – *serve, pass, want*. These are the regular verbs, sometimes called weak verbs.

The irregular verbs, as with most other European languages, include most of the verbs of the highest frequency. Those which change the vowel sound within the stem are often called strong verbs – *swim, break, lead*. Other irregular verbs add [d] or [t] and also change the vowel sound – *hear, sweep*. Verbs of one fairly large class already ending in [d] or [t] make no change – *spread, put*.

*   *   *

● Read the following: (a) in PAST SIMPLE TENSE; (b) in PAST
SIMPLE TENSE, NEGATIVE:

1   I break a cup.
2   It begins to rain.
3   We like oranges.
4   You cut your finger.
5   She comes early.
6   Birds fly high.
7   I lie on the bed.
8   He teaches English.
9   The river flows to the sea.
10 I know his name.
11 You lie to me.
12 The prisoner runs away.
13 He tears his coat.
14 They have a car.
15 We wake up at seven.
16 Your dog bites me.
17 It costs a lot of money.
18 You hide the key.
19 The river freezes in winter.
20 They drink tea every day.
21 I choose a book.
22 The servant sweeps the room.
23 He does his work well.
24 That pudding smells nice.
25 You find your bag.
26 You wear a lovely dress.
27 I say 'No.'
28 Someone steals the money.
29 We ring the bell.
30 You ride a bicycle.
31 The boy throws a ball.
32 The girl catches it.
33 I put the book on the table.
34 Mother makes a cup of tea.
35 She takes a plate from the cupboard.
36 You spend too much money.
37 She tells us a story.
38 I try to be useful.
39 The red light means 'stop'.
40 The little boy falls down.

41   They build a house.
42   The sick man gets better.
43   I eat my lunch quickly.
44   Flowers grow in my garden.
45   The soldier fights the enemy.
46   I want coffee for breakfast.
47   We buy meat.
48   He feeds his horse.
49   She loses her way.
50   A baker sells bread.
51   I bend my arm.
52   We swim in the sea.
53   She understands everything.
54   I see a beautiful tie in the shop window.
55   The wind blows strongly.
56   He thinks hard.
57   I feel ill.
58   We go out every day.
59   The picture hangs on the wall.
60   Her knee hurts her.
61   I use my car every day.
62   We keep our handkerchiefs in the drawer.
63   They meet outside the cinema.
64   He always pays the bill.
65   I play football every Saturday.
66   I read a book before I go to bed.
67   He smokes a pipe after supper.
68   She shuts the door softly.
69   The artist draws a picture.
70   I write letters on Sundays.
71   She lights the fire every morning.
72   You hear a noise.
73   The little boy stands on a chair.
74   She always sits down when she is tired.
75   We let the cat out at night.

24.2
Elementary
PAST TENSE
QUESTION
FORM

She came here yesterday.

  Did she come here yesterday?
  Didn't she come here yesterday?

Notice that most of the second type can be spoken so as
to expect the answer *yes*.

*   *   *

● Read the following: (a) as a question; (b) as a negative question:

1 Jack went to a shop.
2 He bought some eggs.
3 He paid for them.
4 He put them into a bag.
5 He lost the bag.
6 He left it in a tram.
7 Somebody found it.
8 Jack's mother sent him to bed.
9 Mr A rang the bell.
10 A young woman opened the door.
11 She took his hat and stick.
12 He sat down and waited.
13 He looked at the pictures on the wall.
14 He tried to read a newspaper.
15 The young woman came back.
16 She led him into another room.
17 Mr B said good morning to him.
18 He sat down in an armchair.
19 Mr B stood near him.
20 Mr A opened his mouth and shut his eyes.
21 Mr B pulled out three of his teeth.
22 Mr A felt unhappy.
23 A bird made a nest in this tree.
24 It laid five eggs.
25 Tommy saw the nest.
26 He climbed the tree.
27 He held on to a branch with one hand.
28 He took two of the eggs.
29 He put them in his mouth.
30 He needed both his hands.
31 He began to climb down.
32 One of the branches broke.
33 Tommy fell and hurt his arm.
34 The eggs broke, too!
35 They tasted nice.
36 Mr Brown knew Greek.
37 He became a teacher.
38 He taught the boys Greek.
39 They showed him some games.
40 Everybody laughed.

24.3
Elementary
ANSWERING
IN PAST
TENSE

Questions with a question-word demand a complete answer.
Inversion-questions should be answered in short form.

> What did he write? – He wrote plays.
> Did you see him? – No, I didn't.

DRILL. BOOKS SHUT.

* * *

● Answer the following questions:
1 Where did you buy that hat? (book, bag, pen, etc.)
2 How much did it cost?
3 Did you learn English at school?
4 When did you leave school?
5 What time did you get up this morning?
6 What did you have for breakfast?
7 Where did you catch cold?
8 Did you find the last exercise difficult? (hard, easy, interesting)
9 Did you go to the seaside last summer?
10 How long did you spend there?
11 Did our friends go to England by air or by sea?
12 Which of those books did you like best?
13 (Draw a picture.) What did I do just then?
14 How many cups of coffee did you drink yesterday?
15 Did you come here on a bicycle or by bus?
16 When did you last take an examination?
17 When did you last write a letter?
18 When did you last see snow? (the sea, a mountain, me, your own face)
19 When did you last hear some music? (a donkey, the radio)
20 Did you understand the last question?
21 When did you last go to a cinema? What did you see there?
22 Did you learn English here last year?
23 What did you take home to read last week?
24 On what day(s) did you come to your class last month?
25 When did you last drink some coffee? (break something, find some money, ride a bicycle, tell a story, swim, meet your friend, sing a song, etc.)
26 **Collar/Colour.**[1] Did I say 'collar' or 'colour'?

[1] The teacher chooses one of these two words.

27   **Bought/Boat**. Did I say 'bought' or 'boat'?
28   **Call/Coal**. Did I say 'call' or 'coal'?
29   **Pear/Bear**. Did I say 'pear' or 'bear'?
30   **Caught/Coat**. Did I say 'caught' or 'coat'?

24.4   Students should recognize that the answer to a question
Intermediate is always in the same tense as the question itself.
                  Exercise on mixed PRESENT PERFECT and PAST tense
                  questions.
                  DRILL. BOOKS SHUT.

*   *   *

● Answer the following questions:
1   When did you last see me?
2   Where did you write your last homework?
3   What have you done for homework?
4   When did this lesson begin?
5   Did you understand your last grammar lesson?
6   Have you learnt all the English strong verbs by
    heart? (Why not?)
7   What did you drink for breakfast today?
8   How much did that book (pen, pencil, hat, dress)
    cost?
9   Have you lost anything this week? (Have you
    found it yet?)
10 When did you shut your book?
11 Why have you shut your book?
12 Have I asked you to open your books?
13 Where did you buy that lovely tie (dress, hat,
    blouse, pen – those lovely shoes)?
14 How did you come to your lesson last time?
15 Where did you go last night?
16 What did you have for lunch (breakfast)?
17 Have you ever seen a giraffe?
18 Where did you spend your holiday last year?
19 Have you been to the pictures this week?
20 When did you begin to learn English?

25 Frequency or Pre-verb Adverbs

**25.1
Elementary**

Students will probably have noticed that some very common adverbs, usually answering the question *How often?* come immediately before the PRINCIPAL verb of the sentence.

> I often see him.
> I have often seen him.

They come AFTER the verb *be*.

> She is always late.
> You are never to come late again.

The most important adverbs of this type are:

> *often, never, always, sometimes, generally, usually, just.*

See also Exercise 25.2.

Other common adverbs coming in this position are:

> *almost, nearly, quite, hardly, scarcely.*

*   *   *

● Read the following sentences with the given adverb:
1 I go to the pictures (often).
2 I have seen an elephant (never).
3 She is a good student (always).
4 I do my homework (usually).
5 I forget my homework (sometimes).
6 We try to work well (always).
7 We are very busy (generally).
8 My mother goes for a walk on Sundays (often).
9 The buses are full in this town (usually).
10 They have heard of it (never).
11 The student on my left (right) makes mistakes (always).
12 The student on my right (left) answers correctly (never).
13 My friend stays long (never).
14 I am going for a walk (just).
15 She has come in (just).
16 I travel by train (usually).
17 Mary can swim now (nearly).

18   She knows what to say about it (scarcely).
19   I can't understand (quite).
20   The porter was able to carry my luggage (hardly).
21   We have finished this exercise (almost).
22   The children quarrel with each other (often).
23   Her death has upset me (quite).
24   I drink my tea with milk (generally).
25   He gets up before half past nine (never).

25.2
Intermediate
and
Advanced

(1)   Other important adverbs of the type mentioned in Exercise 25.1 are:
ever, scarcely ever, hardly ever, nearly always, seldom, rarely, occasionally, frequently, already.

Ever is used in questions and sentences with a negative modifier or suggestion of doubt.

> Have you ever been here before?
> If you ever come to Spain, you must look me up.

(2)   Adverbs of variable position, like *nearly, only, just,* behave as above when modifying the verb.

> He lent it to me only. (= not you)
> He only lent it to me. (= didn't give it)

(3)   All these adverbs may be used before auxiliaries when emphasizing them.

> Mary is late again. – Yes, she always *is* late.
> Why don't you do your homework in time? – But I always *do* do it in time!
> I never *could* do difficult sentences like these!

(4)   The two auxiliaries taking *to* with the infinite, viz. *used to, have to,* usually have the adverb before them.

> I scarcely ever had to ask him what to do.
> You always used·to agree with me.
> I shall never have to see his ugly face again.

Ought to sometimes behaves as above in spoken English but it is generally held to be slovenly and uneducated to say 'You always ought to get up early' instead of

> You ought always to get up early.

Need to and *dare to* behave as ordinary verbs when used affirmatively.

(5)   When the auxiliaries are used as responses, etc. and imply the full verb they are associated with, they are

spoken with stress and preceded by the frequency adverb
if there is one.

> Do you think we can get something to eat there? –
> Well, we usually can/No, we never can.

(6)   Nowadays *never* is commonly used merely as a re-
inforced form of *not*, e.g. *Never used to*, already referred
to in Exercise 14.3.

> You need never address me as 'Sir'.

And the very colloquial expression of astonishment

> Well, I never *did*! (= 'Well, I never *did* hear any-
> thing like that before!')

*   *   *

(25.2)   ● Read the following sentences, putting in the given adverb:

1   'I have seen a worse piece of work (rarely).' 'I
    have (never).'

2   'Cyril used to call me by my first name (always).'
    'In my opinion he ought to have spoken to you at
    all! (never)'

3   'Were you able to understand mathematical
    problems? (ever)'   'No, I could! (never)'

4   'I've been able to get in for nothing (nearly
    always).'   'I have been so lucky (never); I have
    to pay (always).'

5   I used to have to wait more than half an hour for
    my friend Maisie (nearly always).

6   I've seen you properly dressed (hardly ever).

7   I've met a more ill-mannered man (seldom).

8   You ought to get off a bus when it is moving
    (never).

9   I *do* get off a bus when it is moving (never).

10 He has told me he is in love with me (frequently).

11 He is a little boy (only), but he broke the window
    with his ball (nearly).

12 He isn't late (generally), but he *was* last night
    (nearly).

13 The municipal water-system breaks down (rarely).

14 You can prove it to be true (never) because it
    isn't so (just).

15 None of them had been there before (ever) and
    they wanted to go again (never).

16 Why don't you wear a hat in winter (ever)? You
    did in England (always).
17 I *do* wear a hat in winter (generally).
18 'You ought to write to your mother (always).'
    'Oh, I do (occasionally).'
19 He *does* say rude things like that (always); he
    ought to have been born (never).
20 I had to tell him twice (scarcely ever).
21 'You are to do as your father tells you (always).'
    'I do (always).'
22 I have to do it myself (nearly always).
23 None of you need come (ever) if you have the
    time (so seldom).
24 I should have known the answers (never) if you
    had not whispered them to me (always).
25 He'll have to leave you again (never).

26 Past Tense (Continued)

26.1   *Since* and *for.*   See Exercise 23.3.
Elementary   *Ago.*   Measuring from NOW back to a point in past
SINCE AND   time, it is used with PAST SIMPLE tense.
FOR; *AGO*   For the difference between *ago* and *before* see Exercise
                  29.2, on PAST PERFECT tense.

                            *   *   *

● Put the verbs into a suitable tense:
1 Columbus (discover) America more than 400 years
   ago.
2 I (not see) you for more than a week.
3 I (not eat) caviare since I was in Moscow.
4 Since when (you know) him?
5 How long ago (be) the last moon landing?
6 Old George (not be) here for years!
7 They (come) here a month ago.
8 He (not speak) to me for over three weeks.
9 You (have) a new one every day for the last six
   weeks.
10 How long ago (you arrive) here?

11   We (finish) our supper half an hour ago.
12   She (not have) a holiday for four years.
13   I (not play) the violin since I was a little boy.
14   They (visit) Westminster Abbey a few days ago.
15   My brother (not write) to me for months.
16   My servant (leave) me two weeks ago.
17   I (not see) you since we met a year ago.
18   My youngest brother (get) a new job a week ago.
19   We (not pay) the butcher for over three weeks.
20   I (buy) one like it a month ago.

26.2   *For*, *since*, and *ago*.   See Exercise 26.1.
Intermediate   Remember that *for* is used with the PRESENT PERFECT tense
only when the length of time is up to NOW.

*   *   *

● Complete the following:
1   Our friends haven't been here since . . .
2   Since I last wrote to you, I . . .
3   I finished school in 1965; then for three years
     I . . .
4   For the last five years I . . .
5   At a beauty competition a month ago, Maisie . . .
6   Cyril hasn't ridden a bicycle since . . .
7   Twenty years ago . . .
8   I've been learning the piano since . . .
9   I've been learning English for . . .
10   She has been waiting in the library since . . .
11   Two hours ago I . . .
12   Since I met you I . . .
13   Since last year . . .
14   For two hours now they . . .
15   Seventeen years ago . . .
16   I was very ill last summer, and for two
     weeks . . .
17   Since the beginning of the month . . .
18   For the last ten days we . . .
19   Less than a minute ago . . .
20   I haven't had such an enjoyable time since . . .

26.3
Elementary
PAST
CONTINUOUS
TENSE

When the time of a past action is defined in relation to another action, the one that is a kind of background to the other is put into the PAST CONTINUOUS. We use it to show interest in the action itself as it is actually taking place; we are not interested in its completion.

Compare the following:

> I met him when he crossed the street.
>> – two consecutive acts: he crossed the street and THEN I met him
>
> I met him when he was crossing the street.
>> – the time of 'meeting' is defined as 'in the middle of the act of crossing'

Looked at in a diagram:

TIME LINE

<....was crossing.........was (still) crossing....>

(moment when I met him)

The weak pronunciation of *was* and *were* should be insisted on for the full form of PAST CONTINUOUS; they only take strong pronunciation in short-form responses, etc.

> He was resting all the afternoon. [wəz]
> I was, too. [woz]

*   *   *

● Complete the PAST CONTINUOUS form in the following:

1 I (read) a book when he came in.
2 The sun (shine) when we went out.
3 He (sit) in the garden when the house fell down.
4 When you came in I (write).
5 I came in while he (write).
6 It (rain) this morning when I got up.
7 He (work) all day yesterday.
8 Who you (talk) to in the club last night when I asked you for a cigarette?
9 We (live) in France when the war began.
10 When I arrived at his house he still (sleep).
11 The boy jumped off the bus while it (move).
12 The fire still (burn) at six o'clock this morning.
13 He (walk) across the bridge when his hat blew off.

14   She cut her finger while she (cut) the bread and butter.
15   The bus started while I (get) on.
16   When I (listen) to the radio last night, I heard a loud scream.
17   The light went out while we (have) supper.
18   She finished the housework while she (cook) the lunch.
19   The children (do) their homework when their father came back from the office.
20   I took another cake when you (not look)!

26.4
Elementary

See Exercise 26.3.
Remember that if the actions are consecutive they appear in PAST SIMPLE tense.
This is the same with habitual actions in the past.

> I (always) wear a hat when it snows.
> I (always) wore a hat when it snowed.

The PAST CONTINUOUS is used when we are not interested in the completion of one or more actions, but simply in the fact that they are in progress at the time something else happens.

*   *   *

● Supply suitable past tenses of the verbs in brackets:
1   He (sit) in a café when I (see) him.
2   When I (go) out the sun (shine).
3   The boy (fall down) while he (run).
4   When the war (begin) we (live) in London.
5   The light (go out) while I (have) tea.
6   I (have) tea when the light (go out).
7   My friends (sing) when I (come) into the room.
8   While you (play) the piano I (write) a letter.
9   When I (be) at school I (learn) Latin.   (*To be* has no continuous form.)
10   He (eat) his dinner when I (go) to see him.
11   When my grandmother (go) for a walk she always (wear) gloves.
12   When it (rain) she (carry) an umbrella.
13   She (die) while she (run) after a bus.
14   We (drink) coffee every day when we (be) in France.

15 You (wear) your new hat when I (meet) you
   yesterday.
16 When I (have) a dog I always (take) him out for a
   walk in the evening.
17 When the phone (ring), I (have) a bath.
18 I (lay) the table for dinner while you (wash) your
   hands.
19 When we (live) in that house we (have) three
   servants.
20 Large crowds (wait) at the station when the Prime
   Minister (arrive).

26.5
Intermediate
See Exercises 26.3, 4.
Seeing that in general the continuous tenses are used to
express our interest in the action in progress (i.e. not in its
completion, but only in the fact of its taking place), a
sentence like:

He was reading a book while I was mending his socks.
tells us of two past actions in progress at the same time,
but tells us nothing of their beginning or end. Certain
verbs (Exercises 21.9, 10) are rare in the continuous forms.

* * *

● Put the verbs in the following sentences into a suitable past
  tense; notice where sensible alternatives are possible:
1 I (speak) to her several times, but she always
  (read) and (not hear) me.
2 He (lose) his watch while he (see) the sights of the
  city.
3 He (teach) English for two months when he (live)
  in Germany and (work) as a journalist.
4 I (open) the door just as Cyril (ring) the bell.
5 The house (burn) fast, so we (break) a window to
  get out.
6 Maisie (cook) fish when I first (ask) her to
  marry me.
7 We (walk) to the station when it (begin) to rain.
8 We (run) under a bridge when the storm (break).
9 My sister (drop) two cups while she (wash up)
  last night; neither of them (break).
10 She (put) on her raincoat when it (start) to rain.
11 When the teacher (come) in, the boys (play).

12 The ship (sink), so all the passengers (jump) into the boats.

13 He (think) of something else all the time you (talk) to him.

14 He (eat) three sandwiches while you (talk) to him.

15 When I (see) him, he (sing) and (smoke) a cigar at the same time.

16 Maisie (peel) potatoes when Cyril (ask) her to marry him.

17 The dog (bite) her on the ankle while she (catch) it.

18 While he (get) off the tram, he (fall) and (cut) his face.

19 He (lean) against the door and (listen) to the radio when I first (try) to speak to him.

20 While he (write) a letter the telephone (ring); as he (go) to answer it, he (hear) a knock at the door; the telephone still (ring) while he (walk) to the door; but just as he (open) it, it (stop).

26.6
Intermediate

See Exercises 26.3–5.
The relationship between simple and continuous tenses is often clearer in continuous narration.

*   *   *

● Supply suitable past tenses:

We (enter) Port Said harbour when I (come) on deck. As soon as our ship (come) near enough, a large number of boats (set out) from the shore. We could see that they (bring) money-changers, guides, and men selling all the wonderful things of the East. While I (leave) the ship I (notice) that the rest of the passengers (argue) about the prices in loud voices. I (walk) about for an hour and (watch) the gay street life; men (sell) strange fruits and vegetables, and tradesmen (mend) shoes or (make) carpets in their little shops. I (return) to my ship as the sun (set); the 'market' on the ship still (continue). An old man who (sit) on the deck (offer) me a beautiful Persian rug for only £20. I (talk) hard for ten minutes, and just as the ship (go) I (buy) it for £2. As I (go) to my cabin I (see)

a sailor with a rug like mine. I (ask) him the
price. 'Fifty pence,' he said, 'but I (pay) too
much for it. A man that I (talk) to just now only
(pay) twenty-five pence.' As I (undress) that night,
I (notice) a little piece of cloth which (hang) from
one corner of my rug. On it were the words 'Made
in Manchester'.

26.7
Advanced

See Exercises 26.3–6.
Other uses of the PAST CONTINUOUS.
Repeated actions in the past.

He was always telling me to do things I didn't want
to do.

Reported speech forms.

He is coming this evening.
She said (that) he was coming that evening.

He is going to kill me.
I felt sure he was going to kill me.

* * *

● Put the verbs in the following sentences into the most
suitable past tense:

1 Scenes from the whole of his past life (flash)
through the sailor's mind as he (drown).
2 He (remember) the day he first (go) to school.
3 The other children (go) to their classrooms as his
mother (lead) him into the hall, and everyone
(turn) and (stare) at him.
4 The next thing he (remember) was the face of the
headmaster, who (stand) on the platform.
5 It was a long and stern face, but with eyes that
(twinkle) in a kindly way.
6 Later when he had left school and (look) for a job,
he (meet) a school-friend of his whose uncle was a
merchant seaman.
7 Shortly afterwards he (run) away to sea with his
friend and soon (work) as a cabin boy on the
Saucy Sue.
8 He quickly (discover) that he was expected to do a
good many different jobs.

9   If he (not peel) potatoes, he (wash) up the crockery
    or (scrub) the decks or (clean) the Captain's
    sea-boots.

10 By the time the *Saucy Sue* (reach) New York, her
    first port of call, he (feel) at least ten years older;
    he always (complain) he had too much work.

11 In due course he (marry), and although his wife's
    name was not Sue, he (find) her a saucy thing.

12 She (always nag) him, and she (allow) him no
    peace except when she was asleep.

13 One day, while his wife (stay) at her mother's for
    a weekend, he (run) away for the second time.

14 He forever (grumble) about his fate, and (decide)
    that he was not a lucky man.

15 Like all sailors, he was superstitious, and (feel)
    convinced that something terrible (go) to happen
    to him.

16 He was right, for his ship (strike) a rock and (tear)
    a gaping hole in her side when she (make) for
    America.

17 As the ship (sink) fast he (jump) overboard,
    together with the rest of the crew who were still
    alive.

18 He (cling) to a small raft that (float) in the sea,
    and thus (keep) himself afloat.

19 He (be) bitterly cold, and he (begin) to wish that
    death would come and end his misery.

20 While he (wish) this, a piece of floating timber
    (strike) him on the head, and he was unable to
    hang on to the raft any longer.

**26.8
Advanced**   ● Put the verbs in the following passage into a suitable PAST
    tense form (SIMPLE or CONTINUOUS):

    The afternoon sun (get) low as the Rat (scull)
    gently homewards in a dreamy mood, murmuring
    poetry-things over to himself, and not paying
    much attention to Mole.   But the Mole (be) very
    full of lunch and self-satisfaction and pride, and
    already quite at home in a boat – so he thought –
    and (get) a bit restless besides; and presently he
    (say) 'Ratty! Please, *I* want to row now!'

The Rat (shake) his head with a smile.   But he
(begin) to feel more and more jealous of Rat,
sculling so strongly and so easily along, and his
pride (begin) to whisper that he (can) do it every
bit as well.   He (jump) up and (seize) the sculls so
suddenly that the Rat, who (gaze) out over the
water and (say) more poetry-things to himself,
was taken by surprise and (fall) backwards off his
seat with his legs in the air for the second time,
while the triumphant Mole (take) his place and
(grab) the sculls with entire confidence.

– KENNETH GRAHAME, *The Wind in the Willows*

26.9   ● Put the verbs in the following passage into the most suit-
Advanced   able PAST tense form (SIMPLE or CONTINUOUS):

The gypsies (see) at once that she (be) a little
lady, and were prepared to treat her accordingly.
There was a group round the fire when they
(reach) it. An old gypsy woman (sit) on the ground,
occasionally poking a skewer into the round
kettle that (send) forth an odorous steam; two
small shock-headed children (lie) prone and (rest)
their elbows something like small sphinxes; and
a placid donkey (bend) his head over a tall girl,
who (scratch) his nose and (indulge) him with a
bite of excellent stolen hay. The slanting sunlight
(fall) kindly upon them, and the scene (be) really
very pretty, Maggie (think), only she (hope) they
would soon set out the tea-cups. It (be) a little
confusing, though, that the young woman (begin)
to speak to the old one in a language which
Maggie (not understand), while the tall girl, who
(feed) the donkey, (sit up) and (stare) at her
without offering any salutation.

– GEORGE ELIOT, *The Mill on the Floss*

27 Tense Revision
(Present, Past, Present Perfect)

27.1
Elementary

● Read each of the following sentences twice: first in the PRESENT PERFECT tense, using the first of the given time adverbials, and then in the PAST SIMPLE tense, using the second adverbial.

EXAMPLE

I have cocoa for supper. *always/last night.*
ANSWER 1: I have always had cocoa for supper.
ANSWER 2: I had cocoa for supper last night.

1 I drink tea for breakfast. **always/yesterday.**
2 The class begins at six o'clock. **usually/last year.**
3 His brother lives in Rome. **always/in 1930.**
4 We go to Monte Carlo. **sometimes/for our last holiday.**
5 It rains here. **never/last week.**
6 Miss X buys a new hat. **often/on Monday.**
7 Mr Y pays his bills. **never/last month.**
8 That boy eats too much. **often/at the party last night.**
9 He makes himself ill with ice-cream. **often/yesterday.**
10 The plane starts very early. **always/this morning.**
11 It arrives in the afternoon. **usually/when you were out.**
12 He smokes in bed. **never/when he was ill.**
13 Mother makes a nice cake. **often/for tea yesterday.**
14 She learns quickly. **generally/when she was at school.**
15 These children lose their pencils. **often/at school.**
16 We speak French. **seldom/during Marie's visit.**
17 She shuts the windows. **frequently/when I was out.**
18 Do you write letters? **often/while you were away.**
19 Do you play football? **ever/when you were a boy.**
20 Does the train start at the right time? **ever/before the change of timetable.**

21 Does John forget his books? **regularly/
yesterday.**

22 Do you have coffee after dinner? **always/at the
Smiths'.**

23 He sleeps in the garden. **sometimes/last night.**

24 We don't see a policeman. **often/all last week.**

25 That student doesn't come. **always/last
Wednesday.**

27.2 ● Read the following sentences twice; incorporate the given
Intermediate time adverbials to replace the one in italics in the sentence:
and Advanced

1 He *often* cooks his own breakfast. **yesterday/
every morning since his wife left home.**

2 We are living in the country *now*. **until 1972/since
1972.**

3 The fat lady next door *frequently* practises singing.
**for three hours yesterday/every day since we came
to live here.**

4 Cyril doesn't *often* drink any beer. **at the party
last night/since I first met him.**

5 He was preparing for the examination *last month*.
now/for the last fortnight.

6 I've known all about it *for years*. **at last/days ago.**

7 I was selling a lot of my old books *last month*.
today/lately.

8 You don't often come to see us *nowadays*. **last
year/since you left the district.**

9 Who are you laughing at *now*? **just now/all this
time.**

10 You look like a murderer *in that hat*. **when you
came in with that knife/ever since you grew that
moustache.**

11 *Then* she had to go to the doctor's. **in a minute/
every morning this week.**

12 He has told me that *time and time again*. **two
years ago/every time he sees me.**

13 Maisie was hiding from me *when I called on her
yesterday evening*. **at this very moment, too/for
weeks.**

14 That barber shaves the Prime Minister *whenever*

he visits this town. **before you were born/every day
since he came here.**

15 She *always* keeps us waiting a long time.   **last
night/this evening.**

**27.3
Elementary**
SIMPLE AND
CONTINUOUS
TENSE
REVISION

● Supply the most suitable tense (PRESENT, PAST, or PRESENT
PERFECT):

1 She (go) away every weekend.
2 He (go) abroad last week.
3 No, he isn't here.   He just (go) out.
4 He (go) downstairs when I (meet) him.
5 'Where is Mr Green?' 'He (go) out ten minutes ago.'
6 This boy never (see) the sea.
7 You (see) my bag? I (lose) it.
8 I (see) you yesterday. You (sit) outside a café.
9 He (already write) a lot of letters, but his sister
   (not write) many.
10 He is busy now; he (write) a letter.
11 I (hope) he (get) better now, I (hear) he (have)
   a bad cold all the week.
12 I usually (not take) sugar in my tea.
13 You (see) a good film lately?
14 He (live) in England since 1970.
15 When I last (see) him, he (live) in London.
16 He (sit) in the garden when the storm (break).
17 'You (go) to the cinema last night?'   'No, I (not
   be) for three weeks.'
18 I (hear) the news last night, but I (not hear) it today.
19 'You (read) that book yet?'   'No, I only just
   (begin) it.'
20 I (see) that you (buy) a new hat.   How much you
   (pay) for it?

**27.4
Intermediate**
SIMPLE AND
CONTINUOUS
TENSE ·
REVISION

● Supply the most suitable tense (PRESENT, PAST, or PRESENT
PERFECT):

1 When I (see) him he (sit) asleep in a chair.
2 I suppose you (hear) the latest news : John
   (marry) that horrible Jackson girl yesterday.
3 The sun (shine) for the last half-hour and the
   wind (drop).
4 He (write) a letter now.
5 He already (write) two letters this morning.

6 He (write) a lot of letters yesterday.
7 We (not play) tennis together since last May.
8 I (go) away last weekend.
9 You (see) my fountain-pen? I (lose) it.
10 I (learn) English for the last two years, and now
I (study) Russian, too.
11 When water (boil) the liquid (change) to a vapour
that (be called) steam.
12 He (study) chemistry for three years and then
(give) it up.
13 Cyril never (wash) behind his ears; he (say) the
soap (get) into his eyes.
14 Maisie (paint) her toe-nails and her hair (change)
colour at least three times since last winter.
15 My wife (not come) home yet. She never (come)
home before midnight and last night she (not get)
in till two o'clock.
16 At present he (read) an English novel; it is the
third English novel he (read) this year.
17 When your train (leàve)? You (pack) your bags
yet? Here are some sandwiches I (make) you for
the journey.
18 She never (see) the sea. She (want) to go last year
but she (have) no money.
19 'You (speak) to my sister yesterday?' 'No, I (not
see) her for a long time. I (can) not remember
when I last (see) her.'
20 While I (walk) through the park with Maisie last
night, a man (snatch) her bag from her hand and
(run) away. I (can) not run after him because it
(be) too dark to leave her alone. The police (not
catch) him yet.

27.5
Intermediate
and
Advanced
SIMPLE AND
CONTINUOUS
TENSE
REVISION

● Supply the most suitable tense (PRESENT, PAST, or PRESENT
PERFECT):

1 I (be born) in London but (spend) most of my
childhood in the country.
2 We still (live) there when my father (die).
3 My elder brother (join) the air force when he (be)
seventeen.
4 He (learn) to fly night fighters when the war
(break) out.

5 He (continue) his training for a time, and soon (become) a pilot officer.

6 Afterwards he (fight) on two fronts.

7 I (expect) you (hear) how he (win) a medal for bravery.

8 I once (hear) Tom Jones sing, but I never (hear) Lulu.

9 A few years ago they (pull) down some old houses in that street.

10 Last year they (begin) to build a new block of flats.

11 In my town they continually (pull) down old houses and (put) up new ones.

12 The town (change) its appearance completely since 1968.

13 Two years ago they (call) in an American architect.

14 He already (design) some important public buildings.

15 Now he (prepare) the plans for a new Town Hall.

16 There (be) great improvements in the country too.

17 Until recently there (be) no baths in many of the cottages.

18 Sometimes the roofs (leak) and (let) in the rain.

19 Now they (build) a lot of new workmen's cottages. (Two possibilities.)

20 They already (repair) some of the old ones and (make) them more healthy and comfortable.

27.6
Advanced
SIMPLE AND
CONTINUOUS
TENSE
REVISION

● Supply the most suitable tense (PRESENT, PAST, or PRESENT PERFECT):

1 Lend me your rubber. I (make) a mistake and (want) to rub it out.

2 I (see) you yesterday. You (drink) ginger beer at a café, but you (not see) me.

3 I (go) to Portugal five years ago. Since then I (not speak) Portuguese, and (forget) nearly all I (learn) there.

4 'You (read) *Pickwick Papers*?' 'I (begin) the book last week and just (finish) it.'

5 'I (go) to the Zoo tomorrow. You ever (be) there?'

'Yes, I (be) there last Sunday. I (go) nearly every weekend.'

6   I hear you just (get) married.   When the ceremony (take place)?

7   We (go) to the Valley of Rocks last Sunday. While we (eat) our lunch there a man (fall) from the rocks and (hurt) his head.   We (take) him to the hospital in our car, and (be) to see him twice since then.   He (get) better now.

8   'Hello, who you (bring) with you? He (have) supper yet?'   'No, he (not have).'   'We usually (have) supper at eight, but Mary (not finish) yet.   She still (eat) in the dining-room.   He (not meet) Mary, and she (not know) him, so take him in, introduce him and give him something to eat.'

9   'What you (look for)?'   'I (lose) my purse near here and (want) to find it before it (get) dark.'   'When you (lose) it?'   'I think that I (drop) it when I (go) to school this morning.'

10   'I (look) at your photographs while you (be) out.'   'You (like) them? They (be) not very good.'

11   As he (run) to jump over the ditch, he (fall) and (twist) his ankle.   We (have) to carry him home. He now (lie) on the sofa, and he (read) a book until a few minutes ago.   The doctor just (leave) and (say) as he (go) out that he must rest for a week.

12   'You (like) chess?'   'Yes, but I (not play) for many years.   I (live) with a good chess player for the last six months, but he (play) extremely well and I (not wish) to play with him.'

13   'We (wait) here for half an hour now, so I (not think) she will come.   She always (arrive) late, or you (think) something (happen) to her?'   'I (not know), but I (think) we (wait) long enough.'

14   You (remember) my name, or you (forget) it?

15   Look!   My socks already (wear) out at the heels, even though I (wear) two pairs at once these last few weeks.

28 The Future and Future Perfect

PRELIMINARY NOTE ON THE FUTURE FORMS

Consider the following sentences:

> She is going to know in a minute.
> You are taking your medicine every three hours!
> I'm going to come with you if you like.
> Sometimes the baby's going to cry for hours on end.
> I shall go at once because I can see you will be rude to me.
> Am I going to leave without paying?
> Will you leave without paying?

All these seem to be grammatically correct, but they would all sound wrong, or at best, unnatural in most contexts. Why? The problem of choosing the correct and natural future form is a very vexing one in modern English. The usual grammar-book rules for *shall* and *will* are already antiquated; even the increasingly popular *going to* sounds out of place sometimes, although wishful thinking has tried to make it the solution to all problems; and modern English uses *is doing* and *will be doing* very subtly. The ousting of *shall* and *should* (except in questions) by *will* and *would* is bringing about some simplification of speech and writing. Even *will I?* and *will we?* are frequently heard even in England. But custom has not yet decided in all cases, so that while different forms sometimes give a different sense, at other times no difference can be detected between them.

> He'll buy one if you ask him. (indefinite)
> He's going to buy one. (intention)

But there seems to be little difference between these:

> He won't buy it unless it's cheap.
> He's not going to buy it unless it's cheap.

In the following section on the expression of the FUTURE, some attempt has been made to analyse the customary speech-forms of well-educated people in natural conversation. The preference for particular forms in particular mental situations is noticed, and the exercises try to make these prominent. Notes and examples have had to be copious, and teachers and advanced students should go through them carefully.

Two golden rules have emerged:

1 Beware of the innocent-looking *going to* form.
2 When in doubt use *will*.

THE FUTURE

28.1
Elementary

Going to as a future form.
This is probably one of the commonest ways of expressing futurity in both spoken and written English. It is NOT a pure future. (See notes to Exercises 28.4–6.)

DRILL. BOOKS SHUT.

* * *

● Answer the following questions:
1 What are you going to do now?
2 When are we going to finish this book?
3 When is Mr X going to start work?
4 What are you going to do after the lesson?
5 Where are we going to keep the chalk and duster?
6 When are you going to have your next English lesson?
7 Ask X if he (she) is going to watch TV tonight.
8 Are we going to read *Treasure Island*?
9 Ask Y if he (she) is going to walk home or take a bus.
10 What are we going to have for dinner?
11 When are you going to fill your pen again?
12 Are we going to have a conversation lesson today?
13 When are we going to have another party?
14 What are you going to have for supper tonight?
15 When are you going to write to me?
16 Where are you going to spend your next holiday?
17 How much are you going to give me for this new book?
18 What are you going to do this weekend?
19 Are you going to visit anybody tomorrow?
20 When are we going to meet again?

28.2
Elementary

Normal pure (or uncoloured) future is expressed by *shall* (first person), *will* (other persons), plus verb stem. It must be understood that when talking about people, the possibility of wish, will, promise or intention is always likely to be present. The purest futures are the least personal ones, especially when the future action is made to depend upon some external factors, as with *if* or *when* clauses.

Except in questions, the *will* form is very commonly heard for all persons.

The SOUND-SIGN of futurity is — *'ll* + verb stem. Except as the first or last word of the utterance, the auxiliary *shall* for the pure future is usually pronounced [ʃl].

DRILL. BOOKS SHUT.

● Answer the following questions:

1   Will you have time to do an exercise this week?
2   When will it get dark this evening?
3   Will X come to the cinema with me if I ask him/her?
4   When will you be here again?
5   How'll you get home?
6   Will you come here again next week?
7   Will you soon know English very well?
8   Will you remember these sentences next lesson?
9   Shall I see you next lesson?
10 How will you come to your next English lesson?
11 When will you do me another exercise?
12 Will you be here tomorrow?
13 When shall we see you again?
14 Shall I have time to write a letter before the end of the lesson?
15 Where will you go after the lesson?
16 Will there be a class next Thursday?
17 Will the shops be open at 8 o'clock tomorrow morning?
18 Will they still be open at 10 this evening?
19 Will they be open on Saturday afternoon?
20 Where will you be at midday tomorrow?
21 How long will your friends be here?
22 Do you think the lesson will last much longer? No, it . . .
23 How long do you think it'll last?

24 Will there be an important match this week?
25 What will you do this weekend?

**28.3
Elementary**

Must has future *shall* or *will* + *have to*; *can* has future *shall* or *will* + *be able to*.

But see also earlier exercises on *must* and *can*.

The following exercise is on the *shall/will* future, although some of the sentences might just as well be made with the *going to* future. Notice where *going to* is awkward or inappropriate, especially Nos. 4 and 15, *understand, know*. We found in Exercises 21.9, 10 that certain verbs avoid the continuous forms, probably because they are 'automatic' verbs that can scarcely be called into action at any given moment. Similarly it would be difficult to have any 'intention' regarding them, so that special circumstances are needed to make *going to* possible with them.

> I shall know from his next letter.
> I'm going to know the answer before I let you go.

* * *

● Put the following into the FUTURE SIMPLE tense; use the short form in negative sentences:

1 We always ask that question.
2 You never answer me correctly without the help of the book.
3 I never believe you.
4 You don't understand it.
5 I don't buy cheap things.
6 He never cleans his own shoes.
7 It doesn't cost very much.
8 We don't do any homework in the class.
9 Why doesn't she drink her cocoa?
10 I eat an orange every day.
11 He feels ill.
12 I never have much money.
13 You grow fatter every day.
14 It doesn't hurt you.
15 I know the answer now. (Tomorrow . . .)
16 He can swim. (After six lessons . . .)
17 I never look as pretty as her.
18 You must work harder.
19 I must read more books.
20 He doesn't like it at all.

28.4
Intermediate

Shall/will and *going to*.   See previous Exercises.

Shall/will expresses pure futurity, hence is almost always found when the futurity depends on external circumstances, and not on any person's will or intention.

Try *going to* in these three sentences:

If you go with him, he'll give you a new one.

If you ever go to China, you'll see some queer things there.

You'll always find a welcome here whenever you call.

As a simple affirmative statement of intention, with no external circumstances (time, condition, reason, etc.) mentioned, the *shall/will* future tense is rare; where the futurity depends on the external circumstances, *going to* is rare.

He will sell his house. (rare)
He's going to sell his house. (normal)

He'll sell it if you ask him. (normal)
He is going to sell it if you ask him. (rare)

She'll know the answer. (normal; automatic verb, see notes to Exercise 28.3)
She is going to know. (rare)

The *going to* form is consequently rarely found when other clauses are present, because here the intention of a person is no longer important; it is a pure notional future depending on external circumstances.

More details about *going to* come in Exercises 28.5 and 28.6.

*   *   *

● Read each of the following sentences twice, referring to the future: first in *shall/will* form, and then in *going to* form. Replace the time expression in bold type by a future time expression if necessary.

EXAMPLE

He has *just* finished it.
ANSWER 1: He'll finish it next week.
ANSWER 2: He's going to finish it next week.

1 My sister cleaned my room **yesterday**.
2 We've **already** climbed the mountain.
3 They came here **last year**, didn't they?
4 It didn't cost so much **a week ago**.
5 He cut you a bigger piece of cake **last time**.
6 They didn't do any business with us **in 1970**.

   7   Prices have gone up **during the last few weeks**.
   8   Did he take you with him to the Zoo **last time**?
   9   I have been very busy **today**.
10   He had a tooth pulled out **yesterday**.
11   He looked for you at the party **last night**.
12   Cyril hasn't shaved **since yesterday**.
13   I saw the queen **three days ago**.
14   We took our examinations **in 1972**.
15   Did we go out **yesterday afternoon**?
16   He stayed at home **till six o'clock**.
17   They haven't paid me **since March**.
18   Did Maisie know what to do?
19   Have you written to him **since**?
20   We didn't have time to see them all.

In most of these *going to* sounds better. Why? Why not in No. 18?

28.5
Elementary

See previous exercises and Exercise 28.6.
Going to.   Notice that *going to* does not normally express simple futurity, but colours the future with INTENTION or a FEELING OF CERTAINTY in the mind of the speaker.

> He's going to write to me every week.
> I'm going to climb to the top.
> She's going to have a baby.

(A *shall/will* form would be out of place in these.)
That is why *going to* is more usual with persons than with things. Note use of *going to* in PASSIVE VOICE, where intention or certainty of the agent is implied:

> This room is going to be cleaned.
> All these trees are going to be cut down soon.

*   *   *

● Change the following sentences into the *going to* form of future:

1   He will leave tomorrow.
2   Where will he stay?
3   John will wait for us there.
4   We shall write letters all the afternoon.
5   He will lend me the money.
6   We shall eat them all.
7   The judge will ask you a few questions.

8 My father will build a new house.
9 We shall choose some new dresses.
10 I'm afraid it will cost a lot of money.
11 They will grow beans in their garden.
12 Mr Thomson will sell his house.
13 I'll sing it again this evening.
14 We'll work harder next year.
15 He'll speak to us about it.
16 The dining-room will be painted next week.
17 I shall have three weeks' holiday this year.
18 They will learn Russian.
19 That house will be pulled down soon.
20 I think I shall be sick.

**28.6
Intermediate**

Going to.   There are many people who assert that this is the PURE FUTURE in English. Careful analysis of sentences with this form and *shall/will* form usually shows this to be untrue. There are instances when it MAY be so used, mostly in certain negatives, but the fundamental meaning seems to be as follows. (Try the effect of changing the forms round, and notice which is the natural one.)

WITH PERSONS: *going to* has the meaning of INTENTION or CERTAINTY.

He's going to give me a new one tomorrow.
If you go with him, he'll give you a new one.

So you're off to China, are you? Well, you're going to see some queer things there.
If ever you go to China, you'll see some queer things there.

Surely you aren't going to put him to bed so soon?
If you want to come in for a chat, I'll put him to bed early.

I'm going to drink a glass of water.
I think I'll have a glass of water. (Cf. Exercise 28.5, No. 20; inevitably!)

You won't speak English well unless you go to England.
He says he's going to speak nothing but English when he goes to England.

Shall I leave without paying?
Are you going to leave without paying?

I wonder when he'll do it; I know he's going to.
I wonder when he's going to do it.

I'm going to give you one of these pills.
You'll take one of them every three hours!

WITH THINGS: *going to* has the meaning of probability or inevitability IN THE MIND OF THE SPEAKER.

This bus will take you to George Street.
Look out! The bus is going to overturn!

What's going to happen next?
What'll happen if you light the wrong end?

If there's a slump, things will get much dearer.
Now that there's a slump, things are going to get much dearer.

Malted milk will do you good. (It says so on the tin.)
This lovely malted milk is going to do you good. (I feel it in my bones.)

What time will the sun rise?
The sun's going to shine in a minute. (The cloud has nearly gone.)

It will rain. (Sense incomplete; no meaning.)

It's going to rain. (It seems so to me because I can see a storm coming up.)
As soon as the depression off Iceland gets further south, there will be a belt of rain across southern England.

This book will tell you all about it.
This book's going to be more difficult than I expected.

Notice that these differences, which are more clearly defined with persons than with things, are much less marked in the negative. *Shan't*, *won't* and *not going to* are more easily interchanged than their affirmative counterparts.

I'm afraid I shan't have time to finish it. (OR: I'm not going to)
I hope you're not going to buy any blue ones. (OR: you won't)

It is clear that no hard-and-fast rule can be given, as the difference is notional, not grammatical. In many cases either form is POSSIBLE, but the meaning will not always be the same.

*   *   *

(28.6)   ● Change the following sentences into the *going to* form of future:

1   She'll be married this spring.
2   The strong man will lift all these weights above his head.
3   I'll practise the violin all the afternoon.
4   I know you will like my music.
5   What! You won't come home this afternoon?
6   I won't be treated like that!
7   You won't get a ticket for my next concert.
8   Cyril will walk home with me tonight.
9   Maisie will sew on my buttons for me.
10   The sun will shine in a minute.
11   I won't spend a penny more.
12   Will you be gone long?
13   Won't you kiss me 'good night'?
14   He'll give me a present for my birthday.
15   I think I shall have a cold.
16   There will be a storm soon.
17   Won't you have something to drink?
18   We shall get a new gardener today.
19   He will cut the grass this afternoon.
20   I shall buy some cream cakes for tea.

28.7
Elementary
PRESENT
CONTINUOUS
FOR FUTURE

Like *going to*, the PRESENT CONTINUOUS can express a definite future, and its time is fairly immediate.

We're going to the pictures this afternoon.
She's buying a new one soon.
They're playing some Beethoven next.

This form is scarcely ever used with THINGS, or with verbs of Exercise 21.10..

*   *   *

● Put the following into the immediate future of the PRESENT CONTINUOUS:

1   We shall start strong verbs on Monday.
2   He'll come to see me the day after tomorrow.
3   We shall set out at two o'clock.
4   She will invite seven other people.
5   I shall take her to the Zoo this afternoon.
6   Will you stay at home tonight?
7   They will see to it tomorrow.

8 I'll play tennis this afternoon.
9 He will use it again tomorrow.
10 The children will have cakes for tea today.
11 She will leave by the three o'clock train.
12 He'll give us a new one next week.
13 I shall take the examination on Friday.
14 She will sing a group of songs next.
15 We shall go out at seven.

28.8
Elementary
FUTURE
CONTINUOUS

The simplest use of the FUTURE CONTINUOUS tense is like that of the other continuous forms.

> When I get back, they'll be having supper.
> (in progress at a given future time)

Compare with:
> They are having supper NOW.
> When I GOT back, they were having supper.

* * *

● Using the given future time adverbial, read the following:
1 What are you doing? **in ten years' time**
2 He is sleeping **at four o'clock**
3 She is doing her homework **after supper**
4 It's raining **when you come back**
5 I'm still mending the chair **at seven o'clock**
6 She is talking **for at least another three hours**
7 I'm waiting for you **at the usual time**
8 We're listening to you **at the concert**
9 She's making tea **about then**
10 He's travelling **all night**
11 I'm doing the washing **tomorrow morning**
12 They're studying English **from 6 till 8**
13 He's writing to her **at tea-time**
14 You're swimming in the sea **this time next week**
15 We're working very hard **in the autumn**

28.9
Intermediate
FUTURE
CONTINUOUS

See Exercises 28.7 and 28.8.
Just as the PRESENT CONTINUOUS is used as a definite immediate future, so the FUTURE CONTINUOUS is used as a definite but not-so-immediate future.

> He's playing a violin solo next. (OR *going to*)
> He'll be playing some more later. (OR *going to*)

He's seeing him at once. (OR *going to*)
He'll be seeing him in a few minutes. (OR *going to*)

*   *   *

(28.9)   ● Restate the following, using the FUTURE CONTINUOUS:

1 I'm seeing him tomorrow.
2 They're going to do it again later.
3 He is leaving in a few days.
4 The leaves are going to fall soon.
5 She says she is going to do the washing
  tomorrow.
6 I'm going to have tea in town.
7 I'll write to you later.
8 He's going to meet us at the station.
9 We're going to have crab for supper.
10 You'll hear from Maisie in any case.
11 Are you going to town again this week?
12 We're having coffee after dinner as usual.
13 He's coming home soon.
14 I'm playing in a table-tennis match on Saturday
   with Cyril.
15 He is lecturing on the seventeenth-century poets
   next.
16 We are having dinner in half an hour.
17 I shall see her tomorrow afternoon.
18 You're going to learn more about this tense next
   lesson.
19 Hurry up! the train is leaving in a minute.
20 You'll forget your head next, you absent-minded
   old thing!

28.10
Intermediate
and
Advanced
CONTINUOUS
FUTURE FORMS

He is going to do and *he'll be doing* have approximately
the SAME MEANING, but the different grammatical form
gives a DIFFERENT FEELING to each.
In the sentences:

(*a*) They are going to put on another play (soon).
(*b*) They'll be putting on another play *soon*.

(*a*) tells us the PRESENT intentions of the actors, (*b*) tells us
of events at a future time, *soon* (which MUST be understood); it tells us of the RESULTS of the intention, but by-
passes the intention itself.
From this we get the following second-person question-
forms:

(*a*) Are you going to put on another play soon? (Direct question about intentions.)

(*b*) Will you be putting on another play soon? (The intentions themselves are by-passed and the question concerns future activities. This is more of a pure future, more remote, and therefore more polite.)

(*c*) Will you put on another play soon? (A request: please do so; we've enjoyed this one.)

The form in (*b*) is the modern equivalent of the older '*Shall you* put on another play soon?' (Is it in your prearranged programme?)

*   *   *

● Turn the following into politer[1] questions by using the FUTURE CONTINUOUS form:

1   Are you going to use this spoon?
2   Are you going to need me any more tonight?
3   Are you going to stay here long?
4   Are you going to want any more like this?
5   When are we going to see you again?
6   When are you coming again?
7   What are you going to have for breakfast?
8   When are you going to post your letters?
9   When are you going to have the house painted?
10   When are you going to try the new ones?
11   When are you going to go away?
12   When are you going to have your next lesson?
13   When are you going to want your heater
     turned on?
14   How are you going to get back?
15   Where are you going to stay in Paris?
16   Are you going to spend much more time here?
17   Are you going to make any more cakes like these?
18   Which school are you going to send him to?
19   Are you going to pay for it yourself?
20   Are you going to have a haircut tomorrow?
21   Are you going to stay out all night again?
22   Do you require anything else?

---

[1] But politeness, in English, is very much more a matter of intonation than of words and syntax. A faulty intonation may make the 'politer' form less courteous than the less elaborate form.

23   Where are you spending your honeymoon?
24   When are you going back to college?
25   Are you going to visit Mary again this week?

28.11
Advanced

See Exercise 28.10.
Look at the two forms:

Will you come tomorrow? + *please* etc.
  – a request
Will you be coming tomorrow?
  – no request: a query about the future activities of
  the person addressed

*   *   *

● Make questions from the following statements in TWO
ways: first making a request; then as a polite query on the
statement.

EXAMPLE

You are going to see him tomorrow.
ANSWER 1: Will you (please) see him tomorrow?
ANSWER 2: Will you be seeing him tomorrow (by any
chance)?

1   You are going to do the washing tomorrow.
2   You will come to see me soon.
3   You are going to see to it this evening.
4   Use this one!
5   You are going to have an early breakfast.
6   Have the house painted white!
7   You are going to do it again.
8   You will make all the arrangements.
9   Look after the baby for her!
10   You are going to post these letters soon.
11   Have another one!
12   You are going to keep your luggage in the spare
room.
13   Light a fire in the sitting-room!
14   You are going to have tea soon.
15   You will phone the grocer this morning.
16   Write to her again!
17   You are going to take the dogs for a walk.
18   You are going to the post office today.
19   You are going to have some more coffee.
20   Make a cake for tea.

28.12
Intermediate
COLOURED
FUTURE WITH
will/shall

Will used with first person colours the future with the speaker's intention or promise. But as most of our first person futures are presumably honest intentions, we find that *will* or *'ll* is one of the commonest future forms for all persons.

Shall with other persons colours the future with promise, compulsion or (in negative) restraint. It is not such a commonly used form as grammar books would suggest, its place more frequently being taken by a FUTURE SUBSTITUTE (see Exercises 28.14, 15).

> I won't forget what you've told me. (promise)
> You shan't leave till you promise to come again. (restraint)
> You shall have it back tomorrow. (promise)
> I'll begin again, and you shan't stop me this time.
> He shall never come here again!

And notice, too, the use of *will* when asking for someone's co-operation:

> If you'll wait here a moment, I'll fetch a chair.
> – not to be confused with true condition

* * *

● Use *shall* or *will* in the following sentences:

1 You — not go until I know the truth.
2 You — have a piece of chocolate if you're good.
3 If you — look after the luggage I — buy the tickets.
4 You — have some more in a minute.
5 I'm determined he —n't come here again.
6 — you have a drink? What — it be?
7 I — see to it myself. You —n't pay a penny.
8 You — have a bicycle of your own when you're older.
9 '— you have tea or coffee?' 'I — have some tea, please.'
10 Members — not introduce more than three guests on any day.
11 'Britons never, never, never — be slaves.'
12 I promise you that you —n't lose by it.
13 If he —n't mend that stove, I — have to do it myself.
14 He — have what he asks for, but *you* —n't.
15 — you lend me £1 (a pound)? I — pay you back tomorrow.

28.13
Advanced

See Exercise 28.12 on the *will/shall* future.

* * *

● Use *shall* and *will* in the following sentences, noticing where either is possible:

1   I —n't go to the tea-party unless *you* come with me.
2   I — come with you if you want me to.
3   — you? That's grand!
4   But let me warn you: I —n't stay any longer than an hour or so.
5   That's all right. I —n't stay any longer myself.
6   — there be many people there we know?
7   I can't tell you, but if Tom and Harry decide to go, we — know at least two people.
8   Tom is not the sort of person that enjoys tea-parties, but his mother seems determined he — go.
9   Poor Tom! I'm sure he —n't enjoy himself a bit.
10 Harry, on the other hand, — be in his element.
11 You're right. He — chatter to all the old women and flirt with all the pretty girls.
12 I'm glad you said 'pretty' girls. He —n't look at anyone who's not pretty enough to go on a chocolate-box.
13 Which reminds me: Anne — be there.
14 Why didn't you say so before? Now I know that, I — certainly come with you.
15 Good. By the way, when — Anne be taking her examination?
16 I don't know. · We — probably find out tomorrow when we see her.
17 She's an undecided sort of person, isn't she? Her lecturer should say to her, 'You — take this examination next June, whether you want to or not.'
18 Quite right. People like Anne — only do things they are made to.
19 — there be any dancing after tea? If there is, I might take along with me a record of the old dance-tune, '— we dance the Polka?'
20 Please do. And we — make a point of being there

punctually, so that Tom and Harry —n't say we've let them down.

FINAL NOTES

More advanced students frequently ask why we have both *shall* and *will* (and similarly *should* and *would*), so the following brief historical notes may be of interest.

Originally English had no separate future tense, and used the SIMPLE PRESENT instead. This is still an idiomatic way of expressing futurity in a vivid and flamboyant way, but, apart from a few stock phrases like *The train leaves at 6.30*, it is not very common; and these few stock phrases are often examples of the habitual present, and not futures at all!

There was also a form of the verb *shall*, with the meaning of command, compulsion or obligation; and a form of the verb *will* meaning 'want' or 'wish'. From these developed a PURE FUTURE tense, for both these ideas carry an idea of futurity with them.

But why choose *I* (*we*) *shall* and *you* (*he, they*) *will* for the PURE FUTURE?

Shall originally meant 'command', but as we so seldom need to give ourselves orders, its original force grew weaker in the first person and so became the natural word to use for a future with no particular colour or emphasis. Similarly *will*, meaning 'wish', is obviously sensible with *I* or *we*, but it is not easy to talk about other people's wishes, so in the second and third persons *will* has become the natural auxiliary for an uncoloured future. One should of course notice that the question *Shall I?* still implies 'Is this your command?' and *Will you?* generally has its original meaning of 'Do you wish?' (See also Reported Speech Exercise 51.9.)

There is a growing tendency for *shall* and *should* to be used less in the first person; this is partly due to the natural association of 'wish' or 'want' with a first person future : if I mention my future actions, it is highly probable that my own volition is brought into play regarding them ; and so *I'll* is used quite naturally in statements. The increasing popularity of *will/would* owes something also to the natural desire for uniformity and easily spoken short forms, even to the extent of sacrificing some of the finer grammatical niceties. In some parts of the English-speaking world, notably Ireland, Scotland and parts of America, the use

of *will* is almost universal, even in first person questions –
*What'll I do? Will I be seeing you? We'll have better
weather soon, I'm thinking.* But we still feel the need sometimes of distinct forms of VOLITION, etc., and PURE FUTURE.
This has helped to bring about the popularity of other
unmistakable ways of expressing FUTURE TIME (*going to*),
VOLITION (*want, wish, intend, mean, choose,* etc.), or
OBLIGATION (*have to, am to, ought to*). (See Exercises
28.14 and 28.15.)

There are apparent exceptions to the *will/shall* coloured
future in the petulant expression *Shan't* and in the military
use of *will* in such orders as

> Officers will appear properly dressed in public places.
> Flags will be flown in honour of His Excellency's
> arrival.
> Evening dress will be worn.

Perhaps there is a feeling that nothing can be more definite
than the statement of a plain future fact – there is a feeling
of the inevitable about its use in the above examples.

SUMMARY

Will and *would* are becoming increasingly popular for all
persons in simple statements: they form contractions as
'll and *'d.*

Shall and *should* are still used where it is necessary to avoid
confusion. Look at the following interesting passage and
notice how clearly *should/would* forms can differentiate
between VOLITION, OBLIGATION, or PURE FUTURE.

> I would injure no man, and should provoke no
> resentment; I would relieve every distress, and should
> enjoy the benedictions of gratitude. I would choose
> my friends among the wise, and my wife among the
> virtuous; and therefore should be in no danger from
> treachery or unkindness. My children should by my
> care be learned and pious, and would repay to my
> age what their childhood had received. – From
> Samuel Johnson's *Rasselas.*

The same contrast holds if the passage is put into the
corresponding future forms.

SOME USEFUL WAYS OF EXPRESSING FUTURITY:

(1) *I (we) shall* (or *he,* etc., *will*) *have more time next week,
I expect.* – PURE FUTURE

(2)   *I won't give you any. You (he) shan't have any.* –
FUTURE with full meaning of auxiliary; the COLOURED
FUTURE
(3)   *He is meeting her tonight at eight.* – Definitely agreed
(4)   *He'll be meeting her tonight at eight* – Definitely
agreed
(5)   *He's going to meet her tonight at eight.* – It's HIS
intention to do so.
(6)   *Will you meet her tonight at eight?* – Request
(7)   *Will you be meeting her tonight at eight?* – Is this
event likely to take place? Is it on your programme?
(8)   *Shall he meet her as well?* – Obligation
(9)   *Is he to meet her as well?* – Same as No. 8; more
usual in this form
(10)   *He's about to leave for London.* – on the point of

FUTURE SUBSTITUTES

28.14
Intermediate   Other verbs and turns of expression frequently replace
will/shall to reinforce various coloured forms of the future.

*   *   *

● Read the following sentences with the suggested alternative verb, making any necessary changes:
1   Will you have some more cake? (like)
2   Shall I get you another book? (want)
3   What will you do now? (mean)
4   You shall stay here till I come back. (is to)
5   We won't listen to him. (choose)
6   I'll be going next week. (intend)
7   I won't do what you tell me. (refuse)
8   You shall have a new bicycle. (promise)
9   I won't take up any more of your time. (want)
10   We'll make our presence known to him. (mean)
11   I think I shall go away next weekend. (hope)
12   He says he will get a rise next month. (expect)
13   Maisie will enter for the local singing
     competition. (intend)
14   They won't accept your apology. (refuse)
15   Cyril will be promoted soon. (is to)

28.15
Advanced

See Exercise 28.14.

* * *

● Read the following sentences with the suggested alternative verb, making any necessary changes:

1 They won't answer my questions. (refuse)
2 When will you pay me for my services? (intend)
3 We shall have wine to drink and good things to eat. (promise) (Passive voice)
4 If he won't shave before breakfast (choose), I won't speak to him. (want)
5 Will he listen to my singing, do you think? (like)
6 Do you think they'll follow us all the way home? (mean)
7 When will you learn English properly? (intend)
8 I'll have it done now (want).   I won't be kept waiting. (is to)
9 You shall have time to think it over. (promise)
10 He'll have his own way in the end (intend); he won't listen to us. (refuse)
11 We shall visit all the sights of London. (hope)
12 Why won't he have any dealings with you? (refuse)
13 I shall be in Bournemouth this time next week. (hope)
14 They will buy up all the land they can lay their hands on. (intend)
15 She will go shopping tomorrow (want).   Will you go too? (mean)

28.16
Intermediate

Future (and past) of *can*, *must*, *needn't*. See also Sections 16 and 17.

Can has past *could* or *was able* (see Exercise 17.2), has future *shall/will be able*, or *can* (See Exercise 17.1).

Must has past *had to* (see Exercises 16.1–4), has future *shall/will have to*.

Needn't has past *didn't need to* or *needn't have* (see Exercise 16.3), has future *shan't/won't need to*, or *shan't/won't have to*.

* * *

● Read the following sentences, adding *yesterday* or *to-morrow*, etc.: first in the PAST throughout; and then in the FUTURE throughout:

1 He must be very careful.
2 John can do it very easily.
3 You needn't go away early.
4 Cyril must mend his own jeans.
5 I can finish the work before breakfast.
6 I must always shave before breakfast.
7 I needn't wake up before seven o'clock.
8 He must change his wet clothes.
9 He can swim much better than you.
10 Maisie must walk all the way back alone.
11 You needn't spend so much as that.
12 They can sleep all day long, but must get up before supper.
13 You needn't work so hard after your illness.
14 I must repeat it several times, and then I can remember it.
15 I must pay him £50 down, but I can't.
16 Can you carry the box without help?
17 We must work harder.
18 We must decide immediately.
19 Must you go? Can't you stay?
20 You needn't answer all the questions.

28.17
Elementary
NO FUTURE
AFTER
TEMPORAL
CONJUNCTIONS

Although the main clause is future, the presence of temporal conjunctions such as *when*, *until*, *as soon as*, *before*, *after*, *while* is sufficient to indicate futurity, and such clauses remain in the present tense.

* * *

● Notice the tenses used in the following sentences, and add the missing time conjunction (not *if*):

1 He will stay here — you come.
2 I'll come and see you — I have time.
3 We shall be ready — you are.
4 — you come tomorrow, I will give you a new book.
5 — they show me their homework, I will correct it.
6 We shall go — he is ready.
7 She will speak to you — you come in.

8 You must wait — the light changes to green.
9 I'll write to you — I leave England.
10 He will remain in the south — the cold weather lasts.
11 These brave men will fight — they die.
12 — I live, I shall always remember his face.
13 You will be able to play the piano — you like.
14 They will not climb the hill — the moon rises.
15 Don't buy bananas — they become cheaper.
16 We must buy some shirts — they become dearer.
17 This coat will lose its colour — it's washed.
18 He will sell the cloth — the price rises.
19 I shall wait — the price falls.
20 The corn will grow quickly — the rain comes.

28.18
Elementary
NO FUTURE
AFTER
TEMPORALS

● Put the verb in brackets into a suitable tense:

1 We shall go as soon as you (be) ready.
2 He will tell you when you (get) home.
3 We'll go out when the rain (stop).
4 I (stay) here until he answers me.
5 Wait until I (catch) you!
6 I'll be ready before you (count) ten.
7 He'll eat strawberries until he (look like) them.
8 John must eat his breakfast before he (go) out.
9 Please sit here until my husband (come).
10 See that it is clean before you (touch) it.
11 I'll help her look for it until she (find) it.
12 The house will stay empty till we (return).
13 As soon as you buy the book, I (borrow) it from you.
14 He'll tell you when you (ask) him.
15 I'll tell you a secret as soon as my husband (go) out.
16 I'll believe it when I (see) it.
17 I (get) a new one before tonight.
18 It will be mended by the time you (get) back.
19 She (not come) until you are ready.
20 I'll give it back as soon as he (want) it.

28.19   ●   Supply a suitable tense for the verbs in brackets:

Intermediate 1   Don't get off the bus till it (stop).

NO FUTURE   2   You will be amazed when you (see) the view.

AFTER   3   Let's go to a café when the concert (be) over.

TEMPORALS   4   You had better wait until the police (come).

5   I (have) a suit made as soon as I arrive in London.

6   Cyril says he won't go to bed until I (kiss) him
good night.

7   I won't play cards with you again till you (stop)
cheating.

8   You won't forget to lock up the house before you
(go) out, will you?

9   I'll come and see you before I (leave) for England.

10   I can't express an opinion until I (know) the facts.

11   We must wait until the waiter (bring) the coffee.

12   I don't think he (phone) before he arrives.

13   My little boy will wear short trousers until he (be)
eleven years old.

14   You can stay at home and cook my lunch while I
(go) to the club.

15   I shall expect it to be ready as soon as I (come) in.

16   Do you think Maisie will sew my buttons on for
me when they (come) off?

17   I (not move) from here until you get back.

18   You'll know him when you (see) him.

19   You (have to) explain to Cyril as soon as he
arrives home.

20   Maisie (not believe) me till I show her the ring.

FUTURE PERFECT TENSE

28.20   The FUTURE PERFECT bears the same relation to a future
Intermediate   moment as the PRESENT PERFECT bears to the present
moment, i.e. it tells us that a certain action will be completed by a certain future time. The fact of its completion
by a certain time is what interests us, not the time of the
action itself.

> I've read three of Shaw's plays.
>
> (I KNOW about them NOW.)
>
> I shall have read seven of Shaw's plays by the end of
> the year.
>
> (I SHALL KNOW about them THEN.)

The FUTURE PERFECT CONTINUOUS tense is not very often used.

> By Christmas I shall have been working in this office for ten years.
>> – and I shall presumably continue to work here

* * *

(28.20)   ● Supply a suitable tense of the verbs in brackets:

1 By next June he (write) his second novel.
2 Before his next visit here he (return) from a world tour.
3 Before you go to see them, they (leave) the country.
4 He (finish) this work before you leave.
5 By the end of the summer he (teach) us to speak English.
6 By this time next week you (meet) my friend Cyril.
7 When you come back he already (buy) the house.
8 The meeting (finish) by the time we get there.
9 By next month he (sell) all his furniture.
10 In 1980 he (be) dead for ten years.
11 By next Sunday you (stay) with us for five weeks.
12 He (take) his examination by his next birthday.
13 By the end of this year he (fly) more than a million miles.
14 I hope, when you have finished this exercise, you (not make) many mistakes in it.
15 The horse race (start) before we even leave home.
16 I hope it (stop) raining by five o'clock.
17 I (finish) long before you get back.
18 I expect Maisie (grow up) by the time I return to England.
19 If we don't get there before seven, they (eat and drink) everything.
20 I hope you (not forget) all this by tomorrow!

28.21
Intermediate

Look at this pair of sentences:

> *He won't come till the play begins.*
>> This means that he will come just at the beginning of the play.
> *He won't come till the play has begun.*
>> This means that he will arrive *after* the beginning.

> It is a FUTURE PERFECT idea; 'by the time he comes, the play *will have begun*.' See Exercise 28.20.

In the same way as a FUTURE SIMPLE idea is expressed by the PRESENT SIMPLE in time clauses (Exercises 28.17–19), so a FUTURE PERFECT idea is expressed by the PRESENT PERFECT.

*　　*　　*

● Put the verb in brackets into a suitable tense:

1 I'll wait until he (write) his next novel.
2 Don't come until I (finish) lunch.
3 I shall probably want to see the book before he (finish) it.
4 We (not find) our seats until the concert has begun.
5 When I (be) in this country for ten years, I shall write a book.
6 They (not plant) the cotton until the corn has been cut.
7 The river will not begin to rise until some rain (fall).
8 As soon as Cyril (spend) that money he will try to borrow some more.
9 You mustn't get up until your temperature (go down).
10 You'd better stay in until you (get rid of) that cough.
11 We can't leave until we (eat) our lunch.
12 The country (look) quite different when the leaves have fallen.
13 Until the snow (go), the train will not be able to move.
14 When I (learn) a thousand English words, shall I be able to read a newspaper?
15 Don't ask for another book until you (finish) this one.
16 When Maisie and I (be) married for twenty-five years, we are going for a world tour.
17 They won't come home until they (see) everything.
18 Sit down, and when you (rest) I'll show you the garden.
19 As soon as he (save) £10,000, he will retire from business.
20 Come again when the machine (be cleaned).

28.22   ● Complete the following sentences:
Intermediate 1 Come and visit us when . . .
2 I shall not move from here until . . .
3 You will have to explain everything before . . .
4 I'll put him to bed without his supper as soon as . . .
5 He won't stop running until . . .
6 I hope you will hide the strawberries and cream before . . .
7 Cyril will be terribly angry when . . .
8 When he writes to me again, I . . .
9 She will never understand until . . .
10 Will you stay and talk to me until . . .
11 Will you buy me a pound of tea when . . .
12 I'll keep you in this room until . . .
13 I'll come and see you again when . . .
14 They won't give me any more cucumbers until . . .
15 Your electricity will be cut off until . . .
16 The pears will all be eaten before . . .
17 The doctor will send you the bill when . . .
18 When my newspaper comes . . .
19 Will you always love me, even when . . .
20 I'll leave it out in the sun until . . .

28.23
Advanced
The ideas behind *shall/will* tenses are expressed after TEMPORAL CONJUNCTIONS by PRESENT tenses (SIMPLE or PERFECT).

The ideas behind *should/would* tenses are expressed after TEMPORAL CONJUNCTIONS by PAST tenses (SIMPLE or PERFECT).

You will come as soon as you *can*, won't you?
You will come as soon as you *have finished* dinner, won't you?
You would come as soon as I *needed* you, wouldn't you?
I should/would have come after I *had finished*, if I had had the time.

Notice that *after* (or *when* in the sense of 'after') most frequently has a perfect tense with it.

*   *   *

● Supply a suitable tense of the verb in brackets:

1   He says he will make up the story as he (go) along.
2   I shall ask you to do this when your friend
    (leave).
3   I told the gatekeeper that we wanted to stay in the
    park until he (shut) the gates.
4   Don't leave the house until you (wash) your face.
5   After he (go) will you come and see me?
6   I shan't know whether I've passed or not till I
    (see) the result printed in the paper.
7   I know I ought to finish reading the book while
    I still (have) time.
8   As soon as the ship (reach) port, its dangerous
    cargo will be unloaded.
9   She said she would go on knitting as long as she
    (sit) in the deck-chair.
10 I'll pay for the apples on the day you (deliver)
    them.
11 How can I say what he is like until I (see) him?
12 Obviously I shouldn't dream of asking you before
    I (have) to.
13 After the game (be) over, let's go home together.
14 If I really liked my job, I should work till my
    eyes (drop) out.
15 I shall have done a lot of work while he (be)
    asleep.
16 Will you please give me the football back again as
    soon as the game (be) over?
17 If I were you, I should do it when the opportunity
    (arise).
18 John says he will wait under the clock until
    Rosemary (come).
19 If the plane (arrive) after the fog (clear), it will
    be able to land.
20 We shall try to persuade him to do it before it (be)
    too late.
21 I know that if I told my father all about it as soon
    as he (come) in, he would be on my side.
22 Profiteers will continue to make lots of money
    while the war (last).
23 I shall not speak to him until you (introduce) him
    to me.

24   Don't count your chickens before they (be)
hatched.

25   I know that as soon as he (see) me, he'll call
me a fool.

28.24
Intermediate
and
Advanced
THE FUTURE
OF
ASSUMPTION

The use of FUTURE SIMPLE and FUTURE PERFECT tenses to replace the idea of *I suppose that, take it for granted that, expect that, imagine that,* etc., is a very interesting one. It occurs most frequently in debates, speeches, lectures, and dialectical writing, and is common enough in ordinary speech to warrant an exercise on it for more advanced students.

You'*ll have noticed* from my lecture how complicated this subject really is.
= I imagine you *have noticed* . . .
This *will be* the right way.
= I take it that this *is* the right way.

Of course is often added to emphasize this idea.

*   *   *

● Recast the following sentences, omitting the introductory remark in **bold type**, and using the FUTURE SIMPLE, FUTURE CONTINUOUS, FUTURE PERFECT CONTINUOUS or FUTURE PERFECT tense:

1   **I suppose** you understand why I can't come.
2   **I suppose** you have noticed how often Cyril has to wind his watch up.
3   **I take it** you appreciate my difficulty.
4   **I take it** your friends have got to London by now.
5   **I expect** you wonder why I haven't told you before.
6   **I suppose** you've recovered by now from the shock of meeting Maisie (of course).
7   **I take it** you have heard of Marlowe (of course).
8   **I imagine** you've been wondering all this time how my invention works.
9   **I expect** he knows what I mean (of course).
10   **I take it** he has told you about our plans already.
11   **I imagine** you haven't heard of me (of course).
12   **I imagine** you don't mind, naturally.
13   **I don't suppose** you've forgotten old Jimmy (of course).
14   **I expect** this is the house they're looking for.
15   Did you hear a knock? **I imagine** that's father.

16 **I take it** you've met my friend Maisie before.
17 **I imagine** you haven't read this book before, so take it with you.
18 **Am I not right in supposing** this is the one you want?
19 **I take it for granted** you've come on foot (of course).
20 **I imagine** you've learnt something new from this exercise, haven't you?

29 The Past Perfect Tense

**29.1
Elementary**

The PAST PERFECT tense is related to a moment in the past in the same way that the PRESENT PERFECT is related to the present moment, i.e. it describes an action completed before some special past moment we have in mind.

*   *   *

● Supply a suitable past tense of the verbs in brackets:
1 She told me his name after he (leave).
2 He (do) nothing before he saw me.
3 My friend enjoyed his food as soon as he (taste) it.
4 He thanked me for what I (do).
5 I (be) sorry that I had hurt him.
6 After they had gone, I (sit) down and (rest).
7 Did you post the letter after you (write) it?
8 As soon as you (go), I wanted to see you again.
9 They dressed after they (wash).
10 After I had heard the news, I (hurry) to see him.
11 She told me her name after I (ask) her twice.
12 Before we (go) very far, we found that we (lose) our way.
13 After you (go), I went to sleep.
14 I read the book after I (finish) my work.
15 When we arrived, the dinner already (begin).
16 He died after he (be) ill a long time.
17 My friend (not see) me for many years when I met him last week.
18 He took the money after I (ask) him not to do so.

19   It rained yesterday after it (be) dry for many
     months.
20   Why didn't you go to the doctor after I (tell)
     you to?
21   He had already learnt English before he (leave)
     for England.
22   But before he arrived in England, he (forget)
     some.
23   In England he soon remembered all he (learn).
24   The sun had set before I (be) ready to go.
25   The river became deeper after it (rain) heavily.

29.2   The idea of the PAST PERFECT as a 'Before-Past' leads to its
Intermediate logical use in REPORTED SPEECH (see also later exercises on
                  this topic). When the SIMPLE PAST *I saw him*, is reported in
                  relation to the introduction *he said that*, it takes place
                  notionally before the past *said*, and must therefore be PAST
                  PERFECT.

                  Ago always dates back from NOW. *Before* dates back from
                  any point in past or future, including NOW.

                           *   *   *

● Supply a suitable past tense:
1   They (go) home after they (finish) their work.
2   She said that she already (see) the Pyramids.
3   She just (go) out when I called at her house.
4   You ought to have brought her straight home
    after she (fall) in the river.
5   They told him they (not meet) him before.
6   He asked why we (come) so early.
7   My small brother (eat) all the pie before we got
    back.
8   He told us he (be) to the seaside for a holiday.
9   He wondered why I (not visit) him before.
10 Before help (reach) us, one woman (collapse).
11 We asked him what countries he (visit).
12 We (hear) that a fire (break out) in the
    neighbouring house.
13 When the plane landed, the pilot (find) that one of
    the wings (be damaged) by a shell.
14 He told me he (catch) a young lion and (shoot)
    two others.

15   They drank small cups of coffee after they
     (finish) dinner.

16   The moment after I (tell) her not to, Maisie (do)
     it again.

17   She told her teacher that her mother (help) her
     with her homework the previous evening, and
     (tell) her the words she (not know).

18   The fire (spread) to the next building before the
     firemen (arrive).

19   We were surprised to hear that she (pass) the
     examination at the age of fourteen.

20   Cyril was very angry and said that he (eat) two
     flies in his fruit salad.   The waiter asked him why
     he (eat) them.   Cyril said he (be) short-sighted
     and already (swallow) them when his friend (tell)
     him what he (eat).

29.3   See the two previous exercises
Advanced
                                    *   *   *

●   Supply a suitable PAST tense:

1   He (discover) to his horror that he (eat) half a
     maggot with his last piece of apple.

2   A friend of mine once (write) a detective story
     called *Murder in the Brewery*, although he (never
     visit) a brewery in his life.

3   The little girl (ask) what (happen) to her
     ice-cream.

4   He (can not) help thinking that he (see) that face
     somewhere before.

5   After he (be) taken to see *My Fair Lady* he (tell) all
     his friends that he (never see) a better musical.

6   His mother (worry) a lot about him before she
     (hear) that he was safe.

7   The politician (declare) that his party always
     (stand) for social security.

8   The house (be) much smaller than he (think) at
     first.

9   The archaeologist (say) that the glories of
     Tutankhamen (not be) at all exaggerated.

10   The valley (be flooded) the year before and so it
     (contain) plenty of green pasturage.

11   It (be) the madman who (do) the killing.
12   The wetness of the deck (tell) him that dew (fall) in the night.
13   It (seem) at least twenty minutes since Smith (set) off for the village.
14   He (know) of only one tiger kept as a pet, and this animal, in seven or eight years, (never show) a trace of ill-temper.
15   Beau Nash already (banish) swords from the ballroom because their clash (frighten) the ladies.
16   She (do) her duty in that state of life to which it (please) God to call her.
17   He (refuse) to admit that he (steal) the peaches.
18   The little boy, who (glance) furtively at me more than once, now (crouch) back against his mother.
19   He lives as happily in this cottage as if it (be) a royal palace.[1]
20   He jumped up as if he (be stung).[1]

30   Revision of Tenses

30.1   ●   Supply suitable tenses (but do not use *should/would*):
Elementary   1   They just (decide) that they (undertake) the job.
2   We (go) to the theatre last night.
3   He usually (write) in green ink.
4   She (play) the piano when our guests (arrive) last night.
5   We (do) an English exercise.   (*How many possibilities*?)
6   She just (come) in and (see) you in five minutes.
7   I (come) as soon as my work is finished.   You (be) ready?
8   Where you (go) for your holidays last year?
9   I (not leave) Paris since we (visit) Dieppe three years ago.
10   My mother (come) to stay with us next weekend.
11   We (meet) only yesterday and already (decide) to get married.

[1] See Exercise 31.10 for *as if* construction.

12 Some people never (see) snow before.
13 Violets (bloom) in the spring.
14 We (not live) in England for the last two years.
15 I (lose) my keys; I cannot remember where I last (see) them.
16 He (not arrive) when I (write) my last letter to you.
17 Whenever he (go) to town nowadays, he (spend) a lot of money.
18 I never (forget) what you just (tell) me.
19 They (prepare) the Christmas dinner today.
20 When I last (stay) in Cairo, I (ride) to the Pyramids on a camel that my friend (borrow) the day before.

30.2 ● Supply suitable tenses (but do not use *should/would*):
Intermediate 1 I (finish) the book by my next birthday.
2 Hello! You (make) a cake? (*Two possibilities.*)
3 He (walk) very quickly when I (meet) him yesterday.
4 'Why she (run) away?' 'Because she (know) it is time for bed and (not want) to go.'
5 Yesterday I (buy) a new watch as my old one (be stolen).
6 We (meet) you tomorrow after you (finish) your work.
7 He said he (be) sorry he (give) me so much trouble.
8 I am sorry that I (not know) you (leave) your pipe when you (come) to see me last Thursday.
9 He (be) so good to me when I was a boy, that to this day I (not forget) his kindness, and I hope that I (never forget).
10 He (sleep) and (not understand) what you (say) to him. He (wake) if you (speak) louder.
11 Some animals (not eat) during the winter and only (come out) in spring; we (call) them hibernating animals.
12 After leaving school he (study) French in Paris for two years then (move) to America, where he now (live). He (visit) England once or twice and (know) English well, but (not yet have) the opportunity of visiting European countries.

13   *A game:* One person (think) of a verb, the others
     (ask) him questions.   He must bring his word into
     the answer, but instead of saying it he (use) the
     word 'coffee-pot' in the place of the word he
     (choose); the others (guess) what the 'coffee-pot'
     (be).
14   I (go) there when I (be) told, not before!
15   I (know) him for a very long time.
16   When Cyril grows a beard, even his closest
     friends (not recognize) him.
17   When I (meet) them in the street, they (go) to the
     cinema.
18   I (study) English for six years now.
19   I expect he (go) to Syria as soon as he (get) a
     visa.
20   '(Go) and (hang) yourself!' he said to me.
21   He (visit) his friend yesterday and (find) that he
     (be) out.
22   They (sell) everything before we (get) there if we
     don't hurry.
23   After she (work) at the hospital for two years, she
     (decide) to give up the job.
24   He will come at once because I (tell) him by phone
     that you (need) him urgently. I'm sure he (find)
     his way easily, although he (never visit) this house
     before.
25   By the time you get back I (finish) all my
     correspondence, and then I (can) help you with
     yours.

30.3   ●   Supply suitable tenses:
Advanced   1   I (always have) trouble with my engine these days.
     2   I wonder why I always (have) trouble with the
         engine whenever I (decide) to go home by car.
     3   If I (be) a ghost, I (try) to frighten all the people I
         dislike.
     4   In a few minutes' time, when the clock (strike)
         six, I (wait) here three-quarters of an hour.
     5   He (know) her a long time before he finally (get)
         married to her.
     6   I hope it (not rain) when the bride (leave) the
         church tomorrow.

7 I'm sorry you (get) lost coming here. I (go) to meet
   you at the station if I (know) you (want) me to.

8 I (tell) a lie if I said that I (like) you.

9 I'm worried about my approaching marriage. I
   (wish) I (can) get out of it, but I simply (can) not.

10 These puppets (not be) with us a week before
   Mr Punch (get lost).

11 He (play) the part now if he (not offend) the
   producer at the last rehearsal.

12 You (go) with us to the Zoo tomorrow if you (be)
   a good boy.

13 They (intend) to go there next week, but now they
   (find) they (have not) enough money.

14 I (work) very hard lately.

15 What you (do) just now while I (wash) the dishes?

16 I (read) in yesterday's paper that a boy (steal) a
   watch and (sell) it, and that the police (look) for
   him everywhere but (not find) him.

17 When he grew old he often (think) of all the things
   he (do) when he (be) young.

18 When he grows old he often (think) of all the
   things he (do) when he (be) young.

19 I never (read) a story that (interest) me so much as
   the one I (read) last night.

20 When we (go) to see them last night, they (play)
   cards; they (say) they (play) since six o'clock.

21 By the end of last year he (read) four Shakespeare
   plays, and by next year he (read) two more. I
   (not see) him since last Monday, but I (believe) he
   (write) an essay on *Hamlet* at present.

22 This is the second time you (break) a cup; you
   (break) one yesterday. The last girl (never break)
   anything, but you (break) nearly half the things in
   the house.

23 Mother (just go) to the market; John (see) her just
   now in the main road as he (come) home from
   school.

24 I always (tell) you to comb your hair, but you
   never (do) what I (say).

25 You forever (misunderstand) what I (explain) to
   you! Why you (not listen) while I (speak) to you?

31 Conditions and Unreal Past

**31.1
Elementary**

Like clauses beginning with *when, as soon as*, etc., *if*-clauses also have no *shall, will, should, would*, in them.

English can express THREE important ideas with *if*.

(1) He *will come* if you *call* him. – something will happen if a certain CONDITION is fulfilled.

(2) He *would come* if you *called* him. – the probable result of a certain condition that we suppose or imagine. The *if*-clause names action that is not taking place at this moment, but I can imagine the probable result. We include here all the unreal *ifs*, like: *if you were a fish, the cat would eat you*.

(3) He *would have come* if you *had called* him – but he didn't come! Why? Because you didn't call him.

All No. (3) types are impossible ideas, because we know the condition was not fulfilled, but we like to imagine the result if . . .

So we have:

TYPE (1) Main clause – FUTURE; *if*-clause – PRESENT. (Likely or probable.)

TYPE (2) Main clause – *would*; *if*-clause – PAST. (Unlikely or improbable; imaginary.)

TYPE (3) Main clause – *would have*: *if*-clause – PAST PERFECT. (Impossible.)

Unless is usually close in meaning to *if not* but it cannot be universally substituted for *if not*. It is not an equivalent in TYPE (3) conditions, and even in TYPE (1) conditions there may be a difference, e.g.

> You will hurt yourself *if you are not careful*.
> – so be careful

> You will hurt yourself *unless you are careful*.
> – so it would be better not to do it at all

NOTE: *I should* has largely been replaced by *I would*.

* * *

● Read the following sentences, notice carefully the tenses of the two verbs, and say what kind of condition each sentence is:

1 If I come, I shall see you.
2 You will spoil it if you aren't careful.
3 We would answer if we could.

4　They will get wet if it rains.
5　I would (should) be pleased if you came.
6　If I had known that, I should not have made a mistake.
7　It would have been better if you had waited.
8　If I were[1] you, I should go home immediately.
9　Will you help me if I need you?
10　He would have told you if you had asked him.
11　They would be silly if they did not take this opportunity.
12　If it is fine, I shall go for a swim.
13　If it rained, I would stay at home.
14　I'll help you if I can.
15　It would have broken if you had not caught it.

31.2　　　See previous exercise.
Intermediate　Of the three types of condition given, the first and third are far more important than the second.

*　　*　　*

● State the type of the following conditionals:
1　If you had done as I told you, you would have succeeded.
2　If you did as I told you, you would succeed.
3　You'll succeed if you do as I tell you.
4　If you are good, I'll give you a piece of chocolate.
5　If Maria had known English was so difficult, she would never have taken it up.
6　If the rain failed to come, there would be a famine.
7　If you eat too much, you will be ill.
8　You would be ill if you ate too much.
9　If I hadn't told him, he would never have known.
10　You would catch the train if you left earlier.
11　You will pass your examination if you work hard.
12　If you had left earlier, you would have caught the train.
13　You will catch the train if you leave earlier.
14　If I'd lost my spectacles, I wouldn't have been able to read.
15　If I were an orange, I should be spherical and juicy.

---

[1] Technically speaking, *if*-clauses are in subjunctive mood, but *were* is the only place where it still lives as a different form.

31.3
Elementary

See the Exercise 31.1 note on *unless*.

* * *

● Supply *if* or *unless* in the following sentences, noticing carefully the tense sequence:

1 He wouldn't have waited — you'd been late.
2 He won't speak French — he goes to France.
3 I'll go to the door — I hear the bell.
4 I shan't go to the door — I hear the bell.
5 — you ring the bell, the servant will come.
6 He'll come — you ring the bell.
7 — you don't ring the bell, the servant won't come.
8 He won't come — you ring the bell.
9 — he wrote to me, I should write to him.
10 I shan't write to him — he writes to me.
11 — the clock had been right, we would have caught the train.
12 — my watch hadn't been slow, I wouldn't have been late.
13 He will not learn much — he works harder.
14 — you send a telegram now, he'll get it this evening.
15 — he started immediately, he would arrive by midday.
16 I should never have found the house — the policeman hadn't helped me.
17 — you invited him, he would come[1]
18 He would come — you invited him.
19 — you had invited him, he would have come.
20 He would have come — you had invited him.

31.4
Elementary

Look once more at the three principal types:
TYPE (1)   He will come if you wait. (He'll come . . .)
TYPE (2)   He would come if you waited. (He'd come . . .)
TYPE (3)   He would have come if you had waited. (He'd have . . . you'd . . .)
(Notice in TYPE (2) we can find the last recognizable subjunctive form, *If he (I) were . . .*).

* * *

[1] In the last four sentences the normal spoken English contracted forms (*he would = he'd*, and *he had = he'd*) have been omitted to avoid confusion at this early stage. The teacher might, however, read them to the students with these contractions.

● Now read each of the following sentences first in the form printed and then in the other two forms:

1 He'll come if you wait.
2 If you ring the bell, somebody will come.
3 You'll catch the train if you take a taxi.
4 If he wrote to me, I should write to him.
5 You would have found the book if you had opened the bag.
6 If he saw you, he would speak to you.
7 The streets would be wet if it rained.
8 You'll be ill if you drink that water.
9 What will you do if you meet Mr Robinson?
10 I wouldn't have spoken to him even if he had spoken to me.
11 If a beggar asks you for money, will you give him any?
12 What would happen if the bridge broke?
13 If he had fallen into the river, he would have been drowned.
14 If he had been able to swim, he wouldn't have been drowned.
15 If you buy that big house, you will need several servants.
16 Will you be angry if I steal your pocket-knife?
17 Tommy would be sick if he ate all those chocolates.
18 If he'd been thirsty, he would have drunk some water.
19 I shall come and see you if I have time.
20 If you leave the letter on that table, my sister will post it for you.

31.5   ● Read the following sentences in the form printed, and then
Intermediate   in the other two forms:

1 We won't go out unless it stops raining.
2 If you could come too, it would be very nice.
3 It would have been better if they hadn't come.
4 I'll give it to you if you must have one.
5 If Cyril doesn't object, I shall join you.
6 He'll certainly do it if it's possible.
7 If the sun didn't shine, fruit wouldn't ripen.
8 He would steal it from you if he could.
9 If you go to town, will you buy something for me?

10   Maisie would do it if she wanted to.
11   If they hadn't told us, we shouldn't have found the way.
12   What would you do if a bee stung you?
13   He wouldn't have written if he hadn't heard some news.
14   If I had enough money, I would buy a radio set.
15   I shall have to buy a thick coat if the weather gets colder.
16   If you hit the dog, it will bite you.
17   We shall be pleased if our school wins the match.
18   You'll be able to speak English better if you study harder.
19   If he buys a house for £8,000 and sells it for £11,000, he'll make a good profit.
20   The soldiers will fight bravely if they understand their orders.

31.6
Elementary

It is not necessary for *can*, *must*, etc., to be made future in TYPE (1). See special exercises on *can* and *must* for details.

You can go this afternoon if you like. (permission)
You'll soon be able to swim if you practise hard. (capacity)

*   *   *

● Supply a suitable tense of the verbs in brackets:
1   You will be ill if you (eat) so much.
2   I (go) if I had known.
3   If my car (not break) down, I should have caught the train.
4   If she were older, she (have) more sense.
5   If you (read) that book carefully, you would understand it.
6   If the children (be) good, they can stay up late.
7   I (buy) that hat if it were not so dear.
8   You (kill) yourself if you always work as hard as that.
9   If they had waited, they (find) me.
10   I'm sure she will do well if she (go) to the University.
11   If it (be) fine tomorrow, I shall play tennis.
12   I shouldn't have thought it possible if I (not see) it.

13   I'm sure my sister would go out with you if you
      (ask) her nicely.
14   We (enjoy) the play better if it had not been so
      long.
15   They would do it if they (can).
16   If dinner is not ready, I (go) without it.
17   I (show) you how to do it if I knew myself.
18   If the dog had not woken us, we (never hear) the
      burglar.
19   Blackpool (be) ideal for a holiday, if there were not
      so many people there.
20   If he wants to play the violin, I (play) the piano for
      him.
21   The dog (bite) you if it had not been tied up.
22   If you don't shut that window, we all (die) of
      cold.
23   I shall be very angry if you (break) any more
      plates.
24   The child (be killed) if the train hadn't stopped
      quickly.
25   I would have come yesterday if I (have) nothing
      to do.

31.7 ● Supply a suitable tense of the verbs in brackets:

Intermediate 1 If you (go) away, please write to me.
2   If we (have) some bread, we could have some
     bread and cheese if we had some cheese!
3   We are going to play tennis this afternoon if it
     (stop) raining.
4   If you (be) in, I should have given it to you.
5   If Johnny (eat) another cake, he will be sick.
6   If you (not turn) off that noisy radio, I shall
     scream!
7   If you (can) type, you ought to be able to get a job
     easily.
8   If men (be) only more reasonable, there would be
     no more war.
9   You would be taking a great risk if you (invest)
     your money in that business.
10   We would not have despatched the goods if they
     (not be) in good condition.
11   If it (be) convenient, let's meet at nine o'clock.

12   I wouldn't do that if I (be) you.
13   It will be impossible for me to finish my work if you (not cease) this chatter.
14   If Cyril (take) my advice, everything ought to go well.
15   I would have come sooner if I (know) you were here.
16   If you (want) to have tea ready in time, put the kettle on now.
17   It is easy to paint pictures if one (know) how to.
18   If she (not answer) the telephone, she would never have heard the good news.
19   Tell him he must visit the Tower if ever he (go) to London.
20   My uncle would be able to help us if he (be) here.
21   If I (have) the courage, I would have answered him back.
22   If it (rain), you will get wet.
23   If you (want) me to help you, why didn't you say so?
24   Maisie's mother would have known what to do if she (be) alive.
25   If the sentence that had 'had had' had had 'had' it (be) correct.
     (Be careful of the reading of weak, strong and emphatic forms here.)

31.8
Elementary

Reminder about the last recognizable subjunctive form in the conditional type: *If I (he) were ...*

* * *

● Complete the following sentences:
1   The cake would have been burnt if ...
2   You will get into trouble if ...
3   Your dress would look better if ...
4   She would not have married him if ...
5   Don't give him anything unless ...
6   If I had time, ...
7   If it hadn't been raining, ...
8   I might have learnt more English if ...
9   The teacher would not be angry with you if ...
10 You will lose your money if ...

11 Flowers will not grow well unless ...
12 A violinist must practise if ...
13 You could live more cheaply if ...
14 I don't like tea unless ...
15 I should have won the prize if ...
16 The soup will get cold unless ...
17 We would have gone to the cinema with you if ...
18 You would be ill if ...
19 I cannot wake at six o'clock unless ...
20 She will play the piano for you if ...
21 My friend would have helped you if ...
22 The photograph would have been better if ...
23 If I had plenty of money, ...
24 Get ready quickly if ...
25 I don't like meat unless ...

31.9   ● Complete the following conditionals:
Intermediate 1 If your message had not come, ...
2 If you had worked harder, ...
3 Why didn't you do it if ...
4 He will not come unless ...
5 I should not have lost my money if ...
6 If you don't visit me soon, I ...
7 If I met your friend Maisie in the street, ...
8 If I had been in love with him (her), ...
9 You would be very angry with us if ...
10 You would not have been angry with us if ...
11 If I were you, ...
12 If I had known he was here, ...
13 If he wants to see me, ...
14 If I know the details before next week, ...
15 We shall be very disappointed if ...
16 He wouldn't have listened to me if ...
17 Come before seven o'clock if ...
18 I shall not pay you unless ...
19 Unless someone tells me the way, ...
20 If the Seine overflowed its banks, ...
21 Unless you go to France, ...
22 If she were a good girl, ...
23 If you had been a faithful wife, ...
24 I would not have liked your friend Cyril if ...
25 If our teacher were not so severe, ...

31.10
Advanced
THE UNREAL
PAST

It will be noticed that in TYPES (2) and (3) of the conditional (see Exercise 31.1), the PAST SIMPLE or PAST PERFECT tense is used when we suppose what is impossible. These are really subjunctives, but seeing that *were* is the only visible sign of this form that occurs with any frequency, the student needn't be asked to differentiate between past subjunctive and past indicative. The PAST SIMPLE tense is used for something unreal or wished-for NOW, and the PAST PERFECT when the supposition or wish was all in the past. Other expressions using the past tenses in this way are: *I wish, as if, if only, would to God, suppose, it's (high) time, I'd rather*.

If only I *knew* the answer (now)! If only I *had known* (yesterday)!

     *   *   *

● Supply a suitable tense of the verbs in brackets:

1 I wish I (know) his name.
2 It's time we all (go) home.
3 I'd rather you (go) now.
4 It's about time you (get) the tea ready.
5 Don't you wish you (come) earlier?
6 Suppose I (get) there late!
7 He acts as if he (know) English perfectly.
8 Would to God you (be) a better husband to me!
9 If only he (not eat) so much garlic!
10 If only he (not eat) so much garlic last night!
11 I would have helped you if I (hear) about your trouble.
12 A person who (refuse) to eat would be dead in a month.
13 I'd rather you (pay) me now. Suppose he (ask) me for the money tomorrow!
14 If only he (tell) you the whole story!
15 It's high time you (have) a haircut.
16 I feel as if my head (be) on fire.
17 He said he wished he (never see) me.
18 You look as if you (can) do with a drink.
19 I'd rather you (give) me a new one instead of having it repaired as you did.
20 My wife says she wishes I (be) a thousand miles away; indeed, I wish I (be).

21 If only I (know) earlier, I'd have sent you a
    telegram.
22 I felt as if I (be pulled) through a hedge
    backwards.
23 I wish I (not break) it.
24 He came in, looking as if he (see) a ghost.
25 Isn't it about time you (set to) and (do) some
    work?

**31.11
Advanced**

Other types (apart from the three main types):

(1) CAUSE AND EFFECT: tenses parallel.

   Oil floats if you pour it on water.
   You were a fool if you went out without a hat on.

(2) A DOUBTFUL view of Conditional TYPE 1 is emphasized by the use of *should*; the inverted forms are the more
literary.

   Should he refuse you, refer him to me.
   'If I should die, think only this of me.'
                                    (Rupert Brooke)

(3) In POLITE FORMS where the consent of another person
is sought, *will* and *would* are found after *if*. (See note to
Exercise 28.12.)

   If you will wait a moment I'll fetch a chair.
   I should be very grateful if you would do that for me.

(4) GREATER IMPROBABILITY in Conditional TYPES (1) and
(2) is achieved by using *were to* after *if*, and *should*, *would*,
could, or *might* in the principal clause.

   If you were to come tomorrow, I might have time to
   see you.

This construction must not be confused with the other use
of *is to* = obligation, 'must'. Compare:

   If he was to return at 7 o'clock, why didn't he?
   If he were to return at 7 o'clock, he could take me out.

Conditional conjunctions:
*if, unless, as if, if only, supposing, suppose, provided, pro-
viding, as long as.*

                        *   *   *

● Complete the following sentences:
1 It would be a good idea if . . .
2 He wouldn't treat you unkindly provided . . .

3 The potatoes wouldn't have been burnt if ...
4 If you were to come tomorrow, ...
5 If the sun didn't shine, ...
6 You would never have caught that cold if ...
7 I'd go and see him if ...
8 We won't forget what we have learnt unless ...
9 I shall always like you unless ...
10 He wouldn't have begun to learn English if ...
11 If only you knew what *I* know, you ...
12 If I'd known she wasn't coming, ...
13 I should never have known if ...
14 If you had got up earlier this morning, ...
15 You can walk where you like, provided you ...
16 If he should arrive late, you ...
17 I'll go and call her if you will ...
18 If you would only suggest it to him, ...
19 You won't make any further progress as long
    as ...
20 If the spaces between 'Romeo' and 'and', and
    'and' and 'Juliet' were wider, the book-cover ...
21 He was walking about as if ...
22 I would have married him if only ...
23 He won't tell you anything else unless ...
24 If they were to send us plenty of sugar and fruit,
    we ...
25 I don't know if he (come), but if he does, ...

FINAL NOTES ON CONDITIONS

The inverted forms, *Had I seen you earlier* ... are less
frequently found in modern spoken English than in
classical written style. They should, however, be understood by more advanced students, who will meet them
often enough as they extend their reading in literature. A
useful way to practise this inverted pattern is to read each
of the sentences of Exercise 31.4 as a TYPE (3) condition,
first in the *if*-form, then in the inverted form. Here is
No. 1 done in this way:

> *He would have come if you had waited.*
> *He would have come, had you waited:* or
> *Had you waited, he would have come.*

It is better style if the inverted clause comes first.

32 Question-tags

A very common device in conversation is that of making a statement and at once asking the listener to confirm it. In most languages this is done simply by means of a stereo-typed phrase. (Cf. n'est-ce pas, nicht wahr, non è vero, ¿no es verdad?, nu-i aşa, že ano (ze ne), nie prawda-li, не так-ли, اليس كذ لك etc.)

In English this has to be practised, as we have a variable form.

Positive statement, negative tag; negative statement, positive tag.

The auxiliaries repeat themselves in the tag. Other verbs use *do* in the tag.

He is here, isn't he? (He isn't here, is he?)

You will come, won't you? (You won't tell him, will you?)

He came yesterday, didn't he? (He didn't go, did he?)

See also preliminary Exercise 19.17.

* * *

● Read the following statements, adding the necessary question-tag:

1 He is early this morning.
2 We must go now.
3 You can swim well.
4 I was very quick.
5 It could be done.
6 You won't be late.
7 This winter hasn't been cold.
8 They ought not to be here.
9 You shouldn't smoke.
10 He has finished.
11 I am not so fat as you.
12 They always work hard.
13 He speaks English well.
14 You can help him.
15 You teach English.
16 They are learning English.
17 He has a lot of books.
18 She is too young.

19   You eat very quickly.
20   We must answer the letter.
21   John drinks too much.
22   He is greedy.
23   You have a new dress.
24   George has just left.
25   He lives at the end of the road.
26   He didn't come.
27   You were there.
28   I mustn't be late.
29   Boys don't like to wash.
30   She doesn't play tennis.
31   We got home very late.
32   I didn't hurt you.
33   You answered my invitation.
34   He had been to Switzerland.
35   She sang well.

32.2
Intermediate

The positive forms *need* and *dare* are rarely heard in the affirmative with question-tags, but when so used, are treated as full verbs.

> You need to come earlier, don't you? (= must)

Have and *have to*.   See notes to Exercises 14.3 and 18.1.
I am usually has the tag *aren't I?* (for intonation see Exercise 32.3.)
Used to has a question-tag with *did*.

*   *   *

● Read the following sentences, adding the appropriate question-tag:

1   You broke the window.
2   They didn't see you.
3   That boy ran very fast.
4   My wife cooks well.
5   You don't like sugar.
6   He can do that for you.
7   I am very stupid.
8   I am not stupid.
9   She doesn't want to go.
10   I may come with you.
11   He loves fishing.
12   We ought not to have listened.

13 They should have been able to do it.
14 You knew that before.
15 He plays the violin badly.
16 They went out just now.
17 You'll have some more tea.
18 We had better wait for your friend Maisie.
19 You have your lunch at one o'clock.
20 You don't have to go just yet.
21 You had a swim yesterday.
22 He might be there.
23 You needn't stay long.
24 He used to live here.
25 I am older than you.
26 You will come.
27 You would like to come.
28 I shan't be in your way.
29 I ought to ring him up.
30 He'll fall down.
31 You never used to wear a hat.
32 I'm afraid I'm a little late.
33 He hadn't met you before.
34 He made you do it again.
35 You used to love going out with Cyril.

**32.3
Advanced**

The range of intonation patterns for tag questions is
enormous, but students should be particularly aware of
one general distinction.

(1) The speaker can be sure that the statement is right:

> Tom must know the way to Piccadilly Circus. *He
> lives in* ↘*London,* ↘*doesn't he?*
> – a fall on *London* and *doesn't he*

(2) Or he may really want an answer (Yes or No) from
the person spoken to because he is not sure:

> I wonder what Tom's doing on this train. *He lives in*
> ↘*London,* ↗*doesn't he?*

Imperatives are made into more polite[1] requests by adding
a positive future-tag.

> Stop that noise, will you?
> Let's go for a walk, shall we?

[1] Or more petulant, depending on intonation.

Notice also: *You'd better stay, hadn't you? You'd rather go, wouldn't you?*

* * *

(32.3)   ● Add a question-tag to the following sentences:
1   They arrived yesterday.
2   You have heard about that.
3   You like coffee.
4   I may speak to him. (permission)
5   I ought to visit her.
6   You'd rather I didn't say anything.
7   He didn't have to speak to me.
8   I have to buy some matches.
9   He wasn't to speak to me.
10 He won't fall down.
11 You will come.
12 You wouldn't like the window open.
13 He used to beat his wife.
14 I am very late.
15 She came very late.
16 He has your book.
17 He has his breakfast at nine o'clock.
18 He has got to go now.
19 He couldn't have arrived before the others if he missed the fast train.
20 Come and see me tomorrow.
21 Have another cigarette.
22 I suppose he ought to have known that.
23 I take it you won't be coming then.
24 In that case he'll have to get a new one made.
25 Let's pretend we're not here.
26 Let me have a look.
27 You never used to work so late.
28 Just read it to yourself.
29 Let me read it for you.
30 Let's read aloud.
31 That's the sort of thing you *would* do.
32 You *would* lose it.
33 I'd better go.
34 You love your husband.
35 You shouldn't have been such a fool.

32.4
Advanced

A form of tag is frequently heard in English when one person wishes to pass a truculent, sarcastic or incredulous comment on another person's remark. This is done by repeating the remark and adding a tag, *both* being positive or negative. Correct intonation is important to catch the proper emotional content.

> I've broken a cup. – Oh you have, have you?
> I won't eat it! – Oh you won't, won't you?
> I hate you! – You do, do you?

*   *   *

● Add surprised, angry, truculent or sarcastic tags to the following (the teacher to make the remark, the student to add the comment):

1   I want you to give me some more money.
2   I spoke to the Prime Minister this morning.
3   He had a better collection of stamps than yours.
4   You mustn't talk to me like that!
5   I'm very fond of expensive presents.
6   I'd go quite mad if I had to live with *you*!
7   *Our* teacher speaks English much better than *yours*.
8   I've thrown your homework into the wastepaper-basket.
9   I'd rather go out with John than with you.
10   They'll send you to prison.
11   He thinks you're an old fool!
12   So do I!
13   I shall have to put you into a lower class.
14   I'm going home by myself today.
15   You can do the whole exercise again.
16   He hates her like poison.
17   I think this sentence is too hard for you.
18   They want you to give them better wages.
19   You can have the bits that are left over.
20   I feel very sorry for you.
21   I thought you didn't want any more!
22   You're a very rude person!
23   And so is your friend!
24   I'll tell my wife what you said!
25   No, I won't listen to you!

These tag forms are liable to get a little complicated in uneducated town dialects:

You don't half drink a lot, don't you? – I do, do I? – Not half, you don't!

(It's quite all right, your teacher will explain.)

33   *get* and *got* forms

**33.1
Elementary**

In spoken English the form *I've got* is used very extensively for *I have* (in the sense of 'I own'). *I'd got* in PAST tense, but less frequently; past tense form occurs mostly in reported speech.

* * *

● Say the following sentences, using the form with *got* instead of the simple verb *have*:

1   I have some more at home.
2   He hadn't any like this.
3   Have you a dog?
4   I'm afraid I haven't time to do it.
5   I see you have a new car.
6   Have you the tickets?
7   He has plenty in his shop.
8   She has some lovely flowers in her garden.
9   Have they your address?
10 We have some new photos to show you.
11 The cat hasn't anything to eat.
12 Have you someone to help you?
13 It has a bit broken off the top.
14 Have you anything more to say?
15 I've plenty of time now.
16 That woman has an attractive hat on.
17 We've no more left.
18 Have you everything you want?
19 I hadn't any money on me yesterday.
20 I haven't any now.
21 How many children has she?
22 He asked me for some cigarettes, but I hadn't any.
23 I've enough money to buy two.

24 Has he a job now?
25 My friend has a Rolls Royce.
26 The children have a beautiful dolls' house.
27 Had he the kind you wanted? (Did he have the kind you wanted?)
28 What have you to show me?
29 Haven't they anything better to do?
30 He hadn't a penny when I knew him.

Notice that we avoid the question-form *Had I?* etc., and usually use the *did* form even for simple possession, e.g. in No. 27 above. This is probably because *had* is felt to apply to the past moment only, as in the type:

They didn't have electric light in Ancient Rome.

33.2
Intermediate

The use of *get* as shown in Exercise 33.1 has also spread to the form *have to* = 'must'.

What have I got to do next?

The negative form is not the same as *mustn't*, but replaces *needn't* (i.e. it is the OPPOSITE of *must*). See also earlier exercises on *must*, Exercises 16.1, 2.

I haven't got to go just yet.
= *don't have to*, or *needn't*

When the stress falls on *got* it reinforces very strongly the idea of obligation. The PAST tense form, *I'd got to do it* or *I hadn't got to do it*, is rarely heard without this emphasis (*had to* and *didn't have to* being preferred), except in reported speech, where a parallel form is sought.

I had to get to school by 8.30.
You hadn't *got* to do what *he* said.

'I've got to practise it every day.'
He said he'd got to practise it every day.

Notice that *have* without its object can never change to *have got*.

Have you got the books? – Yes, I have,

which shows it to be a quasi-perfect tense.

* * *

● Say the following sentences, using a form with *got* instead of the simple verb *have*:

1 I don't have to get up so early every morning.
2 Have you anything else to give me?
3 He told me he didn't have to work any more.

4   Does she have to ring you up every time?
5   Why have you to give him so much money?
6   I'm afraid I have to go now.
7   Is this all I have to do?
8   You seem to have plenty to do.
9   Has your friend Maisie to come too?
10 Have we enough money?
11 Do they *have* to travel with us? (emphatic)
12 You didn't have to listen to him.
13 She has a pimple on her nose.
14 Has Cyril the sandwiches?
15 I don't have to sleep there, do I?
16 Did you know she hadn't anything to wear?
17 I wish I knew if she had any money.
18 I had a better one at home.
19 Has he the same edition as the rest of us?
20 Have you the time on you?
21 She said she didn't have to be home before midnight.
22 I have to go to the dentist this morning.
23 They have two dogs and three cats next door.
24 You don't have to do what your sister tells you.
25 Do I *have* to eat all this rice-pudding? (emphatic)
26 Have you time to go to the post?
27 'We have too much to do.' 'Have you really?'
28 What time do you have to get up?
29 She told me she didn't have to earn her living.
30 We have no servant, so mother *has* to do all the work. (emphatic)

33.3
Advanced

The *got*-form of Exercises 33.1 and 33.2 is never found when the verb is in the IMPERATIVE, the FUTURE, or any of the PERFECT tenses.

> Don't have any more!
> I've had no news since Wednesday.

Nor in those phrases where *have* and its object represent a single semantic whole.

> He had a very good journey.
> Do you have breakfast at eight?

But we can say, *I haven't got time to do it.*
See also notes to Exercise 18.1 on the difference between *he doesn't have to* and *he hasn't got to.*

*   *   *

● Say the following sentences, using a form with *got* instead of the simple verb *have* WHEREVER POSSIBLE:

1 Did you have any money when you were in Switzerland?
2 Did you have a good journey back?
3 He has quite a lot of friends.
4 He has a party and invites them all at least once a month.
5 Have you a clean handkerchief?
6 Do you have a clean handkerchief every day?
7 Have you enough clean handkerchiefs for every day of the week?
8 Have some more tea!
9 We don't have to wear evening dress, do we?
10 I have a holiday tomorrow.
11 I shan't have another holiday till Christmas.
12 He has to work overtime for a few weeks.
13 Why didn't you do it when you had the opportunity?
14 Doesn't she have to work on Saturday?
15 Have you a cigarette? Have one of mine!
16 Do you have to go back tonight?
17 Do you have lunch at home?
18 Do you always have a swim before breakfast?
19 He said he had a nicer one at home.
20 He said he had three dances with her.
21 It has to be seen to be believed.
22 She has more money than she knows what to do with.
23 I've no time to play the fool.
24 Do you think he has a chance of passing the examination?
25 I always have difficulty in finding my way here.
26 We never have coffee after lunch.
27 We never have enough money to go to the cinema.
28 He hasn't a leg to stand on.
29 Do you ever have time to read a novel at one sitting?
30 Do you really have a good time at these weekly parties?

33.4
Advanced

Get instead of *become*.   This use of *get* is very common. There is an interesting development of this in the PASSIVE VOICE, where the verb *get* replaces *be* usually to stress the moment of action rather than the resultant state. (Owing to the frequent use of past participles as adjectives, the ordinary passive construction cannot always make it clear whether ACTION or STATE is meant.)

The boy was hurt.
The boy got hurt.
He was married to a beautiful girl. (state)
He got married to a beautiful girl. (action)
I got wet through standing in the rain. (became)
My arms got badly burned in the sun.

*   *   *

● Refashion the following statements using a *get*-form:
1   The razor became rusty.
2   She burned the pudding. The pudding . . .
3   I hope you will become well again quickly.
4   He squashed his finger in the door. His finger . . .
5   We shall soon become tired, waiting here all night.
6   Someone ate the last cake yesterday. The last cake . . .
7   My hands have become dirty oiling my bicycle.
8   My teacher told me off yesterday. I . . .
9   He broke his arm in a fight. His arm . . .
10 If you eat too much you will become ill.
11 The maid broke another cup last night. Another cup . . .
12 The English beat the Australian cricket team. The Australians . . .
13 Your boss will give you the sack. You . . .
14 Mary tore her dress on a nail. Mary's dress . . .
15 The explosion cracked the walls of the house. The walls . . .
16 His friends blamed him for the mistake. He . . .
17 Bad news upsets him very easily. He . . .
18 Some men beat me up last night. I . . .
19 We must become better known to each other. (get to know)
20 She is becoming quite a little lady.
21 A stray dog bit her. She . . .

22   Somebody used to beat the poor animal every day.
     The poor animal ...
23   I have become very sunburnt.
24   A storm damaged the ship.   The ship ...
25   He has known me for some time, and now he
     would like to meet other young men here.   (get to
     know)

34 Predicative *so* and *not*

34.1
Elementary

A useful and important time-saver in English speech is
this use of *so* with *I think, believe, hope, am afraid*, etc., in
responses.

> I think it will be fine tomorrow. – Oh, I hope *so*.
> (affirmative)
> You haven't caught cold, have you? – I *don't* think *so*.
> (negative)

     *   *   *

●   Respond in a similar way to the following statements (the
     statements to be read to the students):
1   Is there time for another cup of tea? (think)
2   He left a week ago, didn't he? (believe)
3   Your mother won't be angry with you, will she?
     (not think)
4   I expect we shall have a good time at the party.
     (hope)
5   It seems that the train is very late. (afraid)
6   Perhaps he has got here before us. (not believe)
7   I'm sure you'll soon get better. (hope)
8   You'll have to pay for it yourself. (afraid)
9   Perhaps he will refuse to pay me. (not think)
10   We shall be home again soon. (hope)
11   Wasn't Nelson a famous admiral? (think)
12   Can't you ask for help? (not think)
13   You had a very unpleasant time, I'm told. (afraid)
14   Athens is on the coast, isn't it? (believe)
15   I think it will rain tomorrow. (afraid)
16   Perhaps she has finished my dress. (hope)

17   You are having a holiday this year, aren't you?
      (hope)
18   I expect this case is too heavy for you. (not think)
19   You are too old to climb mountains any more.
      (afraid)
20   It's time to go, isn't it? (believe)

34.2   *I hope* and *I am afraid* take *not* after them as a negative
Intermediate response.
                  Think and *believe* may also use this device, especially when
                  emphasis is required.

      I wonder if they've got lost? –
      (1)   Oh, I hope not.
      (2)   Oh, I don't think so. (I think not.)
      (3)   I'm afraid so. (I'm afraid they have.)

*   *   *

● Respond in a similar way to the following statements (the
  statements to be read to the students):
1   You haven't used this before, have you? (not
     think)
2   I'm sure we shall be able to go away for at least a
     fortnight. (hope)
3   Do you think it will keep fine today? (afraid)
4   Is this book a good one? (believe)
5   Do you think we shall have to pay a fine? (hope)
6   I suppose you wouldn't like to look after the baby
     for an hour, would you? (not think)
7   Were you very late? (afraid)
8   There aren't any cannibals in Africa now, are
     there? (not believe)
9   Do you think Maisie will win the beauty
     competition? (afraid)
10   Are the shops open on Sundays in London? (not
     think)
11   The newspapers say that it will be a good summer.
     (hope)
12   I suppose we shan't get home till after dark,
     Cyril. (afraid)
13   Grammatical exercises are very dull, aren't they?
     (think)
14   I don't think this will hurt you very much. (hope)

15 The Volga is the longest river in Europe, isn't it?
(think)
16 Will you be at the party tonight? (hope)
17 Have you time to type this for me? (think)
18 It's all right, I won't forget to wipe my feet on the
mat. (hope)
19 Won't they be able to have more than two days'
honeymoon? (not think)
20 Will you be seasick crossing the Channel? (hope)

35 *do* and *make*

**35.1
Intermediate**

These two verbs often depart from their fundamental
meanings of 'act' and 'construct' in idiomatic usage.
Examples of fundamental meaning of *do* and *make*:

> What are you *making*? – A cake.
> What are you *doing*? – Writing a letter.

Idiomatic use of these two verbs can only be learnt by
experience. The following two exercises practise a number
of *do* and *make* idioms.

* * *

● Complete the following sentences with *do* or *make*:
1 He — a lot of money last year.
2 They — peace at last.
3 I always — my best.
4 I shall — all the arrangements for you.
5 It has nothing to — with you.
6 He — a lot of business with us.
7 This is all I have. Will it —?
8 People must — without such luxuries in wartime.
9 He — a good speech yesterday.
10 She — him eat his dinner.
11 I will have nothing to — with such people.
12 My friend Maisie always — fun of me.
13 My friend Cyril can — tricks with his ears.
14 A soldier must — his duty.
15 It is my birthday; — come to tea.

16 I think the train leaves at nine, but you had
    better — certain.
17 I have nothing to — this afternoon.
18 It won't — you any harm to take another week's
    holiday.
19 How do you —?
20 Have you — your homework?

35.2   See Exercise 35.1.
Advanced   Notice the colloquial expressions:

> *Nothing doing* = There's nothing interesting in pro-
> gress *or* I'm not going to help you.
>
> *It doesn't do to* = It's not proper (right; advisable) to

and others in the exercise below.

*   *   *

● Supply a part of the verb *do* or *make*:
1   That glass of wine has — me good.
2   She will — him a good wife.
3   Will you — me a favour?
4   Are you trying to — me out a liar?
5   You must — up for lost time.
6   — up your mind to — what is right.
7   'Will this — for you?' 'I think I can — it —.'
8   It doesn't — your face any good to — up too
    much.
9   I can't — out what he is trying to —.
10 You can't — use of that any more; it's — for.
11 You've only half an hour left, so you'd better —
    the most of it.
12 He — a big mistake in — business with such a
    firm.
13 Why can't you — him — his work properly?
14 I'm afraid this is the best I can — for you; I know
    it's not very big, but you'll have to — it —.
15 I could — with a few more people like you to —
    up for the time I've lost with the others.
16 — your worst! Say what you like and have —
    with it!
17 It was all the pilot could — to — the necessary
    height to clear the mountains.
18 It — not — to — fun of your superiors.

19   I'm afraid half a spoonful won't — at all; he'll
     have to — without it altogether.
20   There's nothing — here; let's — our way out.

36   Infinitive Implied by its Particle

36.1
Intermediate

A very odd but important idiom, particularly in spoken
English, is the habit of finishing a phrase (usually a response) with the infinitive particle *to*, leaving the verb to be
implied.

> Will you show me how to do it properly? – I shall be
> glad to.

*   *   *

● Respond to the following questions or statements, using
the expression given in brackets:

1   Why can't you come to the pictures with me? (not
be allowed)
2   Say 'Sir' when you speak to me! (refuse)
3   Read the letter if you want to. (not wish)
4   'I'm afraid I can't come after all.'   'But . . .'
(promise)
5   Why do you put sugar in your soup instead of
salt? (prefer)
6   'You didn't bring any cabbage from the market?'
'I (mean), but I forgot.'
7   'You must take more care of it.'   'Yes, . . .' (ought)
8   Why haven't you proposed to Maisie yet? (not
have chance)
9   Can't we stop for another coffee? (not be time)
10   'He says you are to see him tomorrow.'   'I
suppose . . .' (have)
11   'He has painted his dining-room bright red.'
'Well, he (have the right).'
12   Why didn't you visit him while you were there?
(not have occasion).[1]

---

[1] See Exercise 40.1 for a note on the difference between
occasion to and *the (an) opportunity of* ——*ing*.

13 'Your friend Cyril spoke very rudely to me last
    night.'   'I'm sure he (not mean).'
14 'Why didn't you dance with him?'   'He (not ask).'
15 'You didn't say goodbye to me.'   'No, I (forget).'

37 *else* and *or else*

37.1 **Elementary**	*Else.* This interesting adverb is now so closely bound to certain pronouns that it is rarely heard apart from them. The *some*, *any*, and *no* compounds are followed by *else* to avoid the clumsy form 'any other person', 'some other thing', etc. All are singular, including *everyone else*. Interrogatives (but rarely *why*, *which*, *when*) are similarly followed by *else*. For possessives see next exercise.

*　　*　　*

● Say the following sentences in a better way, using *else*:
1 Have you **any other thing** to say?
2 You must see **another person**.
3 May I stay **at some other place**?
4 What **other thing** must I do?
5 I have **some other thing** to show you.
6 **What other place** can I go to?
7 **What other person** is coming with you?
8 There's **no other thing** to say.
9 Ask **some other person** to lend it to you.
10 **All the other people have** a green ticket.
11 'Haven't I seen you **in some other place**?'
12 'No, you haven't seen me **in any other place**.'
13 **What other person** did you speak to?
14 **No other person** had a dog like mine.
15 What **other thing** could I do?
16 Has he **some other thing** to tell us?
17 **All the other people have** gone.
18 **What other person** did you see?
19 **At what other place** can I find one?
20 '**What other person** is coming?'   '**No other person**.'

37.2
Intermediate

How else and *when else* are less frequently met with than the forms in the previous exercise, and so are not so important for elementary students.

Since *else* is felt to be firmly tied to the word preceding it, the correct possessive form 'anyone's else' sounds unnatural; the accepted form in current English is *anyone else's*.

The same applies to the interrogatives with *else*. One still hears occasionally, 'What could I do else?' but it seems to be dying out. Perhaps for the sake of clarity, the teacher should insist on *What else could I do?* and for the possessive: *Who else's can it be?*

*   *   *

● Say the following sentences, using *else*:

1 Have you decided on **any other thing** yet?
2 I think this is **some other person's** hat.
3 **At what other time** could we meet?
4 If you can't find my umbrella, **any other person's** will do.
5 **In what other way** can you possibly do it?
6 What **other thing** is there to talk about?
7 **No other person's** room has been paid for.
8 If it wasn't your own father, **what other person's** could it be?
9 Cyril is dancing with **some other person's** partner.
10 **In what other way** can it possibly be mended?
11 I wonder if **any other person's** signature would do instead?
12 I wonder **what other person's** would do instead?
13 Can you tell me **any other place** to visit?
14 I'm afraid Maisie has gone out with **some other person**.
15 I jammed the brakes on and swerved to the left. What **other thing** could I do?
16 Hurry up! **All the other people's** glasses are empty.
17 **What other person** do you want some scandal about?
18 I'm afraid you must put on **some other thing** if you want to bathe here.
19 You must have mistaken me for **some other person**. I've never lived **in any other place** but here.
20 Isn't there **any other person's** time you can waste instead of mine?

**37.3
Elementary
and
Intermediate**

Or else.   This is a very useful connective expressing the condition *if not*. It is very frequently met with in conversation, but rarely learnt and practised by foreigners.

Come early, or else you won't get anything to eat.
= If you don't, you won't get ...

Or can always take its place; *else* acts as a kind of intensifier.

*   *   *

● Join the following pairs of sentences with *or else*:

1   Put your coat on.   If you don't, you'll catch cold.
2   You must hurry.   If you don't, you'll be late.
3   We must look pleased.   If we don't, he'll be cross.
4   Hide it.   If you don't, they will steal it.
5   I must clean it.   If I don't, it will get rusty.
6   Follow him.   If you don't, he'll get away.
7   You must put it on ice.   If you don't, it will melt.
8   Hold it by its neck.   If you don't, it'll bite you.
9   We must keep chickens.   If we don't, we shan't have any eggs.
10   We must tear it up.   If we don't, they'll find out our secret.
11   Shut the door quietly.   If you don't, you'll wake the baby.
12   You must pay him well.   If you don't, he won't work for you.
13   You must build a high wall.   If you don't, you will lose all your fruit.
14   Cook it in butter.   If you don't, it'll be hard.
15   Take it away.   If you don't, I'll scream!
16   Put it down quickly.   If you don't, you'll burn your fingers.
17   We must go now.   If we don't, we'll miss the train.
18   You must finish your work now.   If you don't, you won't be able to go out tonight.
19   I must go home.   If I don't, mother will be cross with me.
20   Do as you are told.   If you don't, you'll be punished.
21   Tell the cook to put the meat in the oven now.   If she doesn't, it won't be ready for dinner.
22   She ought to take more exercise.   If she doesn't, she'll get fat.

23 Milk must be kept in a cool place. If it isn't, it
    will turn sour.
24 Sit down. If you don't, you'll be tired.
25 Help me with my homework. If you don't,
    I won't help you.

38 Infinitive

38.1
Intermediate

Frequently a clause having the same subject as the main
sentence can be more concisely expressed by using an
infinitive.

> I was glad when I heard of your success.
> I was glad *to hear* of your success.

Notice also its use after a superlative.

> He was the first man to climb Mount Everest.

* * *

● Reword the following sentences using the infinitive:

1 He was sorry **when he heard** of your
   disappointment.
2 He hopes **that he will know** by tomorrow.
3 It seems **that it is** improbable.
4 Do you understand what **you have to do**?
5 We should be sorry **if we heard** bad reports of him.
6 The candidate did not expect **that he would pass**
   his examination.
7 Elsie was told **that she must not dirty** her dress.
8 The boys only laughed **when they saw** the little
   girl cry.
9 She asked **if she might leave** the room.
10 I hope **that I shall live** to see my son a successful
   doctor.
11 That was the first picture **that came** by satellite.
12 My friend was delighted **when she learned** of the
   arrival of our baby.
13 Do not promise **that you will do** it, if you are not
   sure that you can.
14 The doctor warned Cyril **that he should not touch**
   alcohol.

15   The last person **who spoke** like that about my
friend Maisie was in hospital for two months.

38.2
Advanced

Read notes to Exercise 38.1.

          *   *   *

● Replace clauses with INFINITIVE phrases:

1   I should be delighted **if I could join** you.
2   He was annoyed **when he heard** that the
Conservative Party had got in again.
3   She was sorry **that she had missed** the beginning of
the concert.
4   I am glad **now that I see** all the mess has been
cleared up.
5   We must wait **till we hear** the examination results
before we make any plans.
6   My daughter will be thrilled **when she wears an**
evening dress as lovely as that.
7   Mary was mortified **when she found** that she would
have to wear a wig.
8   They would be very surprised **if they were to**
receive an invitation.
9   I was afraid **at the thought of going** past the
haunted house alone.
10   You would be foolish **if you dyed** your hair red.
11   I would love it **if I could own** a house in the
country.
12   She was hurt **when she found** that her young man
had forgotten her birthday.
13   Bob was pleased **when he heard** he had been
promoted.
14   I was sorry **that I had to** leave so early.
15   She is happy **that she has found** such a nice place to
live in.

TOO, ENOUGH

38.3
Intermediate

See Section 10 for more elementary examples.
Too = excess; is a kind of negative.

    It was *too* cold (for us) to go out.
      = It was so cold (that)[1] we could*n't* go out.

[1] *That* is usually left out in spoken English.

Enough = sufficiency; is a kind of positive (but see next exercise).

It was cold *enough* to freeze our fingers.
= It was so cold (that) our fingers froze. (It was very cold and . . .)

N.B.—Too comes BEFORE and *enough* comes AFTER the adjective.

* * *

● Reword the following sentences using *too* or *enough*:
1 This coffee is so hot that I can't drink it.
2 He's very tall and can touch the ceiling.
3 His car is so big that Maisie can't drive it.
4 I've got so fat that I can't wear this dress now.
5 The weather was so hot that we couldn't go out.
6 Grandfather Giles is so old that he can't learn French.
7 The student was very clever, and could solve any mathematical problem.
8 This battery is strong, and should last forty-eight hours.
9 This novel is so short that it can be read in a few hours.
10 The fields are still wet, and cannot be ploughed.
11 Your nails are so long that they might scratch anybody's eyes out.
12 I'm so excited that I can't think.
13 This problem is so difficult that I can't explain it.
14 The turkey was so big that mother couldn't put it in the oven.
15 You're quite old and you can ask her yourself.
16 That question is so personal Cyril can't answer it.
17 The accident was so terrible we can't talk about it.
18 She is quite old and she ought to know better.
19 You're so old you could be my grandfather.
20 Maisie is so tall I can't kiss her without standing on a chair.
21 That orange you gave me was so sour I couldn't eat it.
22 They were so empty-headed they couldn't learn a single thing.

23   She was very foolish and she believed everything
      I told her.
24   He was so angry he wouldn't speak to me.
25   The window was so dirty they couldn't see through
      it.

38.4
Intermediate
and
Advanced

See previous exercise.
Note also that a negative *enough to* is the equivalent of two
negative clauses.

> He *wasn't* rich enough (for her) to marry.
>   = He *wasn't* rich and so she *didn't* marry him.

*   *   *

● Reword the following using *too* or *enough*:
1   The policeman could not run very fast, and so was
     unable to catch the burglar.
2   I think you are very strong and can lift this trunk.
3   That tea-cup is so badly broken that it can't be
     mended.
4   Some apples are so sour that we can't eat them.
5   You don't eat much; that amount wouldn't keep a
     sparrow alive.
6   There is not much beer, so you can't all have a
     drink.
7   There was a lot of food left over; it would have fed
     a dozen more people.
8   I have very little petrol; it will not get us there.
9   He is quite well, and can go out again now.
10   The river was so deep they couldn't wade across.
11   The light is so dim that it can't be used for close
     work.
12   He plays the violin so well that he could perform
     at a concert.
13   The photo was so clear that you could see every
     detail of the background.
14   The path was so slippery that we couldn't walk
     along it.
15   An elephant's trunk is so strong it can hold a log
     of wood.
16   The current was so strong he couldn't swim
     against it.

17   You're so young that you don't know about such
     things yet.
18   Mr Tumbrill is so fat he can't tie up his own shoes.
19   He's not very good so I can't marry him.
20   He said he was so thirsty he could drink a well
     dry.

Note the popular expression:
It was too dark (etc.) *for words.*

39   *-ing* form – Gerund and Present Participle

<table>
<tr><td>39.1
Elementary</td><td>The part of the verb that ends in *-ing* has two very important functions.
(1)   It can have the force of an *adjective* as well as that of a verb.</td></tr>
</table>

An old house; a burning house.
A good story; an exciting story.
Exciting the crowd with his angry words, the speaker
moved to the edge of the platform.

We call this the PRESENT PARTICIPLE.

(2)   It can have the force of a *noun* as well as that of a verb.

Swimming is a sport.
Climbing mountains is a sport, too.

We call this the GERUND.

A number of verbs and many verbal combinations like *be
fond of* or *give up* can be followed by the *-ing* form of a
verb instead of the infinitive or a clause. When this is a
GERUND, it can be the object of the main verb, and (as it is
a verb itself) can have its own object.

Do you like *tobacco*?
Do you like *smoking*?
Do you like *smoking a pipe*?

He's fond of *music.*
He's fond of *singing.*
He's fond of *singing pop songs.*

*   *   *

(39.1)   ● Complete the following sentences by putting the given verbs into the gerund form:

1 They started (write) the lesson before the teacher came in.

2 I began (read) a novel yesterday.

3 We don't like (have) to do homework.

4 Do you mind (speak) to John and (ask) him to help us?

5 We enjoyed (see) you and (hear) all your news.

6 We thought of (drive) across France. We're rather tired of (go) by train.

7 It has stopped (rain). I hate (go) out in the rain.

8 I love (eat) oranges, but I dislike (peel) them.

9 I can't help (wonder) whether we should risk (go) without our raincoats.

10 My uncle has given up (smoke) and now prefers (eat) sweets.

11 I hate (practise) (read) aloud without first (learn) the new words.

12 I suggest (do) more sentences on the gerund next time.

13 I began (look) for the missing papers a few days ago, but now I must stop (try) to find them.

14 I like (come) to school by bus, but I hate (stand) in the rain and (wait) for it.

15 Start (do) the exercise now, and stop (write) as soon as I tell you to.

Notice that by leaving out *and* in No. 14, *waiting* becomes a PRESENT PARTICIPLE.

39.2
(Elementary and)
Intermediate
'SUBJECT' OF
THE GERUND

Since the GERUND is a noun, it is logical to find it preceded by a POSSESSIVE PRONOUN or a NOUN IN THE POSSESSIVE FORM.

Do you object to a cigarette?
Do you object to our cigarettes?
Do you object to smoking?
Do you object to our smoking?
Do you object to our smoking cigarettes?

In practice this pattern is restricted almost entirely to pronouns and proper names. Non-personal nouns do not normally have a possessive form, nor can we easily make a possessive form with more complicated subjects. So we also have a parallel pattern using the objective (common) case.

> There was no sign of *the dinner* appearing before I left.
> We insisted on *rich and poor* being treated alike.
> Will you approve of *me and my friend* attending the class as visitors?

Examples of this pattern are very common. They are not participle constructions but true gerunds, since the 'object' in each case is not merely the portion in italics, but the whole phrase to the end of the sentence. Therefore it is not surprising to find the same pattern used when a pronoun or proper noun is in SUBJECT relation to the gerund.

> Do you mind *their/them* coming too?
> I don't like *your/you* coming late every time.
> I'm not very keen on *Mary's/Mary* living there alone.

In general the POSSESSIVE form is considered to be more literary and elegant; the OBJECTIVE form is found mainly in the spoken language, where it is probably just as common as the possessive form.

The following short passage from Dickens's *David Copperfield* is of interest:

> (A dream) of *the pair of hired post-horses* being ready; and of *Dora's* going away to change her dress: of *my aunt and Miss Clarissa* remaining with us; and *our* walking in the garden; and *my aunt* . . . being mightily amused with herself . . .
>
> (The whole of this long description of David's wedding in Chapter 43 is written in gerunds, and is well worth reading carefully.)

*   *   *

● Read the following, replacing the (pro)nouns **in bold type** by possessives:

1 Our teacher won't like **us** coming late to school.
2 I don't mind **you** talking to Cyril, but I always remember **him** complaining of **you** staying too long.
3 Please excuse **us** calling you by your first name.
4 I wonder why Maisie hates **me** wearing this pink shirt and green tie?
5 It's no use **you** asking him to lend you any money.
6 I'm afraid of **John** losing the way.
7 They insisted on **me** going again next week.

8   Nobody minds **you** singing in class, but we can't stand **you** singing out of tune.
9   Do you remember **me** asking for the book before?
10 Cyril doesn't like the idea of **me** learning to ride his motor-cycle.
11 Please forgive **me** asking such a personal question.
12 Maisie can't understand **me** wanting to keep goldfish.
13 Cyril says he doesn't remember **you** lending him any money.
14 We shall miss **you** coming in to talk to us in the evenings.
15 Our friends objected to **us** leaving so soon.
16 I don't remember **you** having said before that you wanted to come.
17 I don't much like the idea of **Mary** going home alone in the dark.
18 You must please forgive **us** interrupting you in this way.
19 Did your uncle agree to **you** coming to see me?
20 I just can't understand **you** wanting to do this exercise again!

39.3   ● Read the following, replacing the possessives **in bold type**
(Elementary   by (pro)nouns:
and)   1 Would you mind **my** opening the window?
Intermediate   2 My friend Cyril can't understand **my** treating him like that.
3   I won't have **your** writing homework in pencil.
4   Did you give it back without **his** asking you?
5   Mother hates **our** eating and drinking between meals.
6   I remember **their** coming in, long after midnight.
7   I don't fancy **his** living with us for six months.
8   Cyril will never forget **my** showing him how I can stand on my hands.
9   I can't help **your** forgetting to bring your books.
10 I can't imagine **their** refusing to pay for it.
11 The teacher dislikes **their** sitting too far from the blackboard.
12 The doctor doesn't object to **my** eating a little meat now and then.

13 I can excuse **Betty's** being rude to me, but I can't forgive **her** being rude to Maisie.
14 My parents don't like **my** going out alone at night.
15 I'll have to insist on **his** not disturbing us before the end of the lesson.
16 I was afraid of **your** leaving without me.
17 Do you remember **his** coming here for the first time?
18 I can't understand **their** forgetting to come to our party.
19 The weather won't stop **your** playing in the match.
20 If you don't mind **my** saying so, I think we should do part of this exercise again.

39.4
Intermediate
and Advanced
SURVEY OF
COMMON VERBS
THAT ARE
FOLLOWED BY
-*ING* FORM
OF VERB

LIST 1.   VERBS FOLLOWED BY GERUND

appreciate	*go on* (= continue)
avoid	*keep* (*on*)
consider	*leave off* (= cease)
delay	*mention*
detest	*mind* (negs. and questions)
dislike	*miss*
enjoy	*pardon*
escape	*practise*
excuse	*put off* (= postpone)
fancy (negs. and questions)	*recollect*
finish	*stop*
forgive	*suggest*
give up[1]	*understand*

can't resist	*deny*[2]
can't stand	*postpone*[2]
can't help	*risk*[2]

I couldn't deny that he'd made a reasonable excuse.
(I couldn't deny his having made . . .)
He denied knowing anything about the missing jewels.
It went on raining for days.
Do you recollect (my) telling John about the new house?

[1] And very many other transitive phrasal verbs, i.e. verb + adverbial (*get off going to prison*; *talk over buying a house*) and verb + preposition (*see through his pretending to be an expert*; *get out of doing something unpleasant*) combinations.
[2] The 'subjects' of the gerunds following the last three verbs can only be in the POSSESSIVE form; but as the effect is very heavy, it is more usual to employ a clause (see first example).

They don't understand your/you needing more money.

I've put off (delayed) writing to him till today.

I don't think anyone mentioned (Mary's/Mary) being there.

I couldn't resist buying such lovely apples.

Avoid drinking too much water with your meals.

We all appreciate your wanting to help us in our difficulties.

You certainly mustn't miss seeing this wonderful film.

What good luck! I've escaped being asked to do another grammar question.

I considered (thought about) painting the ceiling blue.

I gave up smoking when I was a young man.

Please excuse (pardon, forgive) my disturbing you.

OR: Please excuse (etc.) me for disturbing you.

In addition to these verbs, a few other common gerund constructions are *worth noting* here:

worth, *it's no use*, introductory *it* and *there*, the idiom *there is no . . .* , verbal object of all prepositions.

The play really wasn't worth watching. (See LIST 3.)

If it's worth doing at all, then it's worth doing well.

It's no use (your) asking for more when it's all gone.

It's been a pleasure meeting you.

I was surprised at there being no one to meet us.

There's no knowing (*or* telling) what will happen next.

Once (= as soon as) he starts telling stories, there's no stopping him.

We didn't mind your insisting on Mary's coming with us on the trip without paying anything.

LIST 2.   SOME COMMON VERBS FOLLOWED BY EITHER GERUND OR INFINITIVE

advise	*forget*	*prefer*
agree	*hate*	*propose*
allow	*intend*	*regret*
attempt	*leave*	*remember*
begin	*like*	*start*
cease	*love*	*study*
continue	*mean*	*try*
dread	*permit*	

There is often a difference of meaning between the gerund and infinitive constructions; examples will be given in Section 40.

LIST 3. GERUNDS WITH MEANING OF PASSIVE INFINITIVE
The OBJECT of the gerund is the SUBJECT of the main verb,
e.g.

> *Your hair needs cutting.* (. . . needs *to be cut*).

deserve	want
merit	won't/doesn't/didn't bear
need	won't/doesn't/didn't stand

(His success) *is past hoping* (*praying*) *for*
(It's an idea) *worth carrying out.*
My shoes want mending.
His opinions won't bear repeating in public.
His brave action certainly deserves rewarding.

* * *

(39.4) ● Complete the following sentences, using gerunds:
EXAMPLE

> Do you mind (I, smoke) a pipe?
> ANSWER: Do you mind my (OR me) smoking a pipe?

1 I can't help (feel) anxious about the political situation.
2 I don't like (she, read) my letters.
3 I think most people prefer (ride) to (walk).
4 She loves (swim) in the sea.
5 I can't understand (he, forget) to answer my letter.
6 There's no (deny) that he enjoys (listen) to his own voice.
7 Don't keep on (shout) like that; we must avoid (annoy) our neighbours.
8 I enjoy (rest) in the afternoon after (try) to finish (do) my homework.
9 Do you mind (I, see) your photos again?
10 I can't understand (he, be) in love with a bad-tempered girl like Maisie.
11 She likes (begin) pieces of knitting but hates (finish) them.
12 I'm sure the librarian will remember (I, return) the dictionary last week.
13 It won't be any use (you, try) to borrow any more money.
14 I remember (he, ask) for this book last Friday.
15 I dread (take) examinations for fear of (fail).

16 I can't insist on (you, leave) early, but if you're set on (stay) any longer, you risk (lose) the last train home.

17 I didn't mind (they, come) late to the lecture, but I objected to (they, make) so much noise.

18 Last week you mentioned (get) us a different reading-book; we've nearly finished (read) this one.

19 This change of timetable will mean (we, leave) much later every day instead of (get) home before evening.

20 We've gone on (write) to this office regularly for weeks and can't help (wonder) why we never get an answer.

21 Your friend's idea is worth (go into) more carefully.

22 I know you won't mind (I, point out) that very small children need (look after) more than older ones.

23 Please excuse (we, come) a little late without (inform) you beforehand.

24 Your doctor advised (go) to bed early, so I really can't understand (you, want) to stay up late.

25 My wife hates (I, read) a newspaper at breakfast.

39.5
Intermediate

See previous exercise.

LIST 4.   OBJECTIVE CASE PLUS *-ing* (PRESENT PARTICIPLE)
This should not be confused with the true GERUND; the 'subject' of the *-ing* form is never in the POSSESSIVE case with this group of verbs.

*feel	**see*
*hear	**watch*
*listen to	hark at
*notice	smell
*observe	look at
*perceive	have (rare in present tense)

can imagine
he kept me waiting, etc.
we caught them stealing apples, etc.
we'll set/start/get them working, etc.

* These eight verbs can also be followed by the infinitive. (See next two exercises for difference between *-ing* form and infinitive.)

I heard him practising his violin.
I can smell fish cooking.
He didn't notice me waiting for him.
Hark at that woman talking!
He'll have us speaking English in a few months.

*   *   *

● Complete the following sentences by using the -*ing* form of the given verbs:

1 Let's listen to (he, play) the piano.
2 I noticed (the children, talk) together, and later caught (they, climb) my apple-trees.
3 I heard (they all, come) downstairs and (go) into the kitchen.
4 As we were passing your house in the car, we saw (you, cross) the road.
5 We observed (a cat, watch) (a bird, feed) in the garden.
6 I can't imagine (they all, get) to school in time.
7 Just look at (all those dogs, run) across our garden!
8 We didn't mean to keep (they, stand) so long in the rain.
9 We must get (they, work) on a new play while their enthusiasm lasts. I hope we'll have (they, act) in a real theatre before long.
10 For a short while he watched (we, peel) potatoes, then he looked at (the meat, roast) in the oven.
11 I think I can smell (something, burn).
12 Can you imagine (I, wear) a pink and blue tie?
13 I didn't notice (you, watch) (we, have) a swim.
14 They caught (he, open) your letters.
15 I've always liked (see) (they, play) together.

40 Infinitive and Gerund

40.1
Intermediate

The most important verbal constructions using the -*ing* form have been listed and practised in Section 39. Even more verbs require an INFINITIVE construction, either with the particle *to* or without it. There are a few verbs that may

be followed by either the -*ing* form or the infinitive, but as
the meaning may also be different, we shall mention the
more important constructions in these notes.

LIST 4 of Exercise 39.5 gives the first 8 verbs as having both
PRESENT PARTICIPLE and INFINITIVE constructions. The
-*ing* form describes the action in progress (like a CON-
TINUOUS tense); the infinitive is used for a complete act.

> I saw him crossing the road. (On the way to the other
> side.)
> I saw him cross the road. (From one side to the other.)
> I heard him singing in his bath. (Noticed this act in
> progress.)
> I heard him sing at the concert. (I heard his whole
> performance.)
> I watched John and Bill playing chess for a while, then
> I went home. (The game still continued.)
> I watched John take Bill's queen, then I went home.

The verbs of LIST 2 may be followed by a GERUND or an
INFINITIVE, usually with a difference of meaning. The basic
difference is often that the GERUND is more general in
meaning; the INFINITIVE suggests some special occasion
(or series of occasions) with a subject more or less implied.

> Riding is pleasanter than walking. (Comparing two
> activities).)
> You'll find it better to take a bus than (to) walk.
> (Talking of some person's actions for some certain
> journey.)
> I hate telling lies. (The act of lying in general.)
> I hate to tell you this, but ... (This particular thing
> that I must now tell you.)
> I prefer staying quietly at home to going to a cinema.
> (In general.)
> Come and see a film tonight. – No, thanks; I prefer
> to stay at home. (On this occasion.)

Here are some more comparisons between these two constructions:

like, don't like.   With an INFINITIVE the affirmative
means 'I prefer, want'; the negative means 'I am un-
willing'.

> I like to feel independent.
> What would you like to eat?
> John always likes to get to school in good time.
> I shouldn't like to work as hard as he does.

I didn't like to say so, but . . .
I don't like to refuse him, but I'm afraid I shall have to.

With a GERUND the affirmative has the more general meaning of 'I am fond of'; the negative expresses the speaker's DISLIKE (a weak form of *hate*).

I like talking to you. (I always *have* found pleasure in your company.)

(Notice how *should/would* and INFINITIVE is used with the verbs *like*, *love* and *hate* when we wish to express the present single act: *I should like to talk to you.*)

Children like playing more than studying.
I don't like waiting in the rain.

Compare:

I don't like waking up so early as this. (= dislike)
I don't like to wake him up so early as this. (= don't want to)

remember, forget.   These have two meanings:
(1)   the working (or not) of memory (INFINITIVE).
(2)   (not) to have a recollection of something (GERUND).

I must remember to post the letter. (must not forget)
I don't remember posting the letter. (can't recall, bring to mind)
I forgot to come to the exam yesterday. (didn't remember)
I shall never forget taking this exam. (will always have this memory)

With these two verbs, therefore, we find that the INFINITIVE points to the future, the GERUND, to the past. A similar contrast is found when *for* (and the GERUND) has a past meaning, the INFINITIVE a future one:

I paid him for translating my letter. (after the translation)
I paid him to translate my letter. (before the translation)
He was kept indoors for being naughty.
He was kept indoors to do his homework.

afraid to, afraid of.

I'm afraid to make her angry. (I daren't make her angry.)

I'm afraid of making her angry. (I don't want to do this because I think it will make her angry.)

I'm afraid to disturb him at this late hour. (I daren't disturb him.)

I can't play the piano to you now as I'm afraid of disturbing him. (I don't want to play because the noise might disturb him.)

allow, *permit*.   When a personal object is present these verbs take an INFINITIVE; otherwise they take a GERUND.

The librarian doesn't allow (permit) us to talk here.
The librarian doesn't allow (permit) talking here.

mean.   (= to intend) takes INFINITIVE;
(*it*) *means* (= signifies) takes GERUND.

I mean to work harder next year.
We meant to tell you, but we forgot.
Having a party tonight will mean (our) working extra hard tomorrow.
The transport strike meant (their) having to walk to work every day.

try.   With INFINITIVE it has the meaning 'make an effort or attempt'; with GERUND it means to test (by making an experiment).

He tried to speak French to us. (He made an effort to do so.)

He tried speaking French to us. (He spoke French, hoping that we should then understand him better.)

I tried to write with my left hand. (I made an effort to do so.)

I tried writing with my left hand. (I did write with my left hand, being curious to see the result.)

He tried to grow potatoes there. (He did his best to make them grow.)

He tried growing potatoes there. (He actually grew some, to see if they would be a successful crop for that kind of soil and climate.)

regret.   Note the meanings of the three following constructions:

I regretted saying it wasn't true. (*was* sorry that I said . . .)

I regret having said it wasn't true. (*am* sorry that I said . . .)

I regret to say it wasn't true. (*am* sorry that I must now say . . .)

opportunity.   The two usual constructions are:
(1) *to have the (an) opportunity of* (with GERUND).
(2) (There will) *be an opportunity to* (with INFINITIVE).
Construction (2) is nearly always introduced with some part of the verb *be*, and means 'a convenient time'.

> You'll have an opportunity of meeting him later.
> It'll be a good opportunity (for us) to ask for more books.
> Last year I had the opportunity of going to London.
> Let's hope there'll be an opportunity for you to go, too, one day.

occasion.   Always with INFINITIVE: *to have occasion to*. The meaning is 'to have a reason for doing' or 'to find it necessary to do'.

> I had occasion to go to London last year. (business reason)
> I hope I shan't have occasion to punish you. (need to)

Compare:

> If I have an opportunity of speaking to him, I'll give him your message. (meet him by some chance)
> If I (ever) have occasion to speak . . . (if there is some reason why I must speak to him)

✳   ✳   ✳

(40.1)   ● Put the verbs between brackets into their correct form (notice any alternatives that might give a different meaning):

1 I had to ask the boys (stop) (play).
2 Don't start (try) (learn) geometry before you have finished (learn) (do) simple things in arithmetic.
3 We can't consider (buy) a new house before (sell) the old one.
4 Please don't talk of (go) before (see) my album.
5 If you can't unscrew the lid, try (hit) it with a hammer.
6 I saw him (sit) in the park on the way home, and heard him (tell) his friend not to be late.
7 I don't want (you, mention) (I, arrive) late.
8 I appreciate (you, want) (help) my friend, but it's time he learnt (practise) (do) his work alone.
9 I have decided (allow) Maisie (do) as she pleases.
10 I can't understand (he, want) (marry) a girl like that.

11   The police suspect him of (try) (sell) stolen goods.
12   I remember (hear) him (say) the grass needed (cut).
13   Can you manage (finish) (pack) these parcels
     alone?
14   We didn't fancy (live) in that house and regretted
     (move) from our old one.
15   'I've always loved (act).' 'I'd love (see) (you, wear)
     a Roman toga and (recite) Shakespeare.'
16   The manager let us (watch) the actors (rehearse).
17   After (get) (like) English through (hear) it on the
     radio, he finished by (study) it.
18   I should like (he, start) (take) more English lessons.
19   We considered (give) her a book for her birthday,
     but couldn't help (buying) her some flowers, too.
20   I couldn't resist (ask) him why he was trying
     (avoid) (meet) me.
21   I hate (get up) early and (dress) in the dark.
22   We regret (say) that the lecture was very dull and
     wasn't worth (listen to).
23   Our teacher has promised (help) us (prepare) for
     the examinations which he has put off (hold) till
     next week.
24   Cyril's hair wants (cut), but I can't imagine (he,
     spend) either time or money on (get) it done.
25   I'd love (have) an opportunity of (meet) you
     again.

40.2 Intermediate and Advanced PREPOSITIONS

All prepositions are followed by a GERUND, except *to*.
After *to* we sometimes find the INFINITIVE, as if the *to* were
the infinitive particle. The most usual expressions where
we find this confusion are used in the following examples:

> They finally *agreed to* pay half the money in advance.
> We're not *accustomed to* stay up so late.
> He had a *tendency* (an *inclination*) *to* drink tea at all
> hours.
> There was little *incentive to* work harder.

In these sentences the *to* is not strictly part of the infinitive;
a gerund can be used instead. Apart from the five expressions above, *to* is regularly followed by the gerund:

> I'm looking forward to seeing you next week.
> I hope you're not averse to meeting a few foreigners.

Are you opposed to (Do you object to) my leaving early?

* * *

● Put the verbs between brackets into their correct form (notice any alternatives that might give a different meaning):

1 Have you ever watched people (try) (catch) fish?

2 If you dislike (peel) onions, try (hold) them under water while (do) so.

3 There'll be an opportunity (ask) questions before (leave) the hall after (hear) the lecture.

4 His ideas are well worth (listen to) in spite of (they, sound) so unpractical.

5 I hoped (arrange) (come) early (help) (put) the room in order for the party.

6 I know you will pardon (I, say) so, but you keep (give) us too many hard words (spell) in English.

7 I've had occasion (complain) of (he, come) late again.

8 It's silly (risk) (get) your feet wet.

9 Stop (make) a fool of yourself by (keep on) (repeat) the same question.

10 I must remember (remind) Cyril that the garden needs (water).

11 I remember (allow) them (play) in my garden without first (ask) for permission.

12 We mustn't risk (be) late for the concert. I put off (go) last week, and I don't want (miss) (hear) him again.

13 I appreciate (you, not want) (mention) (he, have) been to prison before (come) to work for us.

14 Is it any use (I, ask) you (insist) on (John, be) present without (wait) for any further invitation?

15 I recollect (my grandfather, say) that if a job was worth (do) at all it was worth (do) well.

16 He likes (read) crime stories so I can't understand (he, be) unable to resist (look at) the end of the book first.

17 I don't mind (the children, play) in the garden, but I won't have (they, walk) over my flowers.

18 There's no (know) what might happen if we start
(they, work) on plans that won't bear (look into).

19 Don't (keep) (I, wait) long before (answer) my
question.

20 Listen to (the baby, cry)! He can't stand (have) to
wait for his food, and he won't leave off (cry) till
he gets it.

21 I advise you (wait) before (decide) (accept) the job.

22 Is (boil) or (fry) the best way of (cook) this fish?

23 I should like (watch) these farmworkers (cut) the
corn for a few minutes before (go) any farther.

24 Did you forget (remind) John (ask) his friend (pay
back) the money he owes us?

25 Please (begin) (eat) now without (wait) for the
others to come.   There's no (tell) when they'll
manage (get) here.

26 I can see (you, begin) (smile), so it is no use (you,
pretend) (be) asleep.

27 Maisie says she would love (go) with me to the
cinema tonight; she says she hates (go) out alone.

28 Would you mind (arrange) (travel) with my young
sister?

29 Do you remember (I, ask) you (lend) me a
dictionary?

30 Try (persuade) Maisie (be) more reasonable.

31 If you don't enjoy (eat) sour oranges, try (put)
sugar on them after (peel) them.

32 I'm surprised at (you, have) to work so late. Just
imagine (I, do) the same! No, it doesn't bear
(think about).

33 I observed Cyril (try) (persuade) the children
(watch) (he, dance) a jig.

34 (Stay) at work all day will mean (we, have) only
sandwiches for lunch.

35 If I find you (day-dream) again instead of (work),
I regret (say) I shall have to complain to the
manager of (you, not pull) your weight. It'll be no
good (you, try) (find) an excuse next time.

36 I don't fancy (go on) (wait) much longer for her.
Would you consider (give) her another five minutes
before (give up) (wait) for her altogether?

37 By (get) to school late we escaped (have) an exam.

38 A child can't learn (spell) without (be) helped.
39 On (hear) Maisie (speak), everybody took her (be) a foreigner.
40 I dislike (be) looked at while (attempt) (learn) (ski).
41 I want (you, wait) before (decide) (accept) his offer.
42 Can you imagine (he, study) (be) an acrobat?
43 At all costs we must avoid (treat) him in a way that might mean (he, turn) elsewhere for business.
44 I'm sorry (disturb) you with my sneezes; I've felt this cold (come on) for weeks.
45 They refused (allow) us (go in) without (sign) the book.
46 Why do you keep (object) to (have) the party at the Station Restaurant? Has anyone mentioned (go) there?
47 I usually manage (escape) (be) asked to these meetings, but this time I forgot (think up) a good excuse in time.
48 Forgive (I, ring) you up so late, but I couldn't allow your birthday (pass) without (congratulate) you.
49 'Did you remember (post) my letter on your way home?' 'I remember (go) into the post office for some stamps, but even then I'm afraid I forgot (post) it.'
50 I should like you (know) that it's no use (blame) me for your delay. I can't help (you, not be) allowed (leave) for America without first (finish) (write) your doctor's thesis.

41 Perfect Infinitive of Imaginary Past

41.1
Intermediate

The form *to have eaten* takes the place of the infinitive when certain constructions, notably *is to, ought to, like*, are used for imagined action in the past.

He is to come tomorrow.
He was *to have come* yesterday . . . (but he didn't).

Note that *I should like to go* has the past forms:
(1) I should like to have gone.

(2) I should have liked to go.
(3) I should have liked to have gone.

The type (3) is very clumsy, but strangely enough quite commonly heard. The other two are logically preferable, and the first is the more frequently heard. (See also notes to Exercise 41.2.)

Must, meaning 'is (logically) so', makes its past by adding a perfect infinitive.

> He must be a fool. (= he certainly is!)
> He must have been a fool. (= he certainly was!)

* * *

(41.1) ● Put into the imaginary past:

1 You ought to get here earlier.
2 They are to arrive at seven o'clock.
3 I suppose I ought to be more careful.
4 I should like to see the Pyramids of Egypt on my way home.
5 Maisie ought not to eat so many chocolates.
6 I am to stay away for a whole week.
7 Would you like to win the first prize?
8 How much ought I to give him?
9 Most of us would like to go there again.
10 Is he to repair this one, too?
11 I should like to see Cyril in yellow swimming shorts.
12 This must be the book you're talking about.
13 He is to visit Paris before returning to America.
14 They would like to get here before us.
15 Your wife ought to tell you all about it.
16 You should not give the baby a penknife to play with.
17 Lady Billingham is to open the new hospital.
18 Your grandfather must be a kind old gentleman to give you such lovely presents.
19 I ought to send my aunt a Christmas present.
20 We would like to spend a holiday together.

41.2
Advanced

See Exercise 41.1.

Some people assert that there is a difference of meaning between

(1) I should like to have gone; and
(2) I should have liked to go.

This difference is largely imaginary, but is argued presumably as follows:

They say that in (1) the liking is a present one, and in (2) it is past. This idea is clearer if we consider carefully the following pair:

(1) I should like to have gone. (What a pity I didn't!)

(2) I should have liked to go (if only I had known about it at the time).

The PERFECT INFINITIVE is commonly used to express an unfulfilled hope or expectation:

I hoped to have seen you before now.
We meant to have stayed there a week.
Henry was to have bought some wine ... (but he forgot).

*   *   *

● Put into the imaginary past:

1 I am to go there tomorrow, weather permitting.

2 You ought not to use the electric light more than is necessary.

3 I should like to lend you some books.

4 There is to be a special train to the coast on Thursday.

5 You ought to know better than to do that.

6 He ought not to eat melon if he knows it disagrees with him.

7 According to the weather prophets, it ought not to rain on the day of the race.

8 This dress is to be made with a fashionably short skirt.

9 They would like to leave the cinema before the end of the picture.

10 The ground-to-air missile system ought to be a useful part of the defence.

11 These chocolates ought not to cost more than thirty pence a box.

12 The policeman says he would like to have more evidence before arresting the suspected thief.
(*N.B.* – *says* need not be changed to *said*.)

13 The telegram ought to be sent only if the patient dies.

14 An exhibition of paintings is to be held at the British Institute on July 9th.

15 You ought to buy your hats at a cheaper shop.
16 It would certainly be better not to speak to him at all.
17 I expect to meet you at Interlaken.
18 He would laugh to see you with that funny hat on.
19 It is better to love in vain, than never to love at all.
20 I'm sure she would like to cook it herself.
21 They hope to win the tournament by Thursday.
22 He certainly would be foolhardy to attack them unarmed.
23 I mean to have another try if I can.
24 You might find it easier to leave me out altogether.
25 It would be easier to climb over the mountain than to go round the valley, if there weren't so much snow.

42 Verb, Noun or Adjective

42.1
Elementary

Many common words can be used as both verbs and nouns. Because they occur more frequently as verbs, students are apt to get less practice in their use as nouns.

*   *   *

● Make two sentences with each of the following words: (a) as a verb; (b) as a noun:

cook; bite; swim; walk; answer; drink; rain; rest; work; smell; shave; smile; use[1]; burn; cut; fight; pay; play; brush; dress; sleep; watch; kiss; look.

42.2
Intermediate

● Make sentences with each of the following words: (a) as a verb; (b) as a noun:

burn; cough; fall; fear; copy; fold; light; drive; mark; smoke; sneeze; show; stand; taste; break; call; climb; cover; fly; help; kick; measure; move; colour; water; arm; hand; damage; place; act; dust; iron.

[1] v. [juːz], n. [juːs]

42.3
Advanced

● Make two sentences with each of the following words: (a) as a verb; (b) as a noun:

change; doubt; jump; laugh; lift; start; stop; turn; step; rub; shake; tear; touch; want; bend; catch; draw; hold; leave; make; air; book; shoe; stomach; mouth[1]; finger; thumb; eye; steam; house[2]; match; dog; harbour.

42.4
Elementary

● Make two sentences with each of the following words: (a) as an adjective; (b) as a verb:

dry; open; shut; warm; clean; hurt; wet.

42.5
Intermediate

● Make two sentences with each of the following words: (a) as an adjective; (b) as a verb:

dirty; clear; cut; empty; light; live[3]; mean; free.

42.6
Advanced

● Make two sentences with each of the following words: (a) as an adjective; (b) as a verb:

complete; equal; loose; second; separate[4]; wrong; better; frequent[5]; right.

43 *have a* ——

43.1
Elementary

Some languages, notably the Slavonic group, can make a distinction between an action done once only and an action done repeatedly. In English we have the *have a* plus verb-noun pattern for the 'once only' form.

> We were riding in the car. (when we saw him)
> We rode there in the car. (means of transport)
> We had a ride in the car. (had one experience of this action)

Although this can be a means of defining one particular performance of the action designated by the verb-noun, it must be admitted that the simple tense is usually equally good.

* * *

[1] v. [mauð], n. [mauθ]   [2] v. [hauz], n. [haus]
[3] a. [laiv], v. [liv]   [4] a. [ˈseprit], v. [ˈsepəreit]
[5] a. [ˈfriːkwənt], v. [friˈkwent]

(43.1)　　● Make short sentences in the PAST, FUTURE or IMPERATIVE
form with *have a* plus:

drink; look; rest; ride; walk; talk; smoke; swim;
wash; bath.

43.2　　See Exercise 43.1.
Intermediate

* * *

● Make short sentences with *have a* plus:

sit down; lie down; go; dance; chance; throw.

In some of these expressions *take* is sometimes heard.
Take a walk, look, bath, etc.

44　Interrogatives

44.1　　See also preliminary Exercise 8.1.
Elementary　　SUBJECTIVE CASE:

Who for persons in general – pronoun
What for things in general – pronoun
What for persons or things in general – adjective
Which for restricted persons or things – pronoun and
adjective

Who broke my pencil? (of all possible people)
What has happened? (of all possible things)
What books are these?
What people live in this country?
Which of you can answer my question? (limited
choice)
Which house is it, No. 32 or No. 34? (limited choice)

Of course there are occasions when the general and restricted interrogatives seem equally good, and the choice
then depends on the speaker's point of view.

* * *

● Add the question-word to the following questions:
1 — went with you to London?
2 — of these books is your favourite?
3 — girl won the beauty competition?
4 — is my place?
5 — came in just now?

6 — river flows through London?
7 — will cook the dinner today?
8 — arrived first?
9 — dress is the prettiest?
10 — bus goes to Charing Cross?
11 — asked you to write this?
12 — has taken my scissors?
13 — hotel is nearest to the sea?
14 — is wrong with the clock?
15 — left the light on?
16 — is your friend's name?
17 — is the healthier place, the country or the seaside?
18 — is the answer?
19 — is the largest town in the world?
20 — is your grocer?
21 — of those young men is her fiancé?
22 — language is the easiest to learn?
23 — gave you those flowers?
24 — is wrong with that exercise?
25 — is smoking here?
26 — is the way to the station?
27 — other schools are there in England besides
   private and public schools?
28 — would like a cup of tea?
29 — painted that picture?
30 — is the matter?

**44.2
Elementary**

OBLIQUE CASES. In the spoken language *who* serves for both
SUBJECT and OBJECT, and *whose* for the POSSESSIVE. There
is no possessive for *what* and *which*; for 'of what' and 'of
which' see Exercise 44.6 on prepositions with interrogatives.

See Exercise 44.4 for further note on *who? = whom?*

Who saw you yesterday?
Who did you see yesterday?
   – Note the inversion when anything but the subject
   is placed first.
Whose car is that? (Whose is that car?)

*   *   *

● Add the question-word to the following questions:

1 — do you want?
2 — book are you reading?

3 — is going to the cinema tonight?
4 — of these girls is the youngest?
5 — hat is this, mine or yours?
6 — is the matter with him?
7 — of you can answer that question?
8 — is John doing?
9 — has finished the exercise?
10 — are those people doing?
11 — has broken the window?
12 — dress do you like?
13 — are you meeting at four o'clock?
14 — have they done?
15 — has eaten my sandwich?
16 — did you want to see?
17 — are you writing?
18 — picture do you prefer, this or that?
19 — went to the seaside with you?
20 — asked you to come?
21 — was that noise?
22 — is your hat? (— hat is yours?)
23 — did I say?
24 — opened my letter?
25 — did you send to market?
26 — European language is the easiest to learn?
27 — can I do to help?
28 — pencil is this, Tom's or Harry's?
29 — looked in at the window just now?
30 — are you drinking?

44.3
Elementary

See Notes to Exercises 44.1 and 44.2.

*   *   *

● Turn the following statements into questions, asking about the words in **bold type**:

1 She is wearing **a new hat**.
2 **I** have been to the Zoo.
3 **They** are sitting under the trees.
4 Tom has eaten **some bad fish**.
5 They have seen **her** in that café every day.
6 **This** is my favourite melody.
7 My name is **Mrs Buttons**.
8 **That** tooth is hurting me.

9 I want to see **you**.
10 That lady is **my friend**.
11 The prize for the competition was **a handbag**.
12 **Someone** has used my fountain-pen.
13 This glass is **his**.
14 I can recommend **this one**.
15 **They** have just come in.
16 We saw **the king** yesterday.
17 I want **his** book.
18 **Mary** ate it.
19 I'll give you **the brown one**.
20 I bought him **a present**.

44.4
Intermediate

See Exercises 44.1 and 44.2.

Whom? This form has almost disappeared from spoken British English. It is found only in the most formal kind of writing. Foreign students need not learn it for their own use. It is not required in any of the interrogative exercises in this book if they are done orally.

SUBJECT:	Who?		What? Which?
OBJECT:	Who? (verb inversion)		What? Which?
POSSESSIVE:	Whose?		What (which) ... of?
PREPOSITION:	Who ... to?		What (which) ... to?

* * *

● Add the question-word to the following questions:
1 — left this bag here?
2 — pencil is this? Is it yours?
3 — are you doing tonight?
4 — are we meeting this afternoon?
5 — do you think of my photograph?
6 — is your dressmaker?
7 — shall we do tomorrow?
8 — train shall we take, the 14.15 or the 15.30?
9 — is singing in the next room?
10 — does she want?
11 — dress was she wearing?
12 — hat blew away? Tom's?
13 — would you like me to do?
14 — threw that stone?
15 — is your daughter going to marry?
16 — of these cakes may I take?

17 — is speaking?
18 — pen are you using?   Is it mine?
19 — is your new teacher?
20 — of these people have you met before?
21 — book did I borrow?   Yours?
22 — shut the door?
23 — did he say?
24 — was your first wife's name?
25 — room is the largest?
26 — school did she attend?
27 — shall we have to eat?
28 — did you visit yesterday afternoon?
29 — is wrong?
30 — would you like to drink?

44.5   See Exercises 44.1, 44.2, and 44.4.
Intermediate

* * *

● Turn the following statements into questions, asking about
the words in **bold type:**

1 Cows eat **grass.**
2 **Father** has taken the newspaper.
3 I prefer **apples to oranges.**
4 **Mont Blanc** is the highest mountain in the Alps.
5 The boy learnt **many subjects** at school.
6 **Miss Jones** taught me the piano.
7 They want **to go out.**
8 The dog bit **the little girl.**
9 He asked you **to help me.**
10 **This** shop sells good cakes.
11 The state pays **pensions** to old people.
12 The doctor told her **to stay in bed.**
13 **Somebody** turned off the radio.
14 I spilt **the ink.**
15 **That** one is better.
16 She has broken **a glass.**
17 That house is **mine.**
18 **This** hotel is the best.
19 They saw **John** with Maisie in the park.
20 **He** insulted your friend Cyril.

44.6
Elementary

PREPOSITIONS. When a preposition governs an interrogative, it is placed at the end of the sentence in spoken English.

> I was speaking to him just now.
> *Who* were you speaking *to*?

What and *Which* are treated in the same way.

> A table is made of wood.
> *What's* a table made *of*?
> This is a part *of the table*.
> *What's* this a part *of*? (= Possessive case of things.)

Note also the double use of *what for?* in spoken English.

> What's this money for? (= for what purpose?)
> What are you crying for? (= why?)

* * *

● Add EITHER the missing question-word OR the missing preposition to the following questions:

1 — are you thinking about?
2 — was she dancing with?
3 — chair was I sitting on?
4 What are they looking —?
5 What is she talking —?
6 Who is she talking —?
7 — shall I give this to?
8 What are you listening —?
9 Who is she writing —?
10 — street do you live in?
11 What are you cutting that paper —?
12 — did Joan give my newspaper to?
13 What are they laughing —?
14 — book are you looking for?
15 — do you want me to talk about?
16 — cup were you drinking out of?
17 — did you wash it with?
18 — room shall I sleep in?
19 What town do you come —?
20 Who is this telegram —?
21 — does this car belong to?
22 — dress shall I put on?
23 Who are you waiting —?
24 What year was he born —?

25 — school did your friend go to?
26 What is butter made —?
27 — library did you get this book from?
28 What train shall we go —?
29 Do you know who this parcel is —?
30 — are you laughing at now?

44.7
Elementary
See Exercise 44.6.

* * *

● Turn the following statements into questions, asking about the words in **bold type**:

1 I'm looking at **him**.
2 She wants to speak to **you**.
3 Aunt Jane has put away **your** things.
4 My friend is waiting for **me**.
5 They are staying with **some friends**.
6 I am laughing at **a funny picture**.
7 The policeman was looking for **the thief**.
8 He is sitting on **a chair**.
9 They were drinking out of **bottles**.
10 I am thinking of **the English countryside**.
11 She is writing to **her mother**.
12 He is working for **Thomas Cook and Son**.
13 My sister sold her house to **a millionaire**.
14 The class was reading about **Shakespeare**.
15 He is talking about **politics**.
16 I gave it to **my brother**.
17 We are going to **the Ritz** cinema.
18 She is looking for **a pin**.
19 The children were playing with **some new toys**.
20 Mrs Smith was talking to **the butcher**.

44.8
Intermediate
See Exercise 44.6.

* * *

● Turn the following statements into questions asking about the words in **bold type**:

1 My wife was angry with **me**.
2 I gave that present to **my aunt**.
3 The school-children covered their books with **brown paper**.

4 The man over there asked for **a cup of tea**.
5 Maisie was eating out of **a paper bag**.
6 Miss Sharp sailed on **the 'Queen Elizabeth 2'**.
7 Cyril is playing with **a ball**.
8 The villagers build their huts with **mud**.
9 We went to see **the latest film** yesterday.
10 The clerk rang up **his girl-friend**.
11 The gardener spoke to **the cook** about it.
12 She threw away **some old clothes**.
13 I found out **the reason**.
14 A tailor sews with **a needle**.
15 The old man was listening to **the radio**.
16 Shoes are made of **leather**.
17 I am thinking about **the party tonight**.
18 Mary reads to **an old blind woman** every week.
19 I shall put on **my new evening dress**.
20 You were looking at **the view**.

GENERAL REVISION

44.9
Intermediate

In the same way as explained in Exercise 44.6, prepositions are separated from the interrogative *where*.

　　Where have you come from?

Note the question-form: *What is . . . like?*

*　　*　　*

● Ask questions with interrogatives (including *why*, *when*, *where*, *how*) to which the following statements are the answers. The point of the question appears in **bold type**:

1 A leaf is **part of a tree**.
2 My father is **an engine driver**.
3 That handsome man over there is **Mr Green**.
4 I am coming back **on Friday**.
5 She is singing **because she is happy**.
6 You left your glasses **on the table**.
7 My friend Maisie married **a sailor**.
8 He opened the door with **a key**.
9 Cyril has **only £17** in the bank.
10 I have **two** cigarettes.
11 I intend to remain here **for two weeks**.
12 You can give your old trousers to **the poor**.

13   He has given the book to **his wife**.

14   If you want to know, that is **my** dog.

15   **Clumsy Clara** must have broken it.

16   You ought to have finished the work **last week**.

17   I don't buy a car **because I can't afford one**.

18   Oregon is **an American state**.

19   I am going to London with **my parents**.

20   I gave **£5** for this dog.

21   She says she has **two** brothers.

22   **Everybody** says he is a good writer.

23   She is **a very charming girl**.

24   Well, I really want **both** of them.

25   It took them **about four months** to make this film.

44.10
Advanced

See Notes to Exercise 44.9.

Advanced students might like to see the full table of positionals in literary English.

here	there	where? (= place)
hither	thither	whither? (= to)
hence	thence	whence? (= from)

In the modern spoken language, and to a large extent in modern literary English, only the top three remain, being modified by *from* to express direction away; *to* can be used with *where* but is not strictly necessary.

Notice the use of *Whereabouts?* when asking for approximate position.

Note the colloquial form: *How (What) about —ing*

How about going to the pictures?
– Is it a good idea?

* * *

● Write questions to which the following statements might be the answer. The point of the question appears in **bold type**:

1   I am taking this garden roller home for **my uncle**.

2   My brother is **as strong as a horse**.

3   He stole the money for the sake of **his starving father**.

4   That magnificent car is **my brother's**.

5   They make false teeth **by means of a mould**.

6   Iraq produces **5 per cent** of England's oil needs.

7   The human heart is **about as big as a clenched fist**.

8   Henry lives **about three miles away**.
9   Our conversation was entirely about **business matters**.
10   **All of us** liked your lecture.
11   I was going to get it **from the chemist's**.
12   I was going to put it **in the cupboard**.
13   He jumped on **the policeman**'s foot.
14   He fell into the river **because he forgot he was on a boat**.
15   He is a **very handsome** fellow.
16   You've told him **dozens of times** not to do it.
17   This magnifying-glass is **for counting stamp perforations**.
18   The English for 'zmrzlina' is **'ice-cream'.**
19   You must drink out of the **blue** cup.
20   His apartment is **just about two miles** beyond the bridge.
21   Maisie is **as stupid as they make them**.
22   I put your ear-rings **somewhere near the clock** on the mantelpiece.
23   All this time I've been thinking **how nice it would be to be home again**.
24   **Yes, I think** a short walk before supper **is a very good idea**.
25   Old Tom is **as fat as a porpoise** these days.
26   Well, since you ask me, I took you for **a bigger fool than you appear to be**.
27   As a matter of fact, he scored **seven** out of ten.
28   Since you mention it, you went off with **my** umbrella.
29   He fell **seventy** feet down the cliff.
30   Czechoslovakia is **a fascinating country**.

45 Interrogative Responses

The automatic question responses to statements fall into two main groups:

TYPE (1) Where the agent or prepositional part of the command is missing, and the response asks for further clarification.

Go quickly. – Where to?
Open it. – What with?

These are normally spoken with a falling intonation.
The preposition is always at the end in this pattern; *whom* is never heard.
For TYPE (2) see Exercise 45.2.
The remarks below should be addressed to the student, who should make an appropriate response. Some of the prepositions are suggested.

* * *

(45.1)   ● Respond as above to the following:
1   Listen.
2   Send it at once.
3   Look.
4   Cut the string.
5   Go on, have another dance! **(with)**
6   Don't you ever sit and think? **(about)**
7   Sharpen my pencil, will you? **(with** or **for)**
8   Mother has given all my clothes away.
9   I've just bought a birthday present. **(for)**
10   Address this envelope.
11   Play with me. **(at)**
12   I've just received a big parcel.
13   John's just arrived by air.
14   I've been to the pictures. **(with)**
15   Tell me a story. **(about)**
16   Take it away. **(to)**
17   I'm thinking. **(with)**
18   I've been punched on the nose.
19   He's married at last.
20   I'm writing a book.

45.2
Intermediate
See also Exercise 45.1.
TYPE (2) is a response of surprise, consternation or mere misunderstanding of the complete sense. In Exercise 45.1 the sense was always incomplete, so the emphasis always fell on the PREPOSITION in the final position as the active agent.

Write a letter! Who *to*?
–The whole idea of 'TO what person' is missing, and comes naturally in the strongest position, i.e. the end.

In TYPE (2) we question THE WHOLE IDEA, and repeat it with the accent on the QUESTION-WORD, which now takes the final position. Notice the changed intonation.

TYPE (1): Open the bottle. – What *with*? (falling intonation)

TYPE (2): Open the bottle *with this pin*. – With *what*? (rising intonation)

Why, when, where, and the *how* compounds behave similarly. *Whom* does not occur.

The statements below are to be addressed to the student, who should make a suitable response.

* * *

● Respond, as TYPE (2) above, to the following; the key words are in **bold type**:

1 These chocolates are **for** you.
2 He gave it **to** your mother-in-law.
3 Clean it **with** your handkerchief.
4 I came here **on** a tricycle.
5 I'm going to tea **with** the King.
6 Have you seen the new play **by** my great-aunt Gertrude?
7 Cyril has fallen **on** a cactus!
8 An army marches **on** its stomach.
9 Will you finish off this letter **to** the Home Needleworkers' Socialist Association?
10 In our play I act the part **of** a Grand Duchess.
11 I'm waiting **for** my grandmother.
12 He couldn't come **because** he was drunk.
13 I'm going for a walk **with** your friend Maisie.
14 You can cook a kipper **on** a candle.
15 Send this parcel **to** my great-uncle's youngest brother-in-law.
16 I've had measles **sixteen times**.
17 So I told her **about** your affair **with** that pretty dancer! (two possible responses)
18 I like my breakfast **at half past five**.
19 Mix it **with** lemonade.
20 I bought the whole set **for** five pence!

45.3
Advanced

See notes to Exercises 45.1 and 45.2.

There is a further development of TYPE (2), expressing extreme surprise, consternation, or disbelief. Here the whole of the speaker's remark is echoed to him with the unbelievable section turned into the appropriate interrogative. This interrogative takes a heavy stress and quickly rising intonation.

> So I had the bill sent to my wife. – You had it sent to WHOOO! ! ! ?
>
> Sir, you're nothing but a raving lunatic! – I'm a WHAAAT! ! ? (Note that the indefinite article is retained.)
>
> I dyed my hair green yesterday. – You dyed it WHAAT colour! ! ?

(The teacher reads the statement, the student responds.)

* * *

● Respond similarly to the following remarks:

1 Columbus discovered America in 1764.
2 I love eating raw fish.
3 She wants to be a film star.
4 I'm afraid you'll have to sleep in the bathroom.
5 Mr Poorly has £45,000 in the bank.
6 I had lunch with the Prime Minister yesterday.
7 Nero was a kind-hearted emperor.
8 For my dinner yesterday I had a jar of pickles.
9 Jane is going to marry the dustman!
10 She was wearing a hideous ostrich-feather hat.
11 My brother has twenty-nine children.
12 So I gave your plans of a submarine to a strange-looking foreigner.
13 Baby has swallowed a teaspoon!
14 Schoolmistresses are usually very attractive.
15 The cat has had kittens in father's hat!
16 I left my cigarette-end on the petrol-tin.
17 My sister is going to live at Omsk.
18 She was seen riding on a coal-cart.
19 Just throw the rubbish out of the window.
20 Darling, I've bought this bottle of whisky for your sake!

46 Relatives

**46.1
Elementary**

GENERAL REMARKS

The apparently haphazard English system of relatives is best approached by teaching them from the beginning in their two main groups of DEFINING and NON-DEFINING relatives. Although the following exercises are meant for practice in spoken English, the points they deal with are equally applicable to the written language.

By far the greater number of relatives in general use are of the DEFINING type; this kind should therefore be taught first, though some grammar books deal with the forms of the non-defining relative as the standard, and include the defining relative rather as an after-thought.

For the sake of clarity, the following forms should be taught and practised in writing and speaking. The forms in square brackets [ ] are acceptable alternatives, but are NOT recommended for active teaching; teach contact-clauses by omitting *that* whenever possible. A *that* in round brackets ( ) can be omitted; in spoken English it usually is.

DEFINING RELATIVE

	PEOPLE	THINGS
SUBJECT	*who* [*that*]	*that* [*which*]
OBJECT	(*that*)	(*that*)
PREPOSITION	(*that*)... preposition	(*that*)... preposition
POSSESSIVE	*whose*	*of which* [*whose*]

NON-DEFINING RELATIVE

	PEOPLE	THINGS
SUBJECT	—, *who* —,	—, *which* —,
OBJECT	—, *whom* —,	—, *which* —,
PREPOSITION	—, preposition + *whom* —,	—, preposition + *which* —,
	[—, *who(m)* — preposition,]	[—, *which* — preposition,]
POSSESSIVE	—, *whose* —,	—, *of which* —,
		[—, *whose* —,]

DEFINING RELATIVE

Here the relative clause is an essential part of the idea being expressed, in that it defines or limits its antecedent to one particular selected type.

The man is coming to tea. (Well, what man?)
The man who [that] wrote this poem is coming to tea.

who wrote this poem cannot be omitted, since without it we cannot define *the man.*

Most of the relatives of spoken English – probably at least 90 per cent – fall into this category. In Exercise 46.1, Numbers 1 to 10 are in the simplest form, with the defining relative clause at the end of the sentence, as in:

That's the boy *who broke the window.*
Here's the book *I lost last week.*

It would be convenient to use *that* throughout, but custom prefers *who* in the subject for persons (especially proper names), and inefficient mechanism gives us *whose* and *of which* for the possessive, since *that* has no possessive of its own, and cannot suffer a preposition before it.

We can therefore tabulate the following elementary types:

SUBJECT: The man who [that] wrote this poem is coming to tea.
The book that [which] is lying on the table is mine.

OBJECT: The man you met yesterday is coming to tea. (The man that you met yesterday is coming to tea.)
The book I put on the table is mine. (The book that I put on the table is mine.)
We prefer the contact-clause without *that.*

For Prepositionals and Possessives see next exercise.

The forms in square brackets are possible alternatives, but the main forms as outlined above should be insisted on in the exercises.

N.B. – Defining relative clauses are NEVER preceded by a comma in writing.

*   *   *

(46.1) ● Add the missing relative, but make a contact-clause where possible:

1 I know a man — eats paper.
2 It's a kind of paper — you can eat.
3 He eats only the paper — his wife makes.
4 His wife is a woman — loves a joke.
5 She's one of the people — I really like.
6 You can't write on the paper — she makes.
7 Has this paper got a flavour — pleases you?
8 Have you met anyone else — does such tricks?

9 I'm looking for somebody — I can trust.
10 I want to find a man — will lend me money.
11 The man — you want has just left.
12 The lady — was here yesterday has gone to London.
13 The magazine — you lent me is very interesting.
14 The chair — was broken is now mended.
15 The old man — lives next door has just died.
16 Women — work in hospitals are to be admired.
17 The cigarette — you are smoking is a Player's.
18 The girl — lives opposite my house is very pretty.
19 The fish — I ate yesterday was not so good.
20 The street — leads to the school is very wide.
21 The flowers — I cut this morning are still fresh.
22 The dress — you are wearing is lovely.
23 The person — is sitting next to me is not very clever.
24 The man — cut your hair did it very badly.
25 The letter — we received today had no stamp on it.
26 The music — the orchestra is playing is a Strauss waltz.
27 Was the hat — you were wearing yesterday very expensive?
28 The boy — threw that stone will be punished.
29 The doctor — she visited is famous.
30 The noise — you hear is only our dog fighting.

46.2 The prepositional and possessive forms are as follows:

Elementary PREPOSITIONAL

DEFINING PEOPLE:

RELATIVE The man you spoke to yesterday is coming to tea. (The man that you spoke to yesterday is coming to tea.)
Use of *whom* should be strongly discouraged here.

THINGS:

The book you were looking at just now belongs to me. (The book that you were looking at just now belongs to me.)
Use of *which* should be strongly discouraged here.

POSSESSIVE

PEOPLE:

The man whose name I always forget is coming to tea, or

The man I always forget the name of is coming to tea.
THINGS:
This case is very rare with things; we prefer a way out.

The book with the torn cover is mine.
(= The book of which the cover is torn ... – very clumsy.)

N.B. – A defining relative clause is never preceded by a comma.

*   *   *

(46.2)   ●   Add relatives, WHERE NEEDED:

1 The book — I was reading yesterday was a detective story.
2 The man — you spoke to in the street is my English teacher.
3 I should like to see the trees — you picked these apples from.
4 There's the lady — purse has been stolen.
5 The people — you were living with in London are coming to see you.
6 The picture — you were talking about has been sold.
7 People — live in glass houses shouldn't throw stones.
8 Buy it back from the man — you sold it to.
9 What's the name of that man — wife has run away and left him?
10 Can you remember the person — you took it from?
11 Where is there a shop — sells picture-postcards?
12 That's the knife and fork — I eat with.
13 Where is the man — sold me these sun-glasses?
14 What's that music — you are listening to?
15 I don't like the house — he lives in.
16 The man — made these shoes doesn't know his trade.
17 Here comes the girl — I am hiding from.
18 The people — are looking at that house are my parents.
19 The house — they are looking at is my house.
20 And the girl — you see at the door is my sister.

46.3
Intermediate
DEFINING
RELATIVE

See notes to Exercises 46.1 and 46.2.

Although it was pointed out in Exercise 46.1 that for people custom prefers *who* in the subjective case, the following expressions almost invariably take *that*: SUPERLATIVES; *all*; *any*; *only*; *it is*.

> She is the finest woman that ever lived.
> He is the only American that has swum the Hellespont.
> It's the teacher that decides what to read.

* * *

● Add relatives, WHERE NEEDED (i.e. use contact-clauses where possible):

1 The knife — we cut the bread with is very sharp.
2 The man — I gave the book to has died.
3 The shop — we buy our cakes from is shut.
4 The girl — works in the office is my sister.
5 I'm afraid that's all — I've got.
6 The paint on the seat — you are sitting on is still wet.
7 The ties — Cyril wears are awful.
8 Any man — listens to you is a fool.
9 The old gentleman — lives across the road has got married for the fifth time.
10 The policeman — helmet you knocked off is at the door.
11 The horse — you were telling me about yesterday came in last.
12 The man — is sitting at the desk is the secretary.
13 The man — you see at the desk is the secretary.
14 The girl — mother I was talking to has left the room.
15 The man — I pointed out to you in the street is a crook.
16 The pretty girl — you were speaking to just now slapped Cyril's face yesterday.
17 This is the very room — I first met my wife in.
18 'It's a wise child — knows its own father.'
19 All the people — ever met him have disliked him.
20 The coat — I gave Maisie for her birthday is already wearing out.
21 Any paper — you read will give the same story.

22   The glass — you are drinking out of hasn't been washed.

23   A woman — mind is made up is more obstinate than a mule.

24   She's the most beautiful woman — has appeared on this stage.

25   The meat — we had for lunch was very tough.

46.4 Elementary and Intermediate NON-DEFINING RELATIVES

NON-DEFINING RELATIVES are not very common in speech, but occur quite frequently in the written language. The reason is that speech prefers simple sentences, and the NON-DEFINING relative is a deliberate inclusion of additional matter within the sentence. Often the non-defining clause comes from a stylistic combination of two distinct statements (see Exercise 46.9).

Compare the following examples:

(1) DEFINING: The boy (that) you saw yesterday is coming to tea.

(2) NON-DEFINING: My brother Dick, whom you saw yesterday, is coming to tea.

The relative clause in (2) can be left out without any material damage to the sense, whereas the same omission in (1) robs the sentence of a most essential fact. The normal conversational form of (2) would probably be: 'My brother Dick's coming to tea. You saw him yesterday, you know,' or, 'You remember you saw my brother Dick yesterday? Well, he's coming to tea.'

The non-defining relative is ALWAYS preceded by a comma in writing. This is very important in the written language, because only *whom* belongs exclusively to the non-defining relative, and such sentences as:

NON-DEFINING: My wife, who lives in New York, has just written me a letter.

DEFINING: My wife who lives in New York has just written me a letter.

have startlingly different meanings.

NON-DEFINING: He has two sisters, who work in the Ministry. (= only two sisters)

DEFINING: He has two sisters who work in the Ministry. (= and presumably other sisters who work elsewhere)

The two sentences with NON-DEFINING clauses show the two principal uses of the non-defining relative.

(1) Parenthetic. (2) Connective (= and . . .).

Forms to be used:

	PEOPLE	THINGS
SUBJECT	—, who —,	—, which —,
OBJECT	—, whom —,	—, which —,

N.B. – The non-defining objective case *whom* and *which*, unlike the defining objective case *that*, can NEVER be omitted in this kind of relative clause.

The punctuation referred to above is reflected in speech. The first comma represents the introduction of a separate intonation pattern or 'tune'. The need for students to make this difference in intonation – if only mentally while reading – justifies the inclusion of these exercises in a book largely devoted to spoken English. But notice that the 1st person is avoided in the following exercises since we are usually speaking informally when we are using the 1st person, whereas the non-defining relative is generally a formal construction.

* * *

● Add the necessary relative pronoun to the following:

1 Louis XIV, — we mentioned last week, became king in 1643.

2 The princess, — had been married for ten years, had just had her ninth baby.

3 The author, — has been to Paris, has just returned.

4 See page 33 for a map of the area, — we also printed in our last number.

5 The London train, — should arrive at 2.30, is late.

6 Budapest, — is on the Danube, is a beautiful city.

7 Bernard Shaw, — had a long beard, was a very clever writer.

8 Flies, — come mostly in the summer, carry disease.

9 The B.B.C., — is world-famous, spends millions of pounds every year.

10 Love, — is a wonderful feeling, comes to everyone at some time in his life.

11 Oxford University, — is one of the oldest in the world, has many different colleges.

12 Swimming, — is a good sport, makes people strong.

13 Julius Caesar, — was a great general, was also a writer.
14 Grass, — cows and horses love, is always green in England.
15 Air, — we breathe, is made up of many gases.
16 Wackford Squeers, — everyone feared, was the cruel headmaster of Dotheboys Hall.
17 Whisky, — is very expensive, is the national drink of Scotland.
18 This book is about capital outlay, — is necessary for industrial development.
19 Fear, — is an evil, may lead to sin.
20 The author's last book, — was probably his best, came out in 1972.
21 George Washington, — became President of the United States, never told a lie.
22 Grammar, — students dislike very much, is good for them.
23 Shakespeare, — is the world's greatest dramatist, was born in a little cottage.
24 In Norway, — is a Baltic country, you can see the midnight sun.
25 One should try to stop smoking, — is a bad habit.

46.5
Elementary and Intermediate
NON-DEFINING RELATIVE

The other cases are:

	PEOPLE	THINGS
POSSESSIVE	—, *whose* —,	—, *of which* —,
		[—, *whose* —,]
PREPOSITIONAL	—, *to* etc. *whom* —,	—, *to* etc. *which* —,
	[—, *who(m)* — *to*, etc.]	[—, *which* — *to*, etc.]

The forms in square brackets are alternatives that occasionally occur, but which should not be taught to students.
N.B. – The *whom* and *which* of the non-defining relative is NEVER omitted like the corresponding *that* of the defining relative.

* * *

● Add relative pronouns to the following:
1 The Pope, — many people had never heard before, spoke on the radio last night.
2 He met Prince Henry's mother, from — he got the news of Henry's marriage.

3 It was the last king of Ruritania, — name few people can remember.

4 The elephant, — is an animal that never forgets, lives more than a hundred years.

5 Nicholas II, to — you were referring, was the last czar of Russia.

6 He is a famous scientist, about — many books have been written.

7 The chief of police, — work is very important, takes care of the public safety.

8 Geometry, about — so many books have been written, is not really a dull subject.

9 They developed the hovercraft, — seemed to have a great future.

10 The King, — life has been devoted to his country, deserves his popularity.

11 Parliament, — has just started a new session, is going to discuss the new Bill today.

12 This subject, about — I was speaking yesterday, is an important part of our course.

13 The Tower of London, about — a lecture is to be given tomorrow, is a famous historic building.

14 Beethoven, — music you have just been listening to, was one of the world's finest composers.

15 You should not miss the Iguazú Falls, — are said to be the finest in the world.

16 The lark, — has a very sweet song, builds its nest on the ground.

17 We cannot decide whether tomatoes, — we are all fond of, are a fruit or a vegetable. (See End-preposition note, Exercise 46.10).

18 The science of medicine, in — progress has been very rapid lately, is perhaps the most important of all the sciences.

19 Chess, — is a very old game, is difficult to play.

20 Mme Curie, — discovered radium, is one of the greatest women of our age.

46.6   See notes to Exercises 46.4 and 46.5.

Intermediate

* * *

NON-
DEFINING
RELATIVE

● Combine the following pairs of sentences by means of NON-DEFINING RELATIVE PRONOUNS:

1 Julius Caesar came to Britain in 55 BC. **He** was a powerful Roman general.

2 These cactus plants should not have too much water. **They** will grow in pots indoors.

3 They are still working on the motorway. **Its** completion date was last May.

4 The antiquities of Egypt should not be missed. Such a lot has been written about **them**.

5 The pelican is a very queer-looking bird. **His** beak (says a popular rhyme) can hold more than his belly can.

6 The Irrawaddy flows through countless large swamps. **It** is one of the most important rivers in Asia.

7 The Dover–Calais hovercraft makes the crossing in 30 minutes. **It** carries about 20 vehicles.

8 It is strange that the peacock butterfly has a similar name in most languages. **The peacock butterfly** is found in most parts of Europe.

9 The great fire of London destroyed a large part of the city. **It** broke out in 1666.

10 Dr Johnson often met his friends in the Cheshire Cheese. **His** house was quite near.

11 Helicopters can land near the centre of a large city. **They** do not need a long runway.

12 The shops store food in their deep-freezes. **The deep-freezes**, however, need a constant electricity supply.

13 The world was to be a great adventure for him. He knew very little about **the world**.

14 The programme came by the Indian Ocean satellite. **It** went into fixed orbit in 1969.

15 The Indian Ocean satellite relays hundreds of signals. **The satellite** has been in position since 1969.

46.7
Intermediate
MIXED
TYPES

Two other important occasions where *that* is preferred to *who* are:

After an interrogative.

Who that understands music could say his playing was good? (More usually found in writing than in speech.)

After *much*; *little*; *few*. (Compare *all*, *any*, *only*, Exercise 46.3.)

The few that came were enthusiastic.

* * *

● Combine the following ideas by means of DEFINING or NON-DEFINING relatives, using a contact-clause wherever possible:

1 Is that the new station? You pointed **it** out to me last week.

2 This is the man. I gave money to **him** this morning.

3 Anne Boleyn was Henry VIII's second wife. Henry executed **her** in 1536.

4 Who would look elsewhere, as Henry did? **He** had such a charming wife.

5 An old soldier sits begging on the pavement. **His** legs were shot away in the last war.

6 His stepmother was not very kind to him. He was living with **her**.

7 He had seen only a few policemen. **They** were all young. (Begin with 'The few . . .')

8 Last week I went to see the country town. He used to live in **that town**.

9 Bring me the cigarettes. I left **them** on the table. **The table** stands by the window.

10 Mozart spent the last ten years of his life in Vienna. **His** birthplace was Salzburg.

11 What was the name of the girl? **She** came here last night.

12 This large map belonged to Ptolemy XI. In the middle of **it** you can see part of the Arctic Circle.

13 We now come to Euclid. Readers are well acquainted with **his** work.

14 I'm sure it was Cyril. **He** told her to do it.

15 The matter has been settled. You were arguing about **it** last night.

**46.8
Advanced**

It has been pointed out that the NON-DEFINING RELATIVE is not heard in spoken English, except as a CONNECTIVE. (See next exercise.)

The idea of parenthetical and supplementary remarks is achieved in speech by simple conjunctions like *and, but, because, for, since, as,* etc., or by various speech devices for introducing parentheses and asides, like *by the way, you remember, incidentally,* etc.

> The Lord Mayor, whom you met at the reception yesterday, gave me a handsome present.

The above sentence would never occur in spoken English but is quite a normal written English construction.
In speech it would be expressed as two separate ideas:

Either: You remember you met the Lord Mayor yesterday?

> Well, look what a handsome present he gave me!

or: The Lord Mayor gave me this handsome present. You met him at the reception yesterday (you know).

*   *   *

● Using any simple connective devices, or splitting the material into conversational units, reduce the following series of non-defining relatives to an acceptable spoken form of narrative:

1   The Prime Minister of Ruritania, to whom I introduced you last week, is extremely fond of his national drink.

2   The national drink of the Ruritanians, which (as you know) is mint tea, comes from the neighbouring country of Rusticaria.

3   So the import tax on mint, by which the Ruritanians vastly increase their national income, is a very high one.

4   My friend the Prime Minister, who after all only had the best interests of his country at heart, attempted to cut the tax down by half.

5   The leader of the ensuing revolution, which succeeded in overthrowing the government, dismissed my friend from his post.

6   The return of the old high tax, which now seemed inevitable, would mean that the neighbouring mint-growing country must sell at

rock-bottom prices to enable the Ruritanians (who aren't, on the whole, very rich) to buy the commodity at a reasonable price.

7 The Rusticarians, many of whom had hoped for better selling-prices, were terribly upset by the revolution, which to them meant a return to pinching and scraping.

8 The Ruritanians, most of whom had been looking forward to bigger and better tea-parties, at which of course their own national delicacy, pickled peach-stones, would be consumed in large quantities, were also terribly upset by the revolution, which to them meant a return to pinching and scraping too.

9 The revolutionaries, who had only used the Prime Minister's attempt to reduce the mint import tax as an excuse to get control, were terribly upset by the result, through which they were now compelled to buy their tea at the old high price, which prevented them from celebrating as much as they would have liked.

10 The Rusticarians, in whose minds their neighbours' revolution figured as a blow against their own national prestige as the Land of Mint and Honey, at once broke off all diplomatic relations with the Ruritanians.

11 The impending state of war, which would probably bring about the ruin of both countries, was only less tragic than the cutting off of the supplies of luscious green mint, without which the Ruritanians could scarcely live.

12 The situation was aggravated by the action of the Urticarians (from whose country the Ruritanians import their national delicacy, pickled peach-stones), who suddenly announced a rise in the price of that commodity, which according to them was due to the scarcity of fruit because of drought.

13 The despair of the Ruritanians, for whom life was now scarcely worth living, was so great that the Revolutionary Government, in which nobody now had much confidence, recalled my friend the ex-Prime Minister, who had spent a

happy week trying to grow mint in the stony soil of his country estate.

14   My friend the Prime Minister at once cut the import tax on mint by half, in honour of which Ruritanian flags were flown throughout Rusticaria; and peach-trees began to flourish miraculously throughout Urticaria, whose government were willing to sell their produce to their neighbours at any price.

15   So my friend has brought peace to the Ruritanians, who now consume even more of their national drink, fresh mint tea, which they get from the gratified Rusticarians, and enjoy their national delicacy, pickled peach-stones, which they get from the thankful Urticarians, who would otherwise have half their crops rotting on the trees.

**46.9
Intermediate
and
Advanced
CONNECTIVE
RELATIVE**

The only form of NON-DEFINING RELATIVE found with any frequency in the spoken language is the *who, which,* etc., replacing *and.* It forms a stronger link with the first part of the sentence when we wish to avoid a repetition of either the subject or object or the whole idea of the first part.

It was invented by the Earl of Sandwich, and he gave his name to the thing we eat today.

It was invented by the Earl of Sandwich, who gave his name to the thing we eat today.

He bored a hole in my tooth, and it was very unpleasant.

He bored a hole in my tooth, which was very unpleasant.

Sometimes, however, the non-defining clause is a mere trick of style, as in a number of cases in Exercise 46.8, not to be recommended to students for imitation:

It crashed into a bus-load of children, who were all killed (OR all of whom were killed).
– Better as: They were all killed.

*   *   *

● Reconstruct the following sentences, using a relative pronoun as a connective:

1   He walked along the wall on his hands, and that was a very difficult thing to do.

2 He has three sons, and they all work in the same office.

3 He gave each of the ladies a rose, and this earned him their smiles.

4 He studied hard in his youth, and that contributed to his success in later life.

5 His cousin built several houses, and they are none of them more than five miles from the heart of London.

6 Cyril used to be fond of boxing, and that accounts for his crooked nose.

7 John went fishing last weekend, and that is one of the pleasantest ways of spending one's leisure.

8 There were two spare rooms upstairs, and neither of them had been used for years.

9 They have four children, and they all go to a Comprehensive School.

10 He passed his examination with honours, and this made his parents very proud of him.

11 The soldier on overseas service had a baby girl aged three years, but he had never seen her.

12 He was dropped when he was a baby, and that made him a permanent invalid.

13 They are going on a voyage of exploration to the South Pole, and it will be a dangerous undertaking.

14 There were two dwarfs at the circus, and neither of them was over three feet high.

15 The Professor came home drunk the other night, and that shocked the whole neighbourhood.

46.10
Advanced

DEFINING RELATIVE. Read notes to Exercises 46.1–3 for general remarks on the defining relative.

Advanced students frequently ask why we say such and such a thing. The following brief notes on the relative are added for this purpose to be expanded as required by the teacher.

HISTORICAL. *That* was originally used in relative clauses of all kinds; the *wh*— forms were purely interrogative. Gradually the *wh*— forms came to be used side by side with *that*, and since the eighteenth century have gained great popularity in English, largely through the efforts of classical writers, especially Addison and Johnson, who attempted to make an English imitation of Latin grammatical forms.

Dr Johnson refers to end-prepositions, *that*, and contact-clauses as 'colloquial barbarisms'. Dryden writes of himself, 'I am often put to a stand in considering whether what I write be the idiom of the tongue, . . . and have no other way to clear my doubts but by translating my English into Latin.' Addison has an enlightening essay in the *Spectator* in which he reverses historical development by maligning the 'Jacksprat' *that*, which he asserts has been damaging poor *who* and *which*. All this classical imitation caused a great deal of confusion, and introduced several erroneous ideas and clumsy forms. *That* fell into disuse in written English, but lived happily on in speech. Oddly enough the pendulum swung the other way when things with an archaic flavour became popular through the later Romantics, especially through the works of De Quincey. Partly because of this contrived lapse from use in the written language, and partly because we have come to feel it as a 'neuter' word, it is rarely heard for persons in the subjective case; and as it is the custom to make a contact-clause with the objective and prepositional cases, we don't hear it there either. We have had to borrow *whose* for the possessive.

END-PREPOSITION. The defining relative with *that* or as a contact-clause frequently requires the preposition at the end of the clause. This valuable idiomatic device in the English language should not be forced into the background in favour of the unnatural Latin-English form with the preposition in front of the word it governs. Many hideous phrases are written, and sometimes even spoken, in a misguided effort to avoid what is really a sound English construction. Such phrases as *it's worth waiting for*; *it depends on who you're dealing with*; *we've done the best we could think of*; *that was all it amounted to*, etc., can scarcely be expressed in any other way. Students should beware of trying to use the Latin construction with phrasal verbs i.e. strongly associated verbs and particles (*laugh at*, *wonder at*, *take care of*, *do without*), and when such combinations form one semantic whole (*give up*, *take over*, etc.) where the particle has an adverbial force. A lieutenant once dared to correct a telegram from a superior officer on this point. He received a further telegram reading: 'Insolence is something up with which I will not put.'

OTHER USES OF *that* AS DEFINING RELATIVE

DOUBLE CONTROL. *Which* and *who* are definitely at a disadvantage here, and may cause one to make stupid mistakes, especially when writing with the erroneous idea that *wh—* is better style. *The book you spoke of and recommended to me* cannot be 'the book of which you spoke and recommended to me.' Similarly, *The book I referred to and read out of.*

DOUBLE RELATIVES. We normally find the *wh—* form for the second of two relatives, whether the second one further defines the first or is co-ordinate with it.

> You're the only person I've ever met who could do it.
> The paper I read every day and which I find so enjoyable.
> These are forms that occasionally occur but which should not be taught.

PREDICATIVE *that* (nearly always omitted). *Wh—* forms never found.

> She's not the woman she was before she married.
> I'm not the fool you thought me.

(This is not to be confused with the common colloquial idiom: 'I met Mrs Taylor; Miss Binks that was.')

That + there is. Never *wh—* forms, and nearly always omitted.

> It's the only one there is in the shop.
> The number of mistakes there are in this homework is simply astounding.

All that. We have seen that *all* as an adjective usually has *that*, like other superlative ideas. As a pronoun, however, we now prefer *all who* for persons.

> A welcome is extended to all who (or that) wish to come.
> It was all (that) I could do to keep myself from laughing.

USES OF *that* AS A SHORT CUT IN CLAUSES OF A RELATIVE TYPE.

(1) Ellipsis

> He did it *in* the way (that) I should have done it myself. (= in which)
> You can break it *with* the same ease (that) you can break an egg. (= with which)

N.B. – The preposition implied by *that* must have appeared already.

(2) *That* to indicate time

> By the time (that) you have finished, it'll be too late.
> I met her the year (that) my Uncle William died.

(3)   *That* to indicate place

I'll go anywhere (that) you want me to. (= I'll go to any place (that) you want me to)

N.B. – From this it is but a short step to the forms with introductory *it*.

It was there (OR while at school, at five o'clock, then, at the seaside, etc.) that I first met my wife.
It's to you (that) I'm talking.
It's you (that) I'm talking to.

which lead one to consider *that* a conjunction and not a pronoun. (See note to Exercise 46.4.)

CONNECTIVE RELATIVE

As, same, such, so + as.

I've done the same as you have. (= I've done the same thing that you have)
She was as nice as could be.
You're just the same as you always were.

Wh— CLAUSES, DEFINING AND NON-DEFINING

There are certain cases where the preposition cannot be put at the end of a defining clause, and in such cases the *wh—* form must be used. The clause may, of course, still be a DEFINING RELATIVE, spoken without a pause or written without a comma.

Beyond, round, around, opposite, besides; than whom, than which (the last two never occur in the spoken language)

DEFINING: The man opposite whom I am sitting has a new book.

DEFINING: This is the point beyond which I've never been.

NON-DEFINING: St John's Glacier, beyond which nobody has ever climbed, is only about 8,000 feet high.

Even with these words the 'end-preposition' form of clause is on the increase.

The man I'm sitting opposite.
The fountain they are standing round was built by the Romans.

INSEPARABLE ADVERBIAL PHRASES

The courage with which he faced his enemies was truly inspiring.

(We cannot say 'the courage he faced his enemies with' as

we can say 'The pen I wrote the letter with has a steel nib.')

PARTITIVE USE OF *of*

I have two friends, both of whom are on holiday at the moment.

The train ran into a bus-load of children, many of whom were British.

OVERHEARD IN A CLASSROOM

TEACHER: A preposition is a bad word to end a sentence with.

PUPIL: Please, teacher, you've just ended a sentence with 'with'.

TEACHER: Ah, but what did I end the sentence with 'with' for? Do you know?

PUPIL: No, teacher; and I don't know what you ended that one with 'with with for' for!

* * *

(46.10)   ● Add relatives WHERE NECESSARY, or combine sentences with relatives; use a contact-clause wherever possible:

1 The best play — Shakespeare wrote, but — few people have read, is probably *King Lear*.

2 It was the sergeant-major — told me to fetch the rifle — I had been practising with.

3 The gentleman is the Finance Minister. You trod on his foot

4 The building is the Finance Ministry. I live opposite it.

5 The old man has died. You were talking to me about him and told me to go and see him.

6 He's the person — I meet at the club every day and — I've invited home to dinner tonight.

7 I gave him the one — I wanted to keep, fool — I was.

8 We ate some fish. They must have been very ancient.

9 Miss Harland had several new friends. All of them were atheists. Her father was the vicar of Nether Puddling.

10 The house is mine. In its windows there is a light. (This makes a clumsy relative, what other way can you find?)

11   It's all — there is to last us a week, — is not a
     very cheering thought, is it?

12   It'll be dark by the time — you get to the river,
     so I'm afraid you'll have to go back the same
     way — you came.

13   Mr Trotter was born in Omsk in 1892. He came
     to London three years ago.

14   I appreciate the kind words. You have welcomed
     me with kind words.

15   Boswell wrote a fine biography of Johnson. His
     own life was far from admirable.

16   Put it down anywhere — you like and take
     anything else — you want — you can see.

17   The girl — was at the party is about the only
     friend of yours — I've met — I really like.

18   I'm just the same — I was the day — I first met
     you.

19   O. W. Holmes was one of America's most gifted
     humorists. He said that the American
     constitution could never be used to further private
     interests.

20   The statements were all untrue. He made
     statements concerning his Aunt Tabitha's strange
     disappearance.

21   The tree fell on to a party of fishermen. All of
     them were injured.

22   He repudiated the charge with dignity. His
     dignity greatly impressed the judge. (Begin, 'The
     dignity . . .)

23   The spoon was stolen from a hotel. He was eating
     with it.

24   This is the horse. It kicked the policeman. I saw
     him trying to clear away the crowd. The crowd
     had collected to watch a fight. Two men had
     started the fight.

25   He's the best man — I can find — can mend it
     within an hour.

26   This instrument was in the museum. Its works are
     all rusty.

27   All the while — I'm working, it's you — I'm
     thinking of.

28   He played the piece, — was quite difficult, in the

exact manner — I play it myself, but on an
instrument — I wouldn't even accept as a gift.

29 I have forgotten whether music soothes the
savage 'breast' or the savage 'beast'. According to
Shakespeare music is the food of love. *He* ought
to know.

30 All — applied were given such jobs — were suited
to them; but those — applied first, of — were
selected the best — could be found, were given the
job — they most desired; any — came later could
not always get the jobs — they were looking for.

Note the different uses of *that* in:
'I pointed out that[1] that[2] "that"[3] that[4] that[5] man had
written was in the wrong place.'

	TYPE	HOW PRONOUNCED
1	Conjunction	weak form
2	Demonstrative	strong form
3	Noun	emphatic form
4	Relative	weak form
5	Demonstrative	strong form

Here is a favourite nursery-rhyme:

This is the farmer that sowed the corn
That fed the cock that crowed in the morn
That wakened the priest all shaven and shorn
That married the man all tattered and torn
That kissed the maiden all forlorn
That milked the cow with the crumpled horn
That tossed the dog
That bit the cat
That killed the rat
That ate the malt
That lay in the house
That Jack built. (All DEFINING RELATIVES.)

47 Relative and Interrogative Links

47.1
Elementary   *Who, what, which, where, why*, etc., are very important as
link-words. They form a very elementary type of complex
sentence that is extremely common in both spoken and
written English.

An infinitive phrase is usual when the subjects of both sections are identical, the sense of the infinitive phrase being future. Compare:

> I don't know which to take.
> I don't know which I took.

Note also verbs of request:

> Tell *him* where to go (= where *he* must go).
> *Ask* him what to do (= what *you* must do).

Who is used in both subjective and objective cases.

* * *

(47.1)   ● Add the missing link:
1   I don't know — to do.
2   He has forgotten — to go.
3   I have no idea — to ask.
4   He told me — book to take.
5   Do you know — to make coffee?
6   Ask him — to put the TV set.
7   I don't understand — to drive a car.
8   He wants to know — club to join.
9   You must go — he tells you.
10 Can you suggest — to write?
11 She doesn't know — dress to wear.
12 I can't remember — to do it.
13 We don't know — to show it to.
14 I shan't forget — to find it again.
15 He doesn't know — to open it with.
16 Can you tell me — could advise me in this matter?
17 A lawyer advised me — to do.
18 My friend couldn't remember — way to go.
19 They don't know — your house is.
20 I can't imagine — you are so cross with me.

47.2
Intermediate
Remember *who* is normally used in both the subjective and objective cases.

* * *

● Add the missing links:
1   She doesn't understand — to do the exercise.
2   I can't think — to buy for dinner.
3   Have you decided — to ask to the party?
4   They don't know — to meet us tomorrow.

5 I am wondering — to do with my old clothes.
6 Tell me — to be there, and I shall not be late.
7 It is difficult to know — to choose.
8 He doesn't know — to think of this arrangement.
9 We can't think — to go for our holidays.
10 I don't know — to punish him.
11 They were not sure — room to give you.
12 He wants to learn — to build a boat.
13 Do you know — to get a good meal in this town?
14 Nobody told me — to leave these letters.
15 Tell us — to begin work.

**47.3
Elementary**

When the subjects are different, a clause is always added.

> I don't know who she was speaking to.
> He asked me how I had done it.

The clause in these cases is closely related in form to the reported question (Exercise 51.7). In fact we may see many of the Section 47 clauses AS reported questions. The links are not the same as the relatives considered in Section 46, since they do not relate to an antecedent within the sentence. Compare:

> He proposed a motion, *which* was accepted.
>> – NON-DEFINING RELATIVE *which* related to antecedent *a motion*.

> I don't know *which* they accepted.

Who, what, etc., so used, are for this reason sometimes called INDEPENDENT RELATIVES.

Notice that *who* is invariably heard in place of *whom* in the objective case or with end-prepositions.

* * *

● Add the missing link:
1 I wonder — he means.
2 I have no idea — he arrived.
3 He was telling me — he had fought the champion.
4 Do you know — you are talking to?
5 I have no idea — he will come.
6 Will you please tell me — soon you can finish it?
7 I wonder — hat this is. It's certainly not mine.
8 Aren't you going to tell me — you saw at the pictures?
9 You haven't told me — you did last night.

10 Lots of people don't know — Vladikavkaz is.
11 Can you tell us — road leads to the station?
12 I've forgotten — she gave it to.
13 I wonder — she married.
14 I can't think — she married him.
15 Have they told you — time to come?
16 Can you see — is coming down the street?
17 You must tell the librarian — book you are taking.
18 She hasn't written to tell me — she is coming.
19 The grocer says he doesn't know — he sent it to.
20 I never know — I can trust.

47.4
Intermediate

See Exercise 47.3.

* * *

● Add the missing links:
1 Have you heard — is coming to stay with me?
2 We don't know — she has gone.
3 Can you tell me — this box is so heavy?
4 I remember — you were a little girl.
5 Do you know — makes the sun hot?
6 Nobody knows — you put your shoes.
7 Try to think — you did with my pen-knife.
8 Did anyone see — way Maisie went?
9 I want to know — told you about it.
10 We asked him — he got married.
11 Show me — this machine works.
12 I haven't decided — would be the best thing to do.
13 Do you know — made the tea this morning?
14 Please explain — this is impossible.
15 I am not sure — their train arrives.

47.5
Intermediate
and
Advanced

See Exercise 47.3.
How many, much, long, often, etc. behave similarly.

* * *

● Add the missing links:
1 I inquired — the price of the furniture was.
2 The young couple wanted to know — the rent would be.
3 I've not the slightest idea — you went to see.

4 It is difficult to explain exactly — your project is
   bound to fail.
5 Repeat — I have just told you.
6 Smear the ointment gently — the pain is greatest.
7 The burglar tried in vain to discover — the safe
   opened.
8 She wondered — she had met him.
9 I don't really know — to recommend you to apply
   to.
10 Can you tell me — inches there are in a foot?
11 She was unable to tell us — house she had gone
   into by mistake.
12 The recipe doesn't say — the pudding should take
   to cook.
13 Do you know — tins of salmon I need for a
   hundred sandwiches?
14 Few people realize — tiring it is to teach young
   children.
15 I am trying to find out — her birthday is.
16 Could you tell me — owns that house?
17 I haven't heard — the result was.
18 Nobody seemed to know — the engine wouldn't
   work.
19 I'm surprised — prettier Maisie is than her sister.
20 It wasn't mentioned in the news — people were
   killed.
21 You would be surprised — cheaper it is to live in
   the country.
22 Let us decide — we shall go for our picnic.
23 The dog always knows — the postman is
   coming.
24 It was difficult to understand — the lecturer was
   saying.
25 Please tell me — the width of this material is,
   and — it is per metre.
26 Do you know — is the shortest route to
   Manchester from here?
27 She is going to learn — to make her own clothes.
28 It is uncertain — often he can come.
29 I've often wondered — longer Cyril was going to
   wear that tie.
30 Would you mind repeating — you've just said?

47.6
**Intermediate
and**
Advanced   See Exercise 47.3.

*   *   *

● Complete the following:

1 Have you heard what ...
2 She asked the policeman where ...
3 I was surprised to see how tall ...
4 Children should learn to eat what ...
5 It is difficult to judge how heavy ...
6 Can you tell me who ...
7 My mother could never understand why ...
8 A baby always seems to know when ...
9 The soldier was shown how ...
10 She could not make up her mind which ...
11 The dressmaker asked her how long ...
12 I wonder how much longer ...
13 On reading the newspaper, I was surprised to see
    how many ...
14 Can you remember where ...
15 Tell me whereabouts ...
16 The Prime Minister refused to state when ...
17 The policeman made a note of where ...
18 Can you tell me how ...
19 An employer is sure to ask his typist how
    many ...
20 To this day she has never understood why ...
21 My friend Maisie does whatever ...
22 I am surprised how much more intelligent ...
23 Medical authorities do not agree as to whether ...
24 My mother was astonished when I told her how
    much ...
25 Cyril has become so fat he doesn't know how ...
26 The theory of evolution makes us realize how
    little ...
27 I never realized how few ...
28 The newsboy couldn't remember which ...
29 Anyone can see how thin ...
30 Music tries to express what ...

48 Emphatic Connectives

Who, what, which, whose, when, where, how + *ever*. They are all written as single words, *whoever, whatever*, etc. and usually pronounced with stress on the first syllable of *ever*. Note that *whoever's* is usually preferred to *whosever*. There are two main uses in modern English.

(1) IN THE SENSE 'it doesn't matter who, which, when', etc.

Whoever says that is a liar.
I'll sell it to whoever arrives first.
Eat whatever you like.*
I'll do whatever you tell me to.*
We were warmly welcomed wherever we went.
We shall be pleased to see you whenever you care to call.
Learn whichever poem you find most interesting.
The three of them agreed that whichever (whoever) arrived first should save seats for the other two.

The simple pronoun *what* can usually replace *whatever* (as in the examples marked *); *who* and *which* are no longer used in this way in modern English.

(2) PARENTHETICALLY (suggesting ignorance or indifference).

I'll give the pen back to John or Henry, or whoever it belongs to.
I'll come at 10 or 10.30, or whenever I can get there.

* * *

● Add the appropriate *ever* form to the following:
1 — one of us has got to pay for it, it won't be me.
2 Take — much you want and — you want to.
3 — smashed my glasses shall pay for them, — he's hidden himself.
4 Take this bag, basket or — it is, and hang it up — you can find room for it.
5 — I stay in Brighton, or — else I stay on the south coast, I'm sure to meet that school-teacher fellow Robinson or Robertson or — his name is.
6 — quickly I dry myself after a bath, I always

catch — variety of cold there is going.

7 Please take — one you want and bring it back —
   you like.

8 — told you to keep off meat was quite right; I
   think you should go on doing — he tells you to.

9 Of course you can dance with — you like, but
   don't expect me to introduce you to the glamorous
   Laura, Lorna or — her name is.

10 I'll come — I can and I'll bring — you like with
    me.

11 Eat — one you like and leave the others for —
    comes in later.

12 — told you that Maisie wears a ginger wig is an
    out-and-out liar, — you may care to say in his
    favour.

13 Well I must say this hat fits me, — it is; I nearly
    always find a substitute — I lose my own.

14 — it is you've found, you must give it back to —
    it belongs to.

15 — I try to cook anything, the steak or chop (or —
    it may be) is never quite to the liking of — has to
    eat it.

16 — one of you children disturbs me again, I shall
    punish severely, — it may be.   You always make a
    noise — I try to do my work.

17 — the weather, we go hiking at the weekend with
    — likes to join us.

18 — she does an exercise she makes mistakes, —
    hard she tries.

19 — has time this afternoon, will they please pick
    some roses, or — there is in the garden, for the
    table.

20 — travels will find there's no place like home, —
    he may go; — humble it may be, there will be a
    yearning in his heart — he thinks of it.

49 Emphatic Colloquial Interrogatives

The uses of -*ever* in the previous exercise must not be confused with its very common use in spoken English merely to emphasize the speaker's surprise, consternation or annoyance in question form. *Ever* is written here as a separate word, and usually there is stress on BOTH words: *who, what*, etc., and the first syllable of *ever*. This *ever* has exactly the same meaning as *on earth*.

> Who on earth is that young man in the yellow waistcoat? Who ever can he be?
> What ever are you doing?

COMPARE:

> Whatever he does, he does badly.

In angry or impetuous speech, stronger expressions take their place, notably *the dickens*,[1] *the devil, the blazes, the hell*; all except the last are tolerable in normal society if the situation warrants violent emphasis, though references to the infernal regions should perhaps be avoided in the presence of sensitive ladies.

> What the devil do you mean by that?
> Who the blazes do you think you are?

Whom and *whose* are not used in this spoken form.

* * *

● Read the following remarks, reinforcing them with *ever*, *on earth*, or any of the stronger forms at will. Be careful of stress and intonation:

1 What made you do that?
2 Why are you late?
3 When is Maisie coming?
4 Who broke my pen?
5 Who do you think you're talking to?
6 Why don't you mend it yourself?
7 Where did I pack my toothbrush?
8 How can I see when you're standing in my light?
9 What do you expect me to do about it?
10 Why don't you tell her all about it?

---

[1] No connection with the novelist; even Shakespeare used 'What the dickens.'

11   Who are you?
12   How did *you* get here?
13   Who can I give it to?
14   What have I done with my other trousers?
15   Where have you been?
16   What is she up to now?
17   Who told you *I'd* give you one?
18   How can we get there in time?
19   What did you want to do that for?
20   Why didn't you punch Cyril on the nose?
21   Where can that child have got to?
22   What do you mean by it?
23   How did the cat get through that small hole?
24   When are you going to realize it can't be done?
25   Who put the jam-spoon in the butter?

EMPHATIC CLAUSE INVERSION

**49.2
Advanced**

A fairly common device for emphasis in spoken English is the trick of changing the order of principal and subordinate clauses, in order to lay greater stress on the adverbial phrase. A couple of examples will explain this more easily.

> I don't know how far he's gone.
> He's gone I don't know *how* far.
> I don't know how many things she's broken.
> She's broken I don't know *how* many things.

The majority are *how* ... constructions.

*   *   *

● Change the following into a similar emphatic form. Remember that intonation is important:

1   I don't know how many books I've read.
2   I don't know how many times I've told you.
3   You know who I gave it to.
4   I don't know how deep he had to dive to get it up.
5   I don't know how long I've been waiting for a bus.
6   I don't know how long he's been away.
7   I don't know how many people he's spoken to.
8   I don't know how many years ago I read that.
9   I don't know how many times he has been to see you.

10 I don't know how much money she spent on decorating the house.
11 You know where I've been (to).
12 I don't know how many children she's got.
13 I don't know what she was dressed up like.
14 I don't know how often you've been told that.
15 I don't know how far we walked.

50 *there is* and *it is*

50.1
Elementary
PREPARATORY
THERE

There is, there are. This is the most usual way of denoting existence in English, when the subject has not already been defined.

The two books are on the table. (We know which books.)

There are two books on the table. (Location of two unknown books.)

'Two books are on the table' is a grammatically possible but very rare form.

* * *

● Add the correct form of *There is* to the following:
1 — two dogs in the garden.
2 — a good film on at the Regal.
3 — a lot of people in the park yesterday.
4 — a party in our house tomorrow.
5 — an old friend of yours at the concert last night.
6 — a train coming now.
7 — (negative) another train for at least two hours.
8 — a few changes since you left last week.
9 — a lot of work to do this afternoon.
10 — some chocolates on this plate when I went out just now.
11 — one for you tomorrow.
12 — plenty of knives in the drawer.
13 — only a footpath here last year.
14 — a new moon tonight.
15 — no mistakes in your last exercise.
16 — no fruit on this tree for many years.

17 — a thunderstorm soon, I think.
18 — four hundred children in the school this year.
19 — an accident outside our house last night.
20 — a lot of visitors this morning.

50.2
Elementary
PREPARATORY
IT

It is, was, etc.   These expressions are useful for introducing a complex subject (phrase or clause), which would sound very clumsy if made the real subject.

It's impossible to guess her age.
It is wrong not to do as you are told.

*   *   *

● Add the correct form of *it is* to the following:
1 — a pity (that) she is so stupid.
2 — a shame to spend all this money.
3 — a wonder (that) you didn't hurt yourself.
4 — stupid not to go yesterday.
5 — a great day when he passes his examination.
(Note that 'a great day' is not the true subject of this sentence.)
6 — nice having you to tea last Wednesday.
7 — wonderful to see you again next week.
8 — possible (that) he doesn't understand English.
9 — strange (that) she didn't speak to you.
10 — true (that) Solomon had a thousand wives?
11 — wrong to think (that) all people are greedy for money.
12 — funny that I can see better with one eye than with both.
13 — lovely to go for a sail tomorrow.
14 — cruel to beat a dog like that.
15 — funny seeing you in this place.

50.3
Elementary

See notes on Exercise 50.2. *It* is also the meaningless subject for impersonal verbs and a few expressions of time and distance.

It's raining hard.
It was nearly 10 o'clock.
It's a long way to Timbuktu.

*   *   *

● Add the correct form of *it is* to the following:
1 — a long time ago.
2 — fine tomorrow, I think.

3   — good for you to take exercise.
4   — very wet last month, and now — windy.
5   — raining for three hours without stopping.
6   — a long time since I saw you.
7   — a shame that those trees had to be cut down.
8   — going to snow, isn't it?
9   — snowing since 11 o'clock. When will it stop?
10 — easy for him to find fault, but — not fair.
11 — terribly hot in August last year.
12 The church clock struck.   — exactly 5 o'clock.
13 — probable you'll find it in your pocket.
14 — only 100 kilometres from here.
15 You can get there in an hour, but — not easy to find the way.

**50.4
Elementary**

See notes to Exercises 50.1–3.

* * *

● Add the correct form of *it is* or *there is* to the following:
1   — fine today.
2   — a good thing to be accurate.
3   — a man standing under that tree ten minutes ago.
4   — here that I saw him.
5   — a post office in the village.
6   — nothing left if we don't go soon.
7   — a long time since I had a holiday.
8   — a fact that he is a rich man.
9   — often a rainbow after rain.
10 — a pity (that) you can't come with me.
11 — too early to leave yet.
12 — a beautiful park near my home.
13 — the same film at the Metro for three weeks.
14 — difficult to find a house in the town next year.
15 — a drink for everyone who was thirsty.
16 — a new car in the next street.
17 — not true to say that she is my friend.
18 — a dog running across the road.
19 — a train which leaves at nine o'clock.
20 — not far from my house to the station.

50.5
Intermediate

See notes to Exercises 50.1–3.
Notice the following expressions:

(a) It is time to go. (= The correct moment has arrived.)

(b) It is a long time since . . . (= The time has been long.)

(c) There is time to go. (= We have time; enough time exists.)

(d) It's a long way to Tipperary. (= The distance between here and Tipperary is long.)

(e) There's a long way to go yet before we get there. (= We still have this distance more to go; such a distance still exists for us.)

* * *

● Add the correct form of *there is* or *it is* to the following:

1 — easy to understand why he hasn't come back.

2 — time to go to bed.

3 — many things worse than death.

4 — very strange that we should both arrive together.

5 — no one at home when I called for him.

6 — a few sandwiches left over from yesterday.

7 — fun going up in a helicopter.

8 — two guests coming for the weekend.

9 — no place like home.

10 — impossible to guess where they could have gone to.

11 — a good wheat crop this year.

12 — hard to decide what was the best thing to do.

13 — still several empty seats in the plane when I arrived.

14 — hard times ahead of us.

15 — terrifying to hear a knock on the window at midnight.

16 — not known where he spent his early childhood.

17 — a very good dance band in that restaurant.

18 — time to finish this exercise before we go.

19 — a long time since I saw such a beautiful sunset.

20 — a light in the kitchen when I got home.

21 — crowds of people at the station waiting to greet the film star, so you'd better be there very early.

22 — very few people at his lecture yesterday.

23 — not clear who was responsible.

24 — uncertain why he denied the charge.

25 — no time for tea if we don't hurry.

26 — improbable that the organization will be good.

27 — most unpleasant to have to work twelve hours a day.

28 — time you grew out of such childish behaviour. (See Exercise 31.10.)

29 — a pity you missed that concert.

30 — so much work to get through this morning that I haven't had time to think about the question.

50.6
Advanced

See notes to Exercises 50.1–3 and 50.5.

* * *

● Add the correct form of *there is* or *it is* to the following:

1 — a lot of jobs to be done that morning.

2 — time to go there on foot if you want to.

3 — not the season for bananas.

4 — too soon yet to say definitely.

5 — a sad sight to see a man covered with rags.

6 — a lot to be said for your point of view.

7 — nearly time to say good night.

8 — a fact that he is not at all well.

9 — you (that) I meant.

10 — a time and place for everything.

11 — more important for you at a later date than now.

12 — time to get twice as far as *he* did.

13 — much to be said on both sides.

14 — a place I knew where you could get very good coffee.

15 — a game in some parts of the world called tric-trac, which English people know as backgammon.

16 — time for your medicine in half an hour.

17 — all very well to say you were sorry, but were you really?

18 '— murder,' said the detective calmly.

19 '— a murder, evidently,' said the detective calmly.

20 — a big hole in your stocking.

21 — time for another cigarette before she gets back.

22 — what you do that counts, not what you say.
23 — a long way from the house to the bus-stop.
24 — high time you went home.
25 — an even shorter way to it across the fields if only
    we had known it.

51   Reported Speech

IMPERATIVE

51.1
Elementary
SAY
AND
TELL

Say.   Usually with the actual words spoken. It is never used with the infinitive in reported speech.

Tell.   Never used, in the sense of 'recount', with the actual words spoken. A personal object is always present. Imperatives become infinitive phrases in reported speech, preceded by a verb such as *tell*, *order*, *command*, *ask*, with a (pro)noun for the person addressed.

> Bring me a book.
> He asked her (him, us, etc.) *to bring* him a book.

*   *   *

● Put into REPORTED SPEECH, using the verb indicated:

1   Go away. (He told)
2   Come here. (I asked)
3   Eat it up. (Tell)
4   Run away. (They told)
5   Pay at once. (They ordered)
6   Fold it in half. (She asked)
7   Give me another. (Ask)
8   Write quickly. (Tell)
9   Sit down. (We asked)
10 Have a cup of tea. (She asked)
11 Come at five o'clock. (He told)
12 Pick it up. (He ordered)
13 Wash your face. (He told).
14 Clean my shoes. (I asked)
15 Do it again. (Tell)
16 Open the door. (Ask)
17 Hold this. (She asked)

18 Play the piano. (They asked)
19 Come in. (He ordered)
20 Look out. (I told)

51.2
Intermediate

See notes to Exercise 51.1.
A negative imperative is reported by means of a negative infinitive.

> Don't do it.
> He asked me (her, us, etc.) *not to do* it.

* * *

● Put into REPORTED SPEECH:
1 Clean it yourself.
2 Wrap it up in a piece of paper.
3 Cut the corners off.
4 Fasten your safety belts.
5 Don't sit on my bed.
6 Wait there till I come.
7 Don't speak until you're spoken to.
8 Leave it on the piano.
9 Don't wipe your dirty fingers on my nice clean tablecloth.
10 Don't try to be funny.
11 Brush it off when it gets dry.
12 Don't put your elbow on the table.
13 Look where you're going.
14 Mind the steps.
15 Get your hair cut.
16 Shut the door after you.
17 Hold it round the middle.
18 Don't spill it on the carpet.
19 Pull your socks up.
20 Take a look at yourself in the mirror.

51.3
Advanced

See Exercises 51.1 and 51.2.
This is a revision exercise and contains other REPORTED SPEECH forms in addition to the Imperative.

* * *

● Put the following into REPORTED SPEECH:
1 Go to bed and don't get up till you're called.
2 Eat up your dinner at once or I'll punish you.
3 Write your name clearly at the top and then take down these points as I call them out.

4   Bring in the two accused men and take care they
    don't get away.   (The judge . . .)
5   Don't spend all your money on food and drink.
    Save some for the future.
6   Drive as fast as you can. I don't want to be late.
7   Wait here under the tree until the rain stops.
8   Do what you're told or you'll get into trouble.
9   Imitate my pronunciation if you want to speak
    well.
10 Come and see me whenever you have a few hours
    to spare.   Don't wait for me to ask you every time
    you want to come.
11 Hurry up if you want to go out with me.
12 Tell me when it's quarter past eight.
13 Be a good girl and sit quietly for five minutes and
    Auntie will give you a sweet.
14 Treat other people the way you'd like them to treat
    you.
15 Take a cold shower before breakfast if you want to
    keep fit.

REPORTED SPEECH – STATEMENT

**51.4
Elementary**

When the reporting verb is in the PRESENT SIMPLE, PRESENT
PERFECT, or FUTURE SIMPLE tense, there is no change of
tense in the words reported. Notice only the necessary
change of person.

'I am very sorry.'

He will tell you
He says   (that) he is very sorry.
He has just told me

*   *   *

● Put the following sentences into REPORTED SPEECH, introducing them with a verb in the PRESENT, PRESENT PERFECT,
or FUTURE tense:

1   I am going to town with my sister.
2   You have bought yourself a new hat.
3   We are very late.
4   I want to speak to you.
5   We have finished our work.
6   He is ready to come with us.

7 They do not know you.
8 I will answer the phone.
9 You can do it if you try.
10 She has done her homework well.
11 We are living in another house now.
12 I have been shopping all the morning.
13 I have not told you anything yet.
14 You may see the photographs if you like.
15 She has written me a long letter.
16 I am giving a party this week to all my friends.
17 You have an excellent cook.
18 We have not heard the news.
19 I like oranges better than bananas.
20 They are learning higher mathematics.
21 He is sitting over there.
22 You are not working hard enough.
23 She has given me a present.
24 You play the piano very well.
25 I have flown about a million kilometres.
26 You have been very quick.
27 Elizabeth has gone to school.
28 They are waiting outside.
29 We always try to please you.
30 I have been smoking too much.

51.5
Elementary

When the reporting verb is in the PAST SIMPLE or PAST PERFECT tense, or is a *should/would* form, the words reported are viewed in a different perspective. The speech is now remote, and seen as relating a sequence of events happening in the past, the tenses being changed accordingly.

> 'I am a student, and I have studied for three years.'
> He said (that) he *was* a student and *had studied* for three years.

So the following tense changes are automatic after past tense reporting verbs:

DIRECT SPEECH	REPORTED SPEECH
make(s)	made
is making	was making
has/have made	had made
made	had made
shall/will make	should/would make

should/would make   should/would have made*

* This does not hold for the *should/would* form of polite requests, which usually remains unchanged.

Adverbs of time and place and a few other expressions also change. Here are some examples (to be taken as convenient equivalents, not as 'rules'):

here = there   now = then   yesterday = the day before
this = that   ago = before   next week = the following
                                            week etc.

But these 'equivalents' should be used with common sense:

'This vehicle isn't safe.'

He said that the vehicle was not safe.   (*the*, not *that*, unless *this* is stressed)

And it is not always necessary to use any equivalent at all, as the past tense of the introducing verb is often quite sufficient.

'I am coming to see you now.'

He said he was coming to see me. (*then* is not wanted)

*   *   *

(51.5) ● Put the following sentences into REPORTED SPEECH, introducing them with a verb in the PAST tense:

1   I am ill.
2   I met him last year.
3   They will be here soon.
4   She has finished now.
5   I am living in London.
6   He is going to Berlin tomorrow.
7   I've just been to the butcher's.
8   I can come next week.
9   I don't know what he'll say.
10 They went away yesterday.
11 Wait till I come.
12 I think she is married.
13 I fell downstairs.
14 I'll leave it on the table.
15 I'm sorry I'm late.
16 I am very stupid.
17 She is quite charming but hasn't much sense.
18 He can come in when I have finished my work.
19 The clock will never work again if you try to mend it.

20 I lost my temper yesterday morning.
21 I'll come as soon as I can.
22 I've sold all those you gave me yesterday.
23 I was very ill yesterday.
24 I learnt all this nonsense a long time ago.
25 I have never been here before.
26 I haven't done my homework.
27 You may have to stay in bed for a week.
28 She will be here in half an hour if she isn't late.
29 That is the last time I saw him.
30 I shall try to be in time today. I'm sorry I forgot to come yesterday.

51.6
Intermediate

Read notes to Exercise 51.5.

Must. In ordinary speech *must* has three possible meanings, each of which has a different form when reported. *Can* and *needn't* sometimes behave in a similar way. (See earlier exercises on *must*.)

(1) Necessity or compulsion AT THE MOMENT OF SPEAKING – a TRUE PRESENT. This, of course, becomes a PAST when reported.

	He said he
'I must go now.'	– *had to go at once.*
'I needn't go.'	– *didn't have to go.*
'I mustn't go.'	– *wasn't to go.*

(2) Necessity or compulsion in the future; as a substitute for *shall have to*. This, of course, behaves like a future, and changes to the *should/would* form in reported speech for *must* and *needn't*.

	He said he
'I must go next week.'	– *would have to go the following week*
'I needn't go next week.'	– *wouldn't have to go*
'I mustn't go . . .'	– *wasn't to go*
(has no future form)	

(3) Permanent ruling or prohibition. Here the *must* remains unchanged.

'You mustn't cross the road against the red light.'

He told us we mustn't cross the road against the red light.

All natural laws and eternal truths may remain in the PRESENT SIMPLE.

*   *   *

(51.6)   ● Report the following, putting the introducing verb in the
PAST tense:

1 I would do the same myself if I were in your
place.
2 I tried to ride a bicycle but I fell off three times.
3 I shall expect to see you next Wednesday.
4 These apples won't keep, they are too soft.
5 I haven't had enough time to finish what I
intended to do. I can do some more later on.
6 I expect to hear some news tomorrow; I will tell
you if I do, so that you needn't worry.
7 You must leave the country at once.
8 People mustn't fish in this river.
9 You must decide what you want to do.
10 You must do it all again before next week, though
I must confess it's the first bad repair you've done.
You'll get a new job to do when you've finished it.
11 The football match will take place tomorrow
afternoon. All spectators are requested to obtain
their tickets before five o'clock today.
12 Last night I went to the cinema and saw Peter
O'Toole's latest film. I enjoyed myself very much,
and am going to take my other girl-friend tonight.
(Cyril said that . . .)
13 I am eighteen years old. I was previously
employed in a large shop in this city, and my
employers considered me to be very capable.
14 When I get back I'll give you the five pounds I
borrowed from you yesterday. I hope I shan't
meet with an accident.
15 I can't do it now, but I expect I can do it next
week.
16 By the time we reach the hill, the enemy will have
cut us off from the rest of our men. We shall have
to fight our way back along the coast, where the
enemy has fewer troops.
17 If you can't type any better than this, you had
better not type at all. I can't pay people for
incompetence, so you will have to leave
tomorrow. (He told Maisie that . . .)
18 You must not forget what I told you last lesson.

I shall expect you to be able to repeat it next
lesson by heart. You will have to learn it all
again if you can't.

19[1] I waited for you yesterday till six o'clock, but
you didn't come. I thought you would come later,
so I left a message with the porter.

20[1] I don't believe a word you are saying. I think it
would be better for everybody if you spoke the
truth. This is not the first time you have deceived
me, and I hope it won't occur again.

REPORTED SPEECH (*QUESTIONS*)

51.7
Elementary

The word-order of REPORTED QUESTIONS is the same as a
simple STATEMENT; there is no inversion as in a simple
question. In questions introduced by a question-word
(*who*, *what*, *how*, *when*, etc.), this word serves as a link
between the introducing verb and the reported question.
See also Exercise 47.3.

> 'What is your name?'   ('*My name is X*')
> He asked me what my name was.

* * *

● Put the following sentences into REPORTED SPEECH with the
introducing verb in the PAST tense. Vary the introducing
verb: *he asked, enquired, wondered, wanted to know,* etc.

1 Where are you going? (He asked me . . .)
2 How did you do that? (They wanted to know . . .)
3 Who will come to the pictures with me?
4 When will my dress be finished?
5 Why are you so sad?
6 What is the matter?
7 Which book are you taking?
8 Where ought we to meet tonight?
9 Who showed you my work?
10 How could you be so unkind?
11 When did they tell you that?
12 Why has she not eaten anything?
13 What am I to do?
14 What is the time?

[1] In the second part of these two sentences it is quite convenient
to use the verb *think* (appearing in the words spoken) as introducing verb for that part of the report.

15 How do you know that?
16 Where has he put my pencil?
17 When are you beginning your holiday?
18 Where can I go for it?
19 How do you like this cake?
20 Why does he sing so loudly? (We wondered . . .)

51.8
Elementary

See Exercise 51.7.

If the question has no question-word, but is one of the type that can take *yes* or *no* for an answer, *whether* or *if* is used as a link between the introducing verb and the reported question.

> 'Have you seen him anywhere?'
> He asked me if (whether) I had seen him anywhere.

Whether is a more accurate word to use, since it implies *if* or *if not*, but *if*, being shorter, is more commonly used.

*   *   *

● Put the following sentences into REPORTED SPEECH with the introducing verb in the PAST tense. Vary the introducing verb.

1   Are you enjoying yourself?
2   Did you see the King yesterday?
3   Does she always wear a hat?
4   Have you seen my new hat?
5   Do I look all right?
6   Are the grapes sour?
7   Is it time to go?
8   Will the taxi be here at eight o'clock?
9   Can you hear a noise?
10 Ought the light to be on?
11 Are my shoes cleaned yet?
12 Did the greengrocer have any fresh vegetables?
13 Does your car always make a nasty smell?
14 May I use your telephone?
15 Is it raining very heavily?
16 Do you sleep in the afternoons?
17 Must the door be kept shut?
18 Was the train very full?
19 Have the children put away their toys?
20 Did Bill give you that ring?

**51.9
Elementary
and
Intermediate
SHALL
QUESTIONS**

Shall in REPORTED QUESTIONS requires a special preliminary
exercise if its behaviour has not already been learnt.
Questions beginning *Shall I . . . ?* are of two types.

TYPE 1   PURE FUTURE

    Shall I ever forget her?

TYPE 2   REQUEST (= Do you want me to?)

    Shall I open the window?

In TYPE 1 the *Shall I?* becomes: . . . *if he would* . . .
In TYPE 2 the *Shall I?* becomes: . . . *if he should* . . .

    TYPE 1   'Shall I ever forget her?'
             He wondered if he *would* ever forget her.
    TYPE 2   'Shall I open the window?'
             He asked if he *should* open the window.

*   *   *

● Turn the following into REPORTED SPEECH:

1 Shall I do it before tomorrow?   (He asked)
2 Shall I call for you?   (He asked)
3 Shall I like the concert?   (He wondered)
4 Shall I leave it in the car?   (He asked me)
5 Shall I live to be a hundred?   (He wondered)
6 Shall I lay the table now?   (She wanted to know)
7 Shall we buy your father a present?   (They
   wondered)
8 Shall we know the answer tomorrow?
9 Shall I enjoy the party?   (She wondered)
10 Shall I give you the money now?   (She asked us)
11 Shall I type it again?   (She asked)
12 Shall I remember your name next time?   (He
   wondered)
13 Shall I change the wheel for you?   (He asked her)
14 Shall we succeed in our examinations?   (They
   wondered)
15 Shall I be in your way?
16 Shall I help you pack?
17 Shall I ask the little boy how to get there?
18 Shall we have time to finish?   (They wondered)
19 Shall I marry him?   (She asked her mother)
20 Shall I ever get married?   (She wondered)
21 Shall I be able to hear what he is saying?
22 Shall I hurry on and get the tickets?

23   Shall we wait till the others come?   (They wanted to know)
24   Shall we require new books next time?   (They wondered)
25   Shall I send it to you by post?

**51.10
Intermediate**   See Exercises 51.7–9.

* * *

● Put the following sentences into REPORTED SPEECH with the introducing verb in the PAST tense.   Vary the introducing verb.

1   Where do you live?
2   Have you been to town today?
3   How is your mother-in-law now?
4   Where shall I be tomorrow?
5   Can you tell me where I can find the British Museum?
6   Where are you going?
7   Where did I leave my shirt and trousers?
8   How much did you pay for these overripe tomatoes?
9   Do you speak Russian?   Do you think you can learn it in a year?
10   Can you lend me five pounds?   Do you think you can trust me?
11   Does Cyril wipe his feet on the mat when he comes in?
12   Do you know the way to the station?
13   How old is he now?   Can he read yet?
14   Have you brought your books with you or not?
15   Why didn't you get up earlier?
16   Now do you believe me, or do you still think I'm lying?
17   What do you mean?   Do you think I'm mad?
18   Are you American or do you come from Africa?
19   Must we be here by six or can we come a little later?
20   Did you understand my instructions?
21   Were you very busy yesterday or the day before? Why didn't you come here?

22 When will you come again? Shall I be seeing you next week?

23 Where has Mary put my slippers? Why can't she leave them where I put them when I took them off?

24 How far is it to the National Theatre? Can I walk it in ten minutes or must I take a bus?

25 What's the English for Donaudampfschiffahrts-gesellschaftsbeamter?

26 How many cakes can you get into your mouth at once? Do you think it is greedy to eat more than two at a time?

27 Has Henry got a lawn-mower? Do you think he will lend it to me?

28 How many times have I told you not to do that?

29 Who called while I was out? Did she leave a message?

30 Did Maisie question you about my whereabouts last Friday? What did you tell her? Is she asking you any more questions tomorrow?

51.11
Advanced
REPORTING
A REPORTED
QUESTION

The only point to remember is the change of tense in both parts.

> 'Do you know who is coming?'
> He asked if I *knew* who *was* coming.
> 'Do you know who killed him?'
> He asked if I *knew* who *had killed* him.
> 'Did you wonder why I didn't come?'
> He asked if *I'd wondered* why he *hadn't* come.

But we rarely find a succession of PAST PERFECTS, any other CONTEMPORARY actions being left in the PAST SIMPLE.

> 'Did you wonder why I didn't come when I was wanted?'
> He asked if I'd wondered why he *hadn't* come when he *was* wanted. (*didn't come* is also heard)

* * *

● Put the following sentences into REPORTED SPEECH with the introducing verb in the PAST tense. Vary the introducing verb.

1 Can you tell me why you are so sad?

2 Must you always ask me what I'm doing?

3 Do you know how far it is to the station?

4　Have you any idea when he did it?
5　Will you please find out when he last wrote to me?
6　Did you know what you were doing at the time?
7　Can you see the marks he made on the carpet?
8　Will you please tell me when you expect to come?
9　Have you any idea when you'll be this way again?
10　Won't you find out why he doesn't like us?　(This is really an imperative.　Treat as such.)
11　Where were you when the rain started?
12　Have you sewn on my buttons as I asked?
13　Did you notice whether she was wearing make-up or not?
14　Do you mind if I close the window?
15　Was the Mayor present when the new school was opened?
16　What do you think you are doing?
17　Who do you suppose would believe that story?
18　Do you know if any decision was arrived at?
19　Do you know why he was so cross?
20　Is it true that they were seen alone together?
21　Can you tell me what the time is?
22　Is this the spot where the murder was committed?
23　Can you remember when you last heard that tune?
24　How can one tell if she is speaking the truth?
25　Do you know which is the cup you used?

51.12
Advanced
LATE
RESPONSE

This is a curious but not uncommon trick of conversation combining the principles of direct and reported speech in one. Sometimes a remark is passed, the exact meaning of which is not fully grasped at the moment; after a short lapse of time the listener reverts to the speaker's original subject, asking about the doubtful point, but usually framing his DIRECT question in the tense of a REPORTED QUESTION with a past tense introducing verb. Examples will make this clearer – the words in italics are those the listener is questioning.

Mr A.　I'm supposed to go again *on Friday*.
[Pause, or more miscellaneous conversation.]
Mr B.　When *were you* supposed to go again?
(= When did you say *you were* supposed to go again.)

Mr A.　His name is *Tanner-Whyte*.
[Pause; or conversation.]

> Mr B. What *was* that man's name?
> (= What did you say his name *was*?)

Imperatives take *was* (*were*) *to*, or more rarely *had to*.

> Mr A. Put it *among the papers* in the third drawer down.
>   [Pause for forgetting.]
> Mr B. Where *was I to* put it?
> (= Where did you say I *was to* put it?)

And in the past:

> Mr A. They made *at least seventeen* copies and sold them all.
>   [Pause; or more conversation to confuse the mind of Mr B.]
> Mr B. How many copies *had they made*?
> (= How many did you say they *had made*?)

N.B. – Note the rising intonation from the low-pitched question-word.

* * *

● The teacher reads the statements below. A pause, or further conversation is to be imagined, then the student makes a response, asking about the point in **bold type**, in the manner suggested above:

1 He was **at the pictures** all the time.
2 My husband is very fond of **a piece of pie** for his supper.
3 Take the **pink** cushion with you when you go!
4 He ate **a double helping of meat and potatoes** just before he collapsed.
5 I'm taking the dog **as far as the common** for a run.
6 I packed **three** suitcases before I found I wasn't to go after all.
7 It's **gone half past three**!
8 We're coming again **Monday week**.
9 The cunning old man hid it **under a rose-bush** in his own garden.
10 When you get there, go into **the third** door on your right as you face the building.
11 ... and I shot **five** tigers while I was in India.
12 I'm going to do it all again **on the 15th of July**.
13 My friend cannot come **because she has a touch of flu**.

14 She put it **in the left-hand cupboard**.
15 I'm supposed to have finished it **by five o'clock**.
16 Bring me **that** book **over there**.
17 My husband has gone away for **a week**.
18 Let's go and sit **in the rose-garden**.
19 She cleans her floors with **a special kind of polish**.
20 I am meeting **an old school-friend of mine**
    tomorrow night.

REPORTED SPEECH (MIXED TYPES)

51.13
Intermediate

When statements and questions are mixed, each section must be introduced by an appropriate verb: *tell, say, explain, remark*, etc., for STATEMENTS ONLY; *ask, enquire, want to know, wonder*, etc., for QUESTIONS ONLY. A useful connective device for question plus statement is: *adding that* . . .

> 'I'm off to the pictures. Where are you going?'
> He *said* he was off to the pictures and *wanted to know* where I was going.

*   *   *

● Put the following into REPORTED SPEECH, with the introducing verbs in the PAST tense:

1 It is cold in here.   Is the window open?
2 Do you think it will rain?   It is very cloudy.
3 I must write some letters now.   What date is it?
4 How do you like Maisie's new dress?   I bought it for her at a sale.
5 We are going for a country walk.   Would you like to come too?
6 What time is it?   My watch has stopped.
7 This is a most interesting book.   Have you ever read it?
8 What is the matter?   You don't look very well.
9 That looks difficult to do.   Can I help you?
10 Are you free tomorrow night?   I would like you to come to my party.
11 The dog has stolen the meat.   What are we to do?
12 How far is it to Birmingham?   I hope[1] we can get there before dark.

[1] Use as introducing verb.

13 Who do you think is England's greatest dramatist?
I like Shaw best.

14 How long have you been learning English? Your
accent is very good.

15 It is time to go. Have you got all your things?

16 Is that the postman? I hope he has a letter for me.

17 Would you like to see the garden? It is very
pleasant out there.

18 Where are the Barkers spending their holidays?
They usually go to Bournemouth.

19 You are late home. What have you been doing?

20 Would you like a cup of tea? It's just been made.

21 I am learning English. Can you speak English?

22 I have a headache. Can I have an aspirin?

23 Will you explain what Cyril means? I don't know
what he is talking about.

24 The matter will soon be dealt with. Have you
anything more to ask?

25 Have you a light? I've forgotten to bring my
matches.

26 Do you understand it now? I'll explain it again
if you don't.

27 Why can't you answer at once? You're not always
so slow.

28 I've read this book before. Have you something
else I can read?

29 May I take an apple? They look so nice.

30 Can you tell me the time? I shall have to leave at
five.

51.14
Advanced

See Exercise 51.13.
To report *Yes* or *No* a short-form clause is necessary,
echoing the question-verb.

'Will you come out tonight?' 'No.'
He asked if I would go out with him, but I said I
wouldn't.
'Do you like this?' 'Yes.'
He asked me if I liked it, and I said I did.

* * *

(51.14)   ●   Put the following into REPORTED SPEECH with the introducing verbs in the PAST tense:

1   Have you had anything to eat?   We've just
finished our dinner.

2   I hear that Ann was at the dance last night.   What
was she wearing?

3   The clock has stopped.   Did you forget to wind
it up?

4   'Did you ring me up last night?'   'Yes.'

5   George is taking his exam in June.   Do you think
he will pass?

6   Whatever have you got on?   You look like a
scarecrow.

7   What is the doctor's telephone number?   Mary has
fallen downstairs and broken her leg.

8   The milk is burnt again.   Will you have lemon in
your tea instead?

9   'Did anybody call during my absence?'   'No.'

10   Bob wants to be an insurance agent.   Do you
think it's a good idea?

11   Did you see the fire last night?   Two shops were
burnt to the ground.

12   Your hair is very long.   Are you going to be a
musician?

13   I want a new handbag.   Where is the best place to
get one?

14   May I open the window?   It's rather hot in here.

15   'Can you meet me tomorrow?'   'No.'

16   What have you done with my comb?   I haven't
seen it for days.

17   Are you listening?   I've asked you a question three
times already.

18   The Jacksons live in the most out-of-the-way
place.   Have you ever tried to find it?

19   Why did you lock the door?   Nobody will disturb
us.

20   'Will you have some more strawberries?'   'No,
thank you.'

21   We are very hungry.   What can you give us to eat?

22   'Are you going away for the weekend?'   'Yes.'

23   It's nearly time for tea.   Will you put the kettle on?

24   'Will you come to tea with me next Monday?'   'I

don't know if I shall be free, but I should love to
come if I am.'

25 'Will you take some castor oil?' 'No. I don't like
it. Do you think a medicine I don't like will do me
good?'   'No, I suppose not.'

REPORTED SPEECH (EXCLAMATIONS)

51.15
Intermediate

Reporting an exclamation is usually best achieved by a
circumlocution reflecting the spirit of the original exclamation.

Exclamations are not often reported in spoken English, so
too much time should not be wasted in hunting for the
best expression. The other forms of REPORTED SPEECH are
far more important.

Some exclamatory forms are really questions (rhetorical)
or imperatives.

> 'What a lovely garden (this is)!'
> He remarked what a lovely garden it was.
> 'Hello! where are you going?'
> He greeted me and asked (me) where I was going.
> 'Oh dear! I've torn my frock.'
> She exclaimed bitterly that she had torn her dress.
> or: She sighed and said that she had torn her dress.

*　　*　　*

● Put the following into REPORTED SPEECH with the introducing verb in the PAST tense:

1 What a lovely house!
2 Hello! What do you want?
3 My goodness! You *are* slim!
4 Haven't you ever been here before? (He was
surprised . . .)
5 What a dirty face you have!
6 Oh! I've cut myself!
7 Help me!
8 The house is on fire!
9 What have you done to your hair?
10 Good gracious! It's impossible!
11 What on earth has happened?
12 What ever is the matter?
13 What a terrible noise!
14 Do be quiet!

15   Don't stand there doing nothing!

16   What a fool I've been! Why didn't I think of it
before?

17   What a noise you're making! Do you call that
playing the piano?

18   What a pity we didn't eat up all the figs yesterday!
Now they're all bad.

19   I say, what a charming daughter you have, Mrs
Sidebotham!

20   What a big helping of pudding you've given me!
I shan't be able to eat it all, I'm sure.

51.16   See Exercise 51.15.
Advanced
                                        *   *   *

● Put the following into REPORTED SPEECH with the introducing verb in the PAST tense:

1   Hello! Where are you off to?

2   Oh dear! I've spilt my coffee.

3   Would you believe it! Jane's broken another dish.

4   Help me! Help! Quick!

5   Look out! There's a motor-bike coming.

6   Oh! I've burnt myself!

7   Bother! The light has gone out.

8   Ow! Can't you look where you're going?
You've trodden on my sore toe.

9   Darling! I love you! Will you always love me?

10   Ugh! How I hate touching sticky things!

11   Tut, tut! You *are* a naughty girl!

12   Oh how wonderful! I'd simply love to come!

13   For goodness' sake stop that awful row!

14   What ever shall I do now my wife's fallen ill, what
with looking after the baby and guests in the house
too!

15   Oh John, that's the best news I've heard for a long
time.

16   What a lovely garden you have! How well it is
looked after!

17   Hooray! We're going to have a holiday tomorrow!
Where shall we go?

18   By Jove! That was a good race! How splendidly
they rowed!

19 Good Heavens! Look at the time! I've forgotten all about my cake in the oven. I hope it's not burnt to a cinder.

20 To the bride and bridegroom! May you both be very happy together, and may all your troubles be 'little ones'!

REPORTED SPEECH (REVISION)

51.17
Intermediate
See previous exercises. It is convenient to refer to the 'changes' that occur when speech is reported, and the exercises in this book are in the form of 'translation' of direct to reported speech, but it is important to remember that the forms of reported speech are used in many circumstances besides the reporting of words spoken.

* * *

● Put the following into REPORTED SPEECH with the introducing verb in the PAST tense:

1 I shouldn't do that if I were you. Isn't it very dangerous?

2 When we've finished this game we'll have supper. Will you have time to play again afterwards?

3 Don't you know how to behave? There must be no talking in lessons.

4 Do as you are told! You are a naughty girl.

5 What will you make your new curtains of? Flowered cotton would look very pretty.

6 Please take me home. I don't feel very well.

7 Are you cold? I can soon light a fire.

8 I wonder where I left my scissors. Can you see them anywhere? (He wondered where . . .)

9 Don't do that! Are you mad?

10 What time does the concert start? I'm sure it's time to go.

11 Is that the front-door bell? I'll answer it.

12 This is my engagement ring. Do you like it?

13 Come here! I want to speak to you.

14 It's a lovely day today. I think I'll go for a walk.

15 How can I help laughing? Maisie's hat is so funny.

16   What a dark night it is!   I'm thankful I haven't got
      to go out.
17   Didn't you bring a coat with you? I'm afraid
      you'll be cold.
18   How many kilos of sugar are necessary to make
      ten kilos of jam?   It isn't in the cookery book.
19   We shall be late!   Do hurry up!
20   Do you know it's gone half past eight?   It's time
      for you to go to bed.
21   'Did you visit the Tower when you were in London
      last year?'   'No, I wanted to, but I had no time.'
22   When I go to Paris tomorrow, I shall have been
      there ten times.
23   What a marvellous supper!   I shall get terribly fat.
      Do you always have such magnificent meals?
24   Where did you go the day before yesterday?
      Didn't I see you on the river?   I think you had a
      very charming girl with you.   You won't
      introduce me to her, I suppose?
25   Hello!   What are you doing in this part of the
      world?   What a pity you didn't come yesterday,
      we had a lovely day on the river.   But never mind,
      you must come with us to the hills tomorrow if
      you have time.

51.18
Advanced   ● Put the following into REPORTED SPEECH with the intro-
         ducing verb in the PAST tense:
1   I'm sure we are lost.   Run and ask that policeman
     the way.
2   Did you remember to take your medicine before
     dinner?   If not, you'd better take it now.
3   Do you want to speak to Norah?   I'm afraid she's
     out at the moment.
4   Will you come here, Miss Jones?   I want you to
     take down a letter for me.
5   What a forgetful creature I am!   I've forgotten to
     post your letter.
6   Have you got any shampoo?   I must wash my
     hair.
7   I've just had these shoes made for me.   Do you
     think they're smart?
8   I wonder who is coming on the excursion

tomorrow. I do hope it won't rain. (He
wondered who . . .)

9 Do as I tell you or you will be punished. I'll
teach you who is master in this house!

10 When you have cleaned the sitting-room, will you
please light a fire there? It's rather chilly today.
(It is better to do the request before the
subordinate clause.)

11 I'm glad I've found you out, you dirty little thief!

12 Listen! Can you hear someone coming?

13 Please excuse me. I'm too tired to go out tonight.

14 Have you ever been to the Lake District? It is most
delightful walking country.

15 The lawn-mower is broken again. Go and ask if
you can borrow Mr Jennings's.

16 Are there any ripe blackberries on that bush?
If so, we can take some home for a pie.

17 That picture is crooked. Would you mind putting
it straight?

18 I'm going to the library this morning. Shall I
change your book for you?

19 Stop! Wait for me! I won't be a moment!

20 I'm so sorry! Did I hurt you?

21 I must go home in an hour's time. I must always
be in before eight o'clock.

22 Make me another suit like this. Don't forget to
put in a good lining. I hope to call for it in a
week.

23 If you can supply me with these goods, please let
me know.

24 I've always thought your sister was married. I
must have confused her with someone else. I must
go now, but you must introduce me to her one day.

25 How many pieces of watermelon can you eat?
What! Only five? What a tiny appetite you have!

52 Passive Voice

52.1 Elementary

Simple construction: appropriate tense of verb *be* with the PAST PARTICIPLE.

The PASSIVE VOICE is very important in English. Probably quite 90 per cent of the passive sentences spoken or written are of the type replacing the indefinite pronoun or reflexives in other languages. (Cf. French *on*, German *man*, and the use of reflexive verbs in Slavonic languages.)

In this important class of passive voice sentences we have an unknown or vague active voice subject; it remains unexpressed in the passive voice. The agent with *by* is not needed.

> ACTIVE: Someone has stolen my books.

The indefinite subject *someone* occupies the most prominent place. We prefer:

> PASSIVE: My books have been stolen.

* * *

● Complete the following passive voice sentences in the tenses suggested.

1 This picture (**always admire**). – Present
2 His leg (**hurt**) in an accident. – Past
3 This exercise (**do**) very carefully. – Present Continuous
4 The box (**not open**) for the last hundred years. – Present Perfect
5 The Tower of London (**formerly use**) as a prison. – Past
6 Two of my dinner plates (**break**). – Present Perfect
7 A big battle (**fight**) here 200 years ago. – Past
8 You (**invite**) to lunch tomorrow. – Present Perfect
9 This play (**forget**) in a few years' time. – Future
10 The bridge (**build**) last year. – Past
11 My brother (**never beat**) at tennis. – Present Perfect
12 English (**speak**) all over the world. – Present
13 Any questions (**ask**) about me? – Past

14 The answers must (**write**) on one side of the paper only. – Infinitive
15 These books must (**not take away**). – Infinitive
16 I (**punish**) for something I didn't do. – Past
17 Milk (**use**) for making butter and cheese. – Present
18 You (**want**) to help lay the table. – Present
19 A pupil (**praise**) when he works hard. – Present
20 The stolen car (**find**) in another town. – Present Perfect
21 Hats and coats must (**leave**) in the cloakroom. – Infinitive
22 The piano (**play**) far too loudly. – Past Continuous
23 The matter (**discuss**) tomorrow. – Future
24 Progress (**make**) every day in the world of science. – Present
25 The chickens (**not feed**) this morning. – Past
26 Some ink (**spill**) on the carpet. – Present Perfect
27 She said that some ink (**spill**) on her carpet. – Past Perfect
28 Not a sound (**hear**). – Past
29 This door can (**easily mend**).[1] – Infinitive
30 What (**do**) about this? – Present Perfect
31 The door (**already shut**). – Present Perfect
32 Your question (**answer**)? – Present Perfect
33 The book (**finish**) next month? – Future
34 He saw that the table (**push**) into the corner. – Past Perfect
35 The article (**beautifully write**).[1] – Present Perfect

52.2
Elementary
and
Intermediate

When the verb in the active voice takes two objects, it is more usual in English to make the PERSONAL object the subject of the passive voice.

$$\overset{1}{\underline{\hspace{1em}}}\quad\overset{2}{\underline{\hspace{2em}}}$$

ACTIVE: Someone gave me a book.
PASSIVE: I was given a book.

---

[1] In the passive voice it is more usual to put an adverb of manner immediately in front of the past participle it qualifies: viz.—
This chair is very well made.

The form *A book was given* (*to*) *me* would be used when we need to stress this new subject.

*   *   *

(52.2)   ● Put the following sentences into the PASSIVE VOICE with a PERSONAL SUBJECT:

1 They gave **my little sister** a ticket, too.
2 People will show **the visitors** the new buildings.
3 Someone has already paid **the electrician** for his work.
4 They promise **us** higher wages.
5 Somebody will tell **you** what time the train leaves.
6 Someone ordered **the prisoners** to stand up.
7 Somebody recommended **me** to another doctor.
8 Someone taught **him** French and gave **him** a dictionary.
9 They will allow **each boy** a second plate of ice-cream.
10 The authorities refused **Cyril** a passport.
11 They will ask **us all** several questions.
12 When we first met, they had already offered **me** a job at the bank.
13 Someone will read **you** another chapter next time.
14 They requested **the stranger** to leave the meeting.
15 This is the third time they have written to **us** about this.
16 They still deny **women** the right to vote in some countries.
17 They have made **my uncle** a captain.
18 They asked **the rest of us** to be there at eight o'clock.
19 The others told **the new students** where to sit.
20 Someone is showing **Maisie** how to bath a baby.

52.3
Elementary

See Exercises 52.1 and 52.2.
The general principle governing the use of the passive voice is as follows: when the main interest of the speaker or writer is on the verb activity itself rather than on the active subject, there is a desire to express this idea first. In the sentence *People speak English all over the world* too much weight is given to the vague subject *people*, when our real concern is the SPEAKING OF ENGLISH. The passive voice form

English is spoken all over the world

puts the idea in a much better perspective. The agent *by people* is superfluous – we have just used a passive construction to get rid of it anyway!

WARNING. In all PASSIVE VOICE exercises the use of *by* with an agent must be rigorously suppressed, except in those examples where, although our interest in the predicate has led us to use the passive voice, the active subject has some interest of its own and is necessary for complete sense, e.g.

This poem was written by Keats

shows greater interest in the poem (the speaker is presumably discussing it, or reading it), but mention of the poet is necessary to complete the sense. Such active subjects as *I, we, you, they, one, someone, nobody, people, a man, a boy, the servant*, etc., are very seldom worth mention in the passive construction.

PREPOSITIONS. Prepositions or adverb particles must not be left out with verbs requiring them; there is a tendency to forget them.

ACTIVE: They will look *after* you well.

PASSIVE: You will be well looked *after*. (Note position of adverb of manner.)

* * *

● Put the following sentences into the PASSIVE VOICE, using the part in **bold type** as the subject where shown:

1 She showed **the visitors** the new baby.
2 Someone asked **the student** a very difficult question.
3 We must look into this matter.
4 People speak well of my friend Cyril.
5 They told her to be quick.
6 Someone reads to the old lady every evening.
7 Somebody told the students to wait outside.
8 Someone promised me a bicycle if I passed my examination.
9 You must work for success.
10 Somebody gave her a box of chocolates for her birthday.
11 I told Cyril never to come here again.
12 They gave **me** 10p (ten pence) change at the shop.
13 She promised him a book.

14   It is time they brought the cows in.
15   They told me to go away.
16   Nobody has slept in that room for years.
17   She will look after the little girl well.
18   A car ran over our dog. (AGENT)
19   The teacher promised Mary a prize if she worked well.
20   A friend told me the news this morning. (AGENT)
21   Unkind remarks easily upset Maisie. (AGENT)
22   Somebody must finish the work.
23   Nobody can repair this broken vase.
24   What ought we to do about this?
25   What questions did the examiner set? (AGENT)
26   People play football all over the world.
27   Nobody has made any mistakes.
28   Beethoven composed this piece. (AGENT)
29   A guide pointed out **the Pyramids** to me. (AGENT)
30   Somebody has left the gate open, and so the horses have run away.
31   Somebody must do something for these poor men.
32   She fell into the water because somebody pushed her.
33   People will simply laugh at you for your trouble.
34   They carried her into the house.
35   They showed me a beautiful drawing.
36   Nobody has answered my question properly.
37   They left the wounded behind.
38   Somebody has brought this child up very badly.
39   They didn't tell me the truth about the situation.
40   They asked Maisie why she went about with a silly person like me!

52.4
Intermediate and Advanced

● Put the following sentences into the PASSIVE VOICE using the part in **bold type** as the subject where shown:

1   Somebody has found the boy the people wanted. (2 PASSIVES)
2   People ought not to speak about such things in public.
3   The wind blew his hat down the street.
4   They will take her to hospital tomorrow.
5   The police gave **me** £5 reward. (AGENT)
6   An unseen hand opened the window. (AGENT)

7   They will send Cyril to prison.

8   People should make lessons more interesting for children.

9   They had eaten all the dinner before they finished the conversation. (2 PASSIVES)

10 Somebody left the light on all night.

11 We shall lock the house up for the summer and the old gardener will look after it. (2 PASSIVES)

12 No one can answer your question.

13 Somebody has spilt tea all over the tablecloth.

14 His brother just beat John in the 100-yards race.

15 Has someone mended that chair yet?

16 Nobody has ever spoken to me like that before.

17 A friend lent me this book. (AGENT)

18 We have asked some friends of hers to join us.

19 People talked about Maisie all over the town.

20 They will give you the answer next week.

21 Didn't they tell you to be here by six o'clock?

22 I'd like someone to read to me. (PASSIVE INFINITIVE)

23 You must not throw away empty bottles.

24 No one has drunk out of this glass.

25 The stone struck him in the right shoulder. (AGENT)

26 The fire destroyed many valuable paintings. (AGENT)

27 Someone blew a whistle three times.

28 A huge wave overturned the little boat. (AGENT)

29 He finished his work by eight o'clock.

30 Ladies used to wear their dresses very long.

31 The maid washed the floor only this morning.

32 Lions attacked the travellers. (AGENT)

33 Someone has stolen my collection of stamps.

34 I have sharpened the knives.

35 The same man mended your shoes. (AGENT)

36 They built two new houses last year.

37 They sent letters of thanks to all their friends.

38 We ate up all the biscuits yesterday.

39 People will laugh at you if you wear that silly hat.

40 People were carrying the chairs out into the garden.

41 His friends gave him a cake for his birthday.

42   They took photographs after the ceremony.
43   I hate people looking at me.
44   Do you intend us to take your remark seriously?
45   The police ought to put you in prison.
46   They turned my offer down.
47   This is a good idea, but one cannot carry it out in practice.
48   People shan't speak to me as if I were a child.
49   Somebody has eaten all the food in the house and drunk all the wine.
50   Somebody has locked the box and I cannot open it. (2 PASSIVES)

**52.5
Advanced**

See Exercises 52.1 and 52.2.
People say = It is said
The passive form here only brings in another vague subject, the introductory *it*. So we generally prefer the subject of the clause introduced by *it* as the subject of the passive voice.

> ACTIVE: People say that figs are better for us than bananas.
> PASSIVE (1): It is said that figs are better for us than bananas.
> PASSIVE (2): Figs are said to be better for us than bananas.
> (PASSIVE (2) is the best.)

Another good use of the passive, more usually found in the written language than in speech, is as a device to save changing the subject of a clause sequence.

> ACTIVE: He spoke at great length; people asked him many questions at the end, which he answered satisfactorily.

This is more concisely expressed with the help of the passive voice:

> He spoke at great length, was asked many questions at the end, and answered them all satisfactorily.

*   *   *

● Put the following sentences into the PASSIVE VOICE:
1   Somebody must have taken it while I was out.
2   You must iron this dress for tonight.
3   Did the noise frighten you?

4   They treated us to some ice-cream.
5   Don't let the others see you. (PASSIVE REFLEXIVE)
6   The orchestra played that piece beautifully.
7   He's so good at golf nobody can beat him.
8   The doctor had to operate on him to find out what was wrong.
9   Didn't anybody ever teach you how to behave?
10   They did nothing until he came.
11   I can assure you I will arrange everything in time. (2 PASSIVES)
12   Somebody will meet the visitors at the station.
13   A sudden increase in water pressure would break the dam.
14   Men can shell cities from a distance of several miles.
15   One cannot eat an orange if nobody has peeled it. (2 PASSIVES)
16   They took the collection half-way through the meeting.
17   The police are sure to ask you that question.
18   Her beauty struck me deeply. (AGENT)
19   You needn't think your joke took me in. (AGENT)
20   They should not make the celebration an excuse for bad behaviour.
21   People generally assume that money brings happiness.   (Money . . .)
22   Let me know if there is anything we should do.
23   They gave the thief a fair trial and sent him to prison. (2 PASSIVES)
24   Poverty drove him to desperation.
25   You must account for every penny.
26   A new company has taken the business over.
27   They tell me somebody has shot your uncle. (2 PASSIVES)
28   Somebody can't have shut the safe properly.
29   They can't put you in prison if they haven't tried you. (2 PASSIVES)
30   We'll have to examine you again.
31   People say tortoises live longer than elephants. (Tortoises . . .)
32   I should love someone to take me out to dinner. (PASSIVE INFINITIVE)

33 His grandmother brought him up, and he *got
his education* in Paris. (2 PASSIVES)

34 Naturally one expects you to interest yourself in
the job they have offered you. (3 PASSIVES)

35 It must have disappointed him terribly that people
told him they didn't want him. (3 PASSIVES)

36 They must have given you the paper (that) they
meant for the advanced candidates. (2 PASSIVES)

37 Someone had already promised me a watch for
my birthday when they presented me with one as
a prize. (2 PASSIVES)

38 It surprised me to hear someone had robbed you.
(2 PASSIVES)

39 When women have disappointed you as many
times as they have him, you can truly say (that)
bad luck has dogged you. (3 PASSIVES)

40 We haven't moved anything since they sent you
away to cure you. (3 PASSIVES)

41 You must clear up all these books and papers and
put them away in the cupboards you usually
keep them in. (3 PASSIVES)

42 Nobody would have stared at him if they had told
him beforehand what clothes one had to wear in
such a place. (3 PASSIVES)

43 Ladies usually go to a tea-party more to speak to
other people than *for other people to speak to them.*

44 At the cocktail party people took no notice of **the
famous professor**, but they made a fuss of **his
lovely young wife** from the moment someone
introduced her to the guests. (3 PASSIVES)

45 People ought to tell us how much they expect of
us. (2 PASSIVES)

46 People no longer say that anyone inhabits Mars
any more than the moon. (3 PASSIVES)

47 No one has ever taken me for an Englishman
before, although someone *did* once speak to me as
if I were an American. (2 PASSIVES)

48 I've only used this pen once since the day I had it
mended. (2 PASSIVES)

49 There's a new block of flats they are building
down the road; perhaps you'd like someone to
introduce you to the landlord. (2 PASSIVES)

50 When I was a child, people used to read to me out of a book of fairy tales someone had given me for my birthday. (2 PASSIVES)

FINAL REMARKS ON THE PASSIVE VOICE

A great deal of harm has been done by teaching the PASSIVE VOICE as if it were merely another way of expressing a sentence in the ACTIVE VOICE. Students are asked to put such sentences as:

John likes girls.
Henry can read English and French, etc.

into the fantastic forms of

'Girls are liked by John.'
'English and French can be read by Henry' etc.!

We ought to stress the fact that the passive voice has an important and special place in the language; most sentences that are good in the active voice are just grotesque curiosities when put into the passive voice. The proper uses of the passive voice have been carefully pointed out in the last four exercises. Most of the sentences fall more naturally into a passive form than the form given.

The agent with *by* is unnatural in English; MOST sentences needing it belong rightfully to the active voice, and should never be put into the passive voice, even as an academic exercise.

53 Miscellaneous Exercises

In this section appear several exercises that are not easily brought into the general grammatical outline of the book. Some are on points of stress, intonation, etc., others on points of grammatical usage not dealt with under the main headings of this book; others on points of more importance in writing than in speech.

MUCH (MANY) – A LOT OF; FAR – A LONG WAY

**53.1
Elementary**

There is a very strong tendency in English, where alternatives are available, to use the shorter forms in negatives and questions. Thus 'He has much time', although apparently correct grammatically is NEVER seen or heard in modern English; *plenty of*, *a lot of*, *a great deal of*, replace *much* and *many* in simple affirmative statements. *Much* is particularly objectionable in affirmative statements; *many* is uncommon.

Similarly *far* (= extent of distance) has *a long way*; *far off* (= position at a distance) has *a long way off*; and *far away*, *far back* have *a long way away*, *a long way back* in simple affirmative statements.

* * *

(53.1)   ● Bearing this in mind, read the following statements in the AFFIRMATIVE:

1   He hasn't got much money.
2   It wasn't far off.
3   You haven't done much.
4   They haven't many friends.
5   She hasn't given me much.
6   We haven't gone far.
7   There's not much coffee in this pot.
8   He hasn't got much work to do.
9   I have not invited many people to my party.
10 You haven't had much to eat.
11 They don't live far off.
12 The cook hasn't put much salt in it.
13 It is not far to the police station.
14 We haven't walked far today.
15 My brother does not read many books.
16 She has not many children.
17 You did not make much tea.
18 The bird did not fly very far.
19 There was not much dirt in the hall.
20 I have not heard much about it.

53.2   See Exercise 53.1.
Intermediate   *Long* and *a long time* are a similar pair.

* * *

● Read the following sentences in the AFFIRMATIVE:

1   It wasn't far back, was it?
2   You haven't got much to do, have you?
3   I haven't seen many people here.
4   The sea is certainly not far off.

  5 The children don't make much noise.
  6 Cyril hasn't had much to drink.
  7 You haven't been gone long.
  8 I have not bought many apples.
  9 London is not very far from Liverpool.
 10 Maisie didn't leave me much money.
 11 He hadn't been away long before they arrived.
 12 You were not far away when it happened.
 13 Manchester doesn't have much rain.
 14 I did not find many plums on the tree.
 15 We haven't got far to go.
 16 She hasn't seen much of him lately.
 17 The army didn't march far in one day.
 18 There are not many trees on the mountains.
 19 I haven't got much spare time.
 20 I do not have to go far to school.

ALSO, TOO, AS WELL

**53.3
Elementary
and
Intermediate
*TOO*** *Too* meaning *also* can be used only at the end of a phrase.
It is more frequently used in the spoken language than
also.

* * *

● Read the following sentences, replacing *also* by *too*:
  1 I've also got one like that.
  2 My friend also speaks German. (2 MEANINGS, 2
     INTONATIONS)
  3 You must also buy yourself a new hat.
  4 He also gave me one. (2 INTONATIONS, STRESSING *he*
     OR *me*)
  5 The dog also wants his dinner.
  6 Make me one also!
  7 Mary has also gone away.
  8 My youngest daughter also can swim.
  9 We've also been there.
 10 She has two dogs and also a cat.
 11 I was also in town on Monday.
 12 Can we also come?
 13 Have you also read *Oliver Twist*?
 14 You must also wash the saucepans.
 15 He is mad about golf and also tennis.

16   Did you also go and see your grandmother?
17   I've also had pains in my back.
18   The fruit crops are also good this year.
19   Can't I also go to the theatre?
20   You can't have your cake and also eat it.

53.4
Elementary
and
Intermediate
AS WELL

See Exercise 53.3.
Instead of *too*, the more colloquial *as well* is very commonly heard.

*   *   *

● Do Exercise 53.3 again, with *as well* instead of *too*.

JUST AS WELL, JUST AS SOON, RATHER

53.5
Intermediate
and
Advanced

Might (just) as well, would just as soon, would rather are three very important forms for expressing preference. They are extremely common in speech, but rarely employed successfully by a foreign student.
Consider the ideas:

'Come at six.'   'I want to come at five.'

The response can be given further nuances:

(1)   I *might just as well* come at five.
= It's immaterial to me (as far as I'm concerned); Why not at five? – a counter-proposal.

(2)   *I'd just as soon* come at five.
= I'd like five equally well, if it makes no difference to you. Unlike (1), this type demands the implication 'I'd just as soon do *this* as (do) *that*' (subject to your approval). A weak preference.

(3)   *I'd rather* come at five.
= This is what I'd prefer. Stronger preference than (2). All three are useful vehicles for sarcasm.

*   *   *

● Make three sentences with each of the ideas in brackets: (a) with *might (just) as well*;   (b) with *would just as soon* (short form);   (c) with *would rather* (short form).   It is preferable to go through the exercise with (a), then with (b), then with (c):

1   Let's go to the pictures. (stay at home)
2   Let's have a cup of tea. (have a glass of hot water)

  3   Lend him the money. (throw it away)
  4   You must get up at half past three. (not go to bed)
  5   The radio is making unintelligible noises. (not listen)
  6   Take a few of them, they're very cheap. (buy the lot)
  7   It's rather a long way to walk. (go home on foot)
  8   Shout for help! (save your (my, our) breath)
  9   I wonder if we could buy just one to make it a pair? (throw the other one away)
 10   Here's £50 to give away. (spend it on myself)
 11   I haven't heard a word you said! (talk to a brick wall)
 12   Shall I tell him for you? (tell him myself)
 13   Perhaps we ought to put it in the refrigerator. (eat it all up now)
 14   Sorry my car's out of order. (walk)
 15   I'm giving you £5 for your birthday. (have it now)
 16   I keep asking him for your money. (forget about it)
 17   I know it's raining, but let's go for a walk. (stay here)
 18   Shall we leave the dog behind? (take it with us)
 19   Ask her to do it for you. (do it . . .self)
 20   Come and meet my father. (talk to you for a bit first)

(*Just*) *as well* also has the meaning 'it is advisable (a good thing) that (if) . . .'

> It's very cold. It would be as well to take your coat.
> Look at the rain! It's just as well you came when you did.

CERTAINLY *AND* SURELY

53.6 Advanced

Certainly takes the same position as the frequency adverbs (Exercise 25.1); has the meaning 'I, etc., *know* for a fact,' 'it is definite'.

Surely can replace *certainly*, but is rarely found with this meaning. Coming at the beginning of a sentence, or less frequently at the end, or immediately after the subject if it is a pronoun, it has the meaning: 'I firmly believe, I very much hope, this to be true; it's not certain, but I feel confident it will probably happen.'

You're surely not going out in this rain!

Surely you're not going out in this rain. (= I should be very surprised if you did.)

I'm certainly not going out in this rain.

It's worth going to see, surely. (= I believe it is, don't you?)

It's certainly worth going to see. (= There is no doubt in my mind.)

He surely won't forget to bring it. (= I hope not.)

He'll certainly not forget to bring it. (= I know he won't.)

*   *   *

(53.6)   ● Reconstruct the following sentences, using *certainly* or *surely* according to the sense:

1   I know he'll be there.
2   I expect he'll be there, don't you?
3   I doubt very much if he believes you.
4   I know he doesn't believe you.
5   I can't believe it'll last much longer.
6   You haven't forgotten me, have you?
7   Of course I haven't.
8   I've a strong feeling that's Mr Pubsey over there.
9   I'm quite sure that you can't convince me.
10   I assure you I'm not going to try.
11   I've a strong suspicion I've met you before somewhere.
12   Of course I'm not going to tell you!
13   I doubt very much whether you want another one, do you?
14   It's quite definite I can't buy it at that price.
15   You're not going to buy it at that price, are you?
16   Of course I've never been drunk!
17   I don't believe he lives as far along as this.
18   Quite definitely my children are not going out as late as that.
19   I've a strong feeling that your room was arranged quite differently last time.
20   Do you mean to say he's going to marry the butcher's daughter!
21   I'm sure you are mistaken; at least I hope so.
22   There is no doubt that she led him on.

23   I know his parents will disapprove.
24   It is probable that they will be able to dissuade him, don't you think?
25   I'm sure they will try.

FAIRLY *AND* RATHER

The words *fairly* and *rather* are both used in English to express 'to a moderate degree', but foreign students frequently use the wrong one.

Fairly is used when the speaker or writer wishes to affirm some positive or pleasant idea; *rather* is used when the idea is negative or unpleasant. Or we might say that *fairly* is a step TOWARDS an ideal, but *rather* is a step AWAY from it; or that *fairly* is half-way to *enough*, whereas *rather* is half-way to *too*. (See Exercises 38.3 and 38.4.)

So we say a person is '*fairly* well' because *well* is an ideal we strive for; but a person is '*rather* ill' because illness is an undesirable state to achieve.

To say 'Mary is rather tall for her age' suggests she is on the way to being 'too tall'. She is taller than we should like, she is ungainly, or she is outgrowing her strength. To say 'Mary is fairly tall for her age' expresses a plain fact, something more pleasant than otherwise. The 'tallness' here is an ideal we approve of.

To sum up:

> *Fairly* is used with a positive or pleasant idea; i.e. we approve of the ideal we are approaching.
>
> *Rather* is used with a negative or unpleasant idea; i.e. we disapprove of the 'ideal' we are approaching.

*   *   *

● Put either *fairly* or *rather* in the blank spaces:

1   I hope this exercise will be — easy.
2   Well, I'm afraid it will be — difficult.
3   Let's go by bus; it's a — uninteresting walk.
4   I'm afraid the soup is — cold.
5   Your homework was — good this week.
6   The room looks — clean.
7   He has a — bad cold.
8   The food was — badly cooked.
9   Your hands look — dirty.
10 We had a — enjoyable holiday, thank you.

11   The bread is — stale.
12   Can you carry it? I'm afraid it's — heavy.
13   I live — near.
14   It is — difficult to learn new things when you are old.
15   I'm afraid he's — stupid, and won't understand what you mean.
16   I know him — well.
17   The room is — untidy.
18   I must buy a new hat; this one is — old-fashioned.
19   This pencil seems — sharp.
20   What's the matter? You look — tired this morning.

53.8
Intermediate
and
Advanced

See Exercise 53.7 for fundamental differences.
Fairly is never used with comparatives
    I did it rather better last time.

Fairly is never used with colours, unless the colour is modified by *light* or *dark*.

(a) This one's a fairly light green.
        (I think it's light enough for you.)
(b) This one's a rather light green.
        (It won't do for you; you want something darker.)

(Phoneticians please note the rising tail of (a) and sudden fall on *light* in (b); similarly in all these *fairly-rather* sentences.)

(c) Your nose is rather blue.
        (but you don't want it to be.)

Notice the alternative word-order with *rather*:
    I've got a rather bad cold.
    I've got rather a bad cold.

* * *

● Put either *fairly* or *rather* in the blank spaces:

1   The last exercise was — easier than I thought it would be, but this one is — more difficult.
2   The sentences all seem too easy for *you*. Ah! this one seems — difficult.
3   I can't hold it any longer. It's — hot.
4   Have another cup of tea. It's still — hot.

5   This room's — big.   Haven't you anywhere
    smaller?

6   This room's — big.   I think it'll do.

7   The straw is — dry.   Be careful you don't set light
    to it.

8   This wood is — dry.   I think it'll burn all right.

9   I'm afraid that box is — small.   You won't get
    more than half of them in.

10 That box looks — small.   I think it'll easily go in
    my pocket.

11 'This flat looks — tiny for six people.'   'Yes, I
    suppose you'll want a — large one.'   'At all
    events I'll need something — bigger than this.'

12 I don't think I can buy that. It's — expensive.

13 The buses are — full at five o'clock, so come later.
    You'll find them — empty at about six.

14 I'm sorry if the meat is — hard. I'm afraid it's been
    cooked — more than necessary.

15 Mend it with this piece; it seems — hard, and
    shouldn't break easily.

16 I shan't be able to read the whole play in one
    evening; it's — long.

17 You should have a — long dressing-gown to keep
    your ankles warm.

18 I'm afraid I've written it — quickly, but I think
    you'll find it — correct.

19 I can finish it — quickly if you keep quiet for a
    few minutes.

20 I've got a — good memory for names, but I'm —
    bad on dates.

53.9   See Exercises 53.7 and 53.8 for fundamental differences.
Advanced   *Rather*   as an understatement for *very*. Sentences like:

> I've got some rather good news for you.
> That's really rather clever of you.
> I must confess I thought she was rather charming.
> He showed me some rather fine landscapes by Con-
> stable.

obviously do not conform to the fundamental patterns of
Exercises 53.7 and 53.8. This use of *rather* is part of the
English love of understatement, a national characteristic
that has affected our language idiom in many ways.

It wasn't at all a bad play.
They weren't half glad to be home again.
Similar mistakes are not uncommon.
(and other such double negative ideas)
QUESTION: Would you like another cup of tea?
RESPONSE: Not half!
Well, I wouldn't say no.
I shouldn't object.
Ra-ather! (wave-intonation)
I don't mind (if I do).

This understatement use of *rather* is a diffident way of expressing *very*, especially where the Englishman hates to be definite on a subject of a complimentary, eulogistic or emotional nature.

* * *

(53.9)   ● Put *fairly* or *rather* into the blank spaces:
1 Don't you think my friend Maisie is really — pretty?
2 Surely it's — obvious that you can't carry more than one at a time.
3 Don't whisper to me now, it looks — obvious!
4 You must agree that I look — well in this suit.
5 I should go and see that film; it's really — good.
6 I think I'll buy it. The price seems — reasonable.
7 Read this book. I think you'll find it — interesting.
8 School teachers generally get — long holidays.
9 Your hair is — long, Cyril! Go and get it cut!
10 It is — easy to get a secretarial job these days.
11 It was — unkind of Cyril to be so rude to you.
12 It's really — cheap; quite a bargain, in fact!
13 I thought her little girl was — sweet. Didn't you?
14 These yellow apples aren't very good, but I think you'll find the red ones — sweet.
15 The left shoe is a bit tight, but the other one fits — well.
16 That blue hat suits you — well!
17 It was — clever of you to do it all by yourself!
18 I can't say he's a brilliant student, but he's — intelligent.
19 Your little boy seems really — intelligent for his age.

20 What's that — remarkable-looking building over there?

TAILPIECE. The correct use of *fairly* and *rather* involves a psychological choice rather than a grammatical one. Thus we see from the notes to Exercise 53.7 that we normally expect something to be *fairly easy* or *rather difficult* to do. But if our 'ideal' is the difficulty, as in Exercise 53.8, No. 2, it is quite natural to speak of a suitable sentence as *fairly difficult* and an unsuitable one as *rather easy*.

54 Phrase Openings

**54.1
Intermediate**

We include here many of those stock phrases that lead easily into our thoughts. They are commonly followed by an infinitive or a *that*-clause, and it is a very valuable conversational exercise for more advanced students to be given such an opening and be asked to finish the sentence.

A WORD OF ADVICE TO TEACHERS. In exercises where a student has to make a sentence of his own (as, for example, in this exercise, or freely on opposites or derivatives, etc.), ALWAYS give the next question to the next student to think about. If necessary, keep yourself two students ahead of schedule, but at all costs avoid wasting time.

Examples of phrase openings:

It's good for you to eat plenty of vegetables.
It's wrong for a student to neglect his homework.
It was the fault of the teacher that he didn't understand.
The time has come for us to say goodbye.
He was sometimes heard to swear.

Here are some openings to be completed by intermediate students; hundreds of others can be invented by the teacher when required.

* * *

● Complete the following skeleton sentences:
1 It's silly to —
2 We found it very boring to —
3 It's unhealthy to —

4   I think it would be best to —
5   There'll be plenty of time to —
6   He thought it was immoral to —
7   It was due to — that —
8   It was on account of — that —
9   It's easy for you to —
10   It would be useless for — to —
11   Everything is ready for — to —
12   It's all very well to —, but —
13   He was never known to —
14   It's foolish to think that —
15   Is it too much to ask you to —
16   I suppose it's too much to hope that —
17   I didn't stop to —
18   You've only got to — to —
19   If you want to —, you must —
20   It was through — that —
21   It was in — that —
22   It was because of — that —
23   It will be impossible for — to —
24   It's only right for — to —
25   It would be no use for — to —
26   It is well known that —
27   We couldn't help —
28   She has been known to —
29   It is unlikely that —
30   It is a fact that —

54.2
Advanced

See Exercise 54.1.

Some useful openings require inversion of subject and verb; in general, this type of opening is more frequently found in writing than in speech.

Examples of more difficult openings:

Only in this way could I manage to see him.
At no time have I ever been more frightened than now.
The essentials of good government *are* sound administration and honest officials.
We are not so considerate for the feelings of others *as we should be*.
It's not the words *that matter so much as* the way you say them.

*   *   *

● Complete the following skeleton sentences; the first 9 ALL require inversion of subject and verb, and so does one other sentence.

1 Not only — but —
2 Not even once —
3 On no account —
4 Only by running at full speed —
5 On no occasion —
6 So badly —
7 Seldom —
8 In no circumstances —
9 Nowhere —
10 One of the best ways of — is to —
11 I had almost completely — when —
12 He was half-way through — when —
13 If ever I'd — I'm sure I'd have —
14 Even if we had (not) — we couldn't have —
15 The more (adverb) the (noun+verb) —
16 It would be absurd to suppose that —
17 However quickly —
18 Is it too much to insist that —?
19 It's outrageous to be told that —
20 Only by paying double the money —

**54.3
Very
Advanced**

See Exercises 54.1 and 54.2.
The following are very difficult sentence beginnings, probably too difficult to be done impromptu.

* * *

● Complete the following sentences:

1 Apart from the actual —
2 For reasons already stated —
3 Not only are —
4 That there were —
5 As a consequence of his —ing —
6 If you would only —
7 If you will only —
8 It wasn't until —
9 This was due not so much to — as to —
10 So much is this the —
11 According to —
12 It would hardly be necessary to —
13 As for these so-called —

14 In view of the great —
15 It was as though —
16 Let's assume that —
17 The members have agreed in principle —
18 He didn't even have the grace to —
19 That's why —
20 What matters to us is —
21 Nor is this the only —
22 Never before —
23 In neither case —
24 It should be the first duty of —
25 Allowing for —

55 The Comparison Game

**55.1
Elementary**

A simple free-construction exercise can be made by taking objects of a similar nature and asking the following two questions:

1 How is X like Y?
2 How does X differ from Y?

The student then makes a few sentences on those points of similarity or difference he can find.

*   *   *

● Using the following pairs of words, make a few sentences on:

(1) How is X like Y?
(2) How does X differ from Y?

1	chair	table
2	pen	pencil
3	glass	cup
4	house	flat
5	dress	suit
6	orange	apple
7	car	bus
8	king	president
9	newspaper	magazine
10	cow	sheep
11	butcher	grocer
12	arm	leg

13	tennis	football
14	cigar	cigarette
15	horse	dog
16	café	restaurant
17	soldier	sailor
18	butter	cheese
19	chicken	duck
20	cabbage	lettuce
21	tea	coffee
22	watch	clock
23	kettle	teapot
24	ice	snow
25	boot	shoe

55.2
Intermediate

See Exercise 55.1.

1	radio	television
2	moustache	beard
3	dream	nightmare
4	gate	door
5	box	tin
6	sock	stocking
7	salt	pepper
8	chair	sofa
9	worm	caterpillar
10	jacket	waistcoat
11	road	street
12	fog	mist
13	cinema	theatre
14	fruit	vegetable
15	tram	train
16	doctor	dentist
17	cat	dog
18	ignorance	stupidity
19	umbrella	sunshade
20	table-knife	carving-knife
21	nail	screw
22	saucepan	frying-pan
23	rabbit	hare
24	trumpet	trombone
25	record-player	tape-recorder

55.3
Intermediate

See Exercise 55.1 for explanations.

1	race	nation
2	plane	helicopter
3	paw	hoof
4	boot	slipper
5	wages	salary
6	cupboard	sideboard
7	sports car	racing car
8	raspberry	blackberry
9	empire	republic
10	map	globe
11	dustman	postman
12	ditch	gutter
13	tour	cruise
14	beetle	spider
15	dictionary	encyclopedia
16	bandage	sling
17	poetry	prose
18	beer	whisky
19	jam	marmalade
20	spoon	fork
21	motorway	speedway
22	pliers	pincers
23	puppy	cub
24	coffee	instant coffee
25	silk	wool
26	sand	soil
27	lake	pond
28	boxing	wrestling
29	violin	viola
30	expedition	excursion

56 Prepositions and Adverbial Particles

56.1
Elementary
and
Intermediate

PREPOSITIONS usually come before the words they control. They indicate various relationships between words or phrases, the most usual being those of time, space (position, direction, etc.), and mental or emotional attitudes.

They can also come AFTER the words they govern, notably in questions and in relative clauses.

> What can I cut the bread *with*?
> This is the book I was telling you *about*.

Many verbs get strongly associated with certain prepositions in one of two ways:

(1)   verb and preposition keeping their basic meanings.
(2)   as a compound having an idiomatic meaning (we cannot guess the meaning from the two parts).

> TYPE (1)   Take the book *in* your hand and open it *at* page 4.
> He's sitting *on* a chair and looking *out of* the window.
> He spoke *about* his holidays.
>
> TYPE (2)   I didn't *take to* him at first. (like)
> He *took after* his father. (resembled)
> She *set about* preparing dinner. (began to prepare)
> The ship *made for* the harbour. (went towards)

Any good dictionary will list, under the verb, these compounds made with prepositions or adverbial particles. Two very useful works containing such idioms are Palmer's *Grammar of English Words* (Longman) and *The Advanced Learner's Dictionary* (Oxford).

The following two lists contain the commonest English PREPOSITIONS; all those in LIST (1) should be known to students within their first two years of study.

LIST (1): about, after, along, among, at, before, behind, beneath, between, by, down, for, from, in, in front of, into, like, near, next to, of, off, on, out of, over, past, round, since, through, till (until), to (towards), under, up, with, without.

LIST (2): above, across, against, below, beside, beyond, concerning, despite, except, inside, in spite of, opposite, outside.

*   *   *

● Put in suitable PREPOSITIONS:

1   We don't go — school — Sundays.
2   Wait — me — the bus-stop!
3   We arrived — Winchester — exactly six o'clock.
4   Come — 10 — Friday morning.

5   I bought this hat — fifty pence.
6   He hasn't been here — Monday.
7   Our cat was bitten — a dog.
8   My home is — London, but I was born — Lynton, a small village — Devonshire.
9   Put your books — the table.
10   You may write — pencil.
11   There's no bus; we'll have to go — foot.
12   We went — the seaside — car.
13   Get — the bus here, and get off — the third stop.
14   Many planes fly — the Atlantic nowadays.
15   We've been waiting — over an hour.
16   I'll call — you — a more convenient time.
17   Hold it carefully — your thumb and first finger.
18   I couldn't hear what they were talking —
19   A girl — blue eyes has just gone — the door.
20   Here's a present — you; don't forget it and go home — it.
21   The teacher was sitting — a desk — the class.
22   — him was a blackboard.
23   As he was coming — me, he threw some orange-peel — the fence — his way — the garden.
24   They were standing — the two houses.
25   We had to go — the hill — a little house — the top.
26   She was looking — the window — the busy street.
27   We walked — the main road, turned left — the railway station, and went as far as the third turning — the right.
28   Read — line 10 — line 20 — page 7.
29   You can use my knife to cut it —.
30   The stream ran — a little tunnel — the roadway.
31   He spoke — me — his hands — his pockets.
32   I walked — one end of the street — the other.
33   You can reach the station — bus — ten minutes.
34   The pictures will be — show — one week longer.
35   I'm bringing an old book — leather covers — you — the evening — dinner.
36   Don't look — me like that!
37   A brick has fallen — the well and knocked the bucket — the rope.

38 I must look — the postcard I got — my teacher last week.

39 Most children remain — school — the ages of six and sixteen.

40 The first space vehicle travelled — the world hundreds of times — a few weeks.

41 I fell — a rock when I was climbing — a mountain last week.

42 It's farther than I thought; it's — ten kilometres — the shortest route.

43 Switzerland lies — Germany, France and Italy.

44 I'm staying — friends not far — the station.

45 Please come — me — the theatre tonight.

46 Who did you give the money —?

47 Children — four years — age do not often go — school.

48 My school was founded — Edward VI — 1553.

49 Come and sit — this sunshade — a comfortable deck-chair.

50 Do you want to speak — me — anything?

51 There's a knock — the door. Who can be calling — us — this late hour?

52 Don't go out — the rain — a hat.

53 I like to smoke a cigarette and listen — the radio — half an hour or so — dinner.

54 The cat is hiding — us — the table.

55 I must work hard — history because I'm not very good — it.

56 I wonder if I shall get — my history examination.

57 You can cut the apple — two — this knife.

58 I go — the post office every day — my way — work.

59 Let's go — a walk — the garden — dinner-time.

60 When we get back — our walk, we're going to sit — the fire — our books — half an hour.

56.2
Elementary
and
Intermediate

ADVERBIAL PARTICLES combine with verbs even more often than prepositions to form idiomatic compounds. Most of them have the same form as their corresponding prepositions, but the following seven are adverbial only and never used as prepositions:

away, back, out; backward(s), downward(s), forward(s), upward(s).

Adverbial particles are most commonly found as part of COMPOUND VERBS (or PHRASAL VERBS). As with similar compounds made with prepositions, these are of two kinds:

(1)   verb and adverb keeping their own basic meanings:
      go in; *walk away*; *come out*; *pay back*, etc.
(2)   combining to give a new idiomatic meaning:
      keep on (continue); *bring about* (cause); *give in* (yield); *take off* (leave the ground OR imitate); *blow up* (explode), etc.

Some of these compounds can be followed by a preposition to make a further combination: *go in for* (practise for pleasure); *come out with* (say suddenly); *get down to* (apply oneself); *put up with* (suffer, bear), etc.

It isn't always easy for a foreign student to distinguish between a PREPOSITIONAL and an ADVERBIAL compound verb. He probably *looks upon* (prep.) these little words as annoying mysteries and then *looks up* (adv.) their meaning in a dictionary. These are the main differences.

A PREPOSITION is closely tied to the (pro)noun it controls.

He looked/ *at the boys*. He spoke/ *to them*. He spoke/ *about his travels*. He looked/ *out of the window*.

An ADVERB PARTICLE is closely tied to its verb (as if by a hyphen):

Please *put-out/* the light.
We *blew-up/* the bridge and the rebels *gave-in*.

WORD-ORDER.   Except as indicated in the notes to Exercise 56.1, a PREPOSITION must precede its (pro)noun object. An ADVERB PARTICLE always FOLLOWS a pronoun object. It usually follows the object even when this is a noun, unless the noun-phrase object is a long one, which would leave the verb too far from its particle.

Look the word up in the index.
Look up the word in the index.
Look up all the difficult words and phrases in the index.
(the particle *up* can only precede such a long object)

The distinct word-orders of PREPOSITION and ADVERB can be seen when the object is a pronoun.

ADVERB PARTICLE: Look the word up.
Look it up.
PREPOSITION: Look up the chimney.
Look up it.

ADVERB PARTICLE: He couldn't get his talk across.
(= manage to communicate)
He couldn't get it across.
PREPOSITION: He couldn't get across the river.
He couldn't get across it.

STRESS.   The difference is quite clear in speech. At the end
of a phrase a VERB WITH PREPOSITION has a final stress on
the VERB:

Give it to the man you '*spoke* to.
Who does he '*take* after?

At the end of a phrase a VERB WITH ADVERB PARTICLE has
a final stress on the ADVERB:

Which word are you going to look '*up*?
This is the book he brought '*back*, and here's the one
he wants to take '*out*.

PHRASAL VERBS with prepositions also take their final stress
on the adverb when in this position:

We have a lot of troubles to put '*up* with.
Chess is a good game to go '*in* for.

*   *   *

(56.2)   ● Put in suitable PREPOSITIONS or ADVERB PARTICLES:

1   He put — his coat and took the dog — for a walk.
2   Run — the corner! Someone is following close —
     us.
3   Look — Cyril! He's got a yellow waistcoat —.
4   Do you always get — — 6 o'clock — the
     morning?
5   It was silly of you to go — — the rain — your
     raincoat —.
6   Please go — the post office and bring — a book —
     stamps — me.
7   I'm fed — — this kind — work.
8   It would be bad — you to stay — late — night too
     often.
9   He had to choose — staying — the country and
     staying — the seaside.
10   Maisie has just rung — to ask me to go — — a
     walk — her — going — bed.
11   The London plane takes — — midday.
12   They were — war — their neighbours.

13 When you grow —, you will be allowed to go —
— yourself — night, but not — then.

14 If you don't want to sit here — the dark, you had
better put the light —.

15 Cats sleep — day and wake — — night.

16 He hid a banknote — the pages — a novel —
Dickens.

17 Most — us stayed — your party till it was — 2
o'clock — the morning, — your sister, who left —
midnight.

18 The enemy took — positions exactly — ours.

19 People say it is lucky to put — an article of
clothing — —.

20 The fire has gone —, my family has gone —, and
now the light has gone —; so I must sit here all —
myself — the dark — anyone to talk —.

21 If you happen to come — my lost papers while
you're looking — your book, please let me
know — once — telephone.

22 These nails may come — handy — hanging —
pictures.

23 My watch has run — because I forgot to wind it —
— going — bed last night.

24 — lack of help the plans fell —.

25 Today's examinations have tired me — so I think
I'll turn — early tonight.

NOTE: It is possible for the same verb-adverb compound to
have more than one meaning according to context:

This box is heavy; I must put it down. (*place on
ground*)
Shall I put his name down, too? (*make note of*)
The riot was put down by the police. (*suppress*)
I should put him down as a student. (*reckon, consider*)
He said nothing; we put it down to shyness. (*attribute*)
You can't get through this door with your umbrella
up; you'll have to put it down. (*shut*)

An amusing contrast between preposition and adverb
particle is found in this well-known children's riddle:

QUEST. What can go up a chimney down, but can't go
down it up?
ANS. An umbrella.

56.3

Intermediate ●   Fill in the blank spaces:

1   He orders me — as if I were his wife!
2   I came — it quite — chance as I was looking — some old papers.
3   Lean it — the wall if you don't want it to fall —.
4   Do you think there is enough food to go —?
5   I don't get — very well — him.
6   That machine digs — earth — high ground and carries it — to build the motorway — — low ground.
7   What do you think — dividing it — the rest — them?
8   I wouldn't dream — being so rude as to answer you —.
9   I don't like people who show —, especially — public.
10   She bought a beautiful cloth, measuring three feet — two feet, all embroidered — hand.
11   We were — a loss to know what you meant — your remark.
12   If you leave your things — all — the place again, I shall punish you — your untidiness.
13   I don't understand; what are you getting —?
14   You shouldn't look — — people who aren't as well — as you are.
15   I know her — sight, but not to speak —.
16   The entertainer took — Tom Jones and made fun — Sacha Distel, but Maisie didn't catch —.
17   Cyril wants to take me — — his car, but it isn't — — much, and he usually runs — — fuel.
18   He shook me — the hand and helped me — with my coat.
19   Everyone was afraid to go out — dark until the rebellion had died —.
20   This is no time for playing —, it is a serious matter.   You are always — — some mischief.
21   It was thanks — you that he was successful — carrying — his project.
22   It's no use keeping — telling me to give — smoking; I can't cure myself — a habit so easily.

23 The house was locked — as all the family was —
— home.

24 The notices say 'Keep —', but there isn't a
doorman to throw — anyone who tries to get —
— a ticket.

25 The notice says 'Keep — the grass.' You'd better
look — — case a park-keeper comes.

26 I wanted to heat — the coffee but it boiled —, and
then I had to clean — the mess.

27 — all his faults you must admit that he's easy to
get — —; he's always — a good temper.

28 Speak —, I can't hear you. You let your voice die
— at the end of every sentence.

29 — spite — many difficulties, the show went —
very well.

30 Don't be — such a hurry, I can't keep — — you.

31 You can rely — me to stand — you if you are —
trouble.

32 I don't know how to get — touch — Mrs Green,
she's not — the phone.

33 We've given — going — that pub. The landlord
tries it —: he waters — the drinks and puts — his
prices.

34 The rocks were worn — by wind and weather.

35 I can see — that clever scheme of his; he can't
deceive me, I know what he's playing —.

36 They will have to do — such luxuries if they want
to pay — all they owe.

37 An epidemic of influenza broke — last winter, and
did not die — — many months.

38 If you paint the figures — bright colours they will
stand — more clearly.

39 We set — as soon as the old man pointed — the
way to us.

40 I have nothing — common — him, so we have put
an end — our friendship once and — all.

41 Make yourself — home, help yourself — anything
you want — waiting to be asked.

42 If you have quarrelled — her, don't worry — it.
Put it completely — — your mind, it will be
sure to turn — all right — the end.

43 They were already — — sight beyond the next hill,

so it was impossible to catch — — them.

44 'Give me — the money you stole — me!' he
burst —.

45 You must account — the manager — the money
you used.

46 The police accused him — murder.

47 You must accustom yourself — the hot summer.

48 I will be sure to act — your instructions — future.

49 This agent is acting — Barclays Bank.

50 The razor can be adapted — any voltage.

51 The committee has agreed — your proposals —
reserve.

52 My wife never agrees — me — anything.

53 You had better allow — a few extra — supper
tonight and cater — ten.

54 His arguments amount — nothing — hot air.

55 This dog answers — the name of Fido.

56 I do not approve — your walking — the street
alone.

57 We will try to arrange — an old lady to go — you.

58 I do not ask very much — you, only a little
courtesy.

59 Their dirty clothes and long hair put me — —
first, but I found — that they had hearts — gold.

60 I can put — — fools, but I am put — — liars.

61 Does this animal belong — you, — any chance?

62 I don't believe — brandy as a cure — colds.

63 Don't run — — the idea that you can run — my
friends and get — — it.

64 The horses broke — a trot — a touch — the whip.

65 The rude man burst — a roar — coarse laughter.

66 The police van will call — you — the morning.

67 I will now call — Mr Higginbotham — a speech.

68 She does not care — me any more.

69 All change here — Epsom; cross the lines —
platform three — the footbridge!

70 How much did they charge you — putting — the
shed?

71 If I can scrape — a few pounds, I'll pay — it.

72 Don't be afraid — him. Speak — and stand — —
yourself.

73 Hydrogen combines — oxygen to produce water.

74 If you compare your version — mine, you'll see
    what is wrong — it.

75 The poet compared his love — a flower.

76 The neighbours are complaining — the smell —
    your kitchen.

77 The invalid complains — pains in his thigh; he
    attributes it — rheumatism, caught — running —
    — a wet swim-suit.

78 Concentrate — doing a little work — a change.

79 The car struggled — — three cylinders, throwing
    — clouds — smoke.

80 Let's look — the Smiths and talk the matter — —
    them.

81 I can't work — the cost — six meals — £1 each.

82 — all your patent medicines you haven't cured me
    — this cold.

83 This wall defends the town — attack — the west.

84 The success — our venture depends — our skill.

85 I hope this cold will not develop — pneumonia.

86 No man can dictate — me — any circumstances.

87 I wonder what this cow died —

88 This man was dismissed — his job — idleness.

89 Mix it — sugar and dissolve it — a glass of water;
    drink it — — one draught.

90 It is cruel to separate children — their parents.

91 I would not dream — disturbing you so late.

92 The speaker enlarged — the difficulties — the
    undertaking.

93 England exchanges machinery — foodstuffs —
    abroad.

94 What has happened — this poor man?

95 I am not interested — modern art — all.

96 You may join your truck — the back of our train.

97 These trousers will last — donkeys' years —
    wearing —.

98 It is bad psychology to laugh — children — their
    mistakes.

99 He was leaning — a tree — a cigarette — his lips.

100 I am looking — my little lost sister; I hope she
     hasn't fallen — bad company.

101 The pickpocket mixed — the crowd — coming —
     — the station.

102 Does the old lady object — my smoking a cigar?
103 Who is going to pay — all this damage — my car?
104 It is very rude to point — people — that way.
105 The soldier poured the beer — the jug — the glass.
106 If you want peace, prepare — war.
107 Don't worry, I will protect you — harm.
108 Your scheme does not provide — accidents — the journey.
109 I never interfere — my staff — their work.
110 I'm fed — — this exercise, and my pencil is worn —.

56.4 See introductory remarks to Exercise 56.1.
Advanced

* * *

● Fill in the blanks:
1 They abandoned their comrade — the wolves.
2 The treasurer has absconded — the funds of the club.
3 You must not absent yourself — the class — any circumstances.
4 The accused was absolved — all blame.
5 He is terribly absorbed — his work — bacteria.
6 Abstain — alcohol. It's dangerous — you — your condition.
7 The young king acceded — the throne — public acclamations.
8 My toothache has worn — and I'm ready — anything.
9 You must accommodate yourself — his needs.
10 The result does not accord — my original conception — the matter.
11 Just acquaint this gentleman — the facts — the case — question.
12 I refuse to acquiesce — this plot — the government.
13 He assured me — his full co-operation — the business.
14 My aunt has been addicted — hashish — years.
15 Do you adhere — any special political opinions, young man?

16   He whiled — an hour jotting — some ideas — his
     next TV script.
17   Kindly advise us — any change — address — your
     stay here.
18   The girl is afflicted — a curious twitching — the
     eyes.
19   Our newspaper aims — having a million readers —
     next year.
20   Twenty pounds are allocated — the purchase of
     books — botany.
21   Fifteen pounds are allotted — us — furniture, so
     we must lay it — carefully — the purchases we
     have — mind.
22   I must ask you not to allude — my past
     indiscretions.
23   Bangs alternated — crashes.
24   I appeal — you — mercy — the prisoner.
25   The husband has been apprised — the good
     news — his son.
26   The boy is apprenticed — Mr Smith, a carpenter
     — trade.
27   We have not arrived — any decision — the matter
     — question.
28   His stupidity can be ascribed — his extreme age.
29   Thanks are also due — all those working — the
     scenes — their kind co-operation — this show.
30   The books are — loan — us — a private library.
31   Everybody should assist — the performance —
     these tasks.
32   Let me assure you — my honest intentions — your
     daughter.
33   I'm a what? You take that — or I'll knock your
     head —!
34   He'll never pay —. You'd better write his debt —.
35   She averted her face — the sight — his suffering.
36   The beast was baulked — his prey — the last
     moment.
37   I refuse to bargain — you — the price — those
     conditions.
38   Please don't tidy — — my room. You always put
     things — where I can't put my hand — them.
39   It is no use your begging — mercy — me.

40 I expect the bill will add — — about £5. We can
each put — £2 and square — later.

41 His surprise — her turning — — such lovely
clothes left him entirely bereft — speech.

42 I'm not going to put — — any more interruptions.
Shut — or get — — the hall!

43 You've knocked your drink —? Soak it — — this
cloth.

44 If you go — — your glasses, you'll trip — or get
run —.

45 Do not bicker — trifles or squabble — yourselves.

46 A very good price was bid — my old oak chest —
the auction sale.

47 The loudspeaker was blaring — pop music —
the hour.

48 You cannot blame me — the mistakes — others —
this affair.

49 CALLER: Smith & Co.? I'm trying to get hold —
Mr John Smith. OPERATOR: Just hold —, please,
and I'll put you —.

50 The band struck — but was horribly — — tune;
the players had forgotten to tune —.

51 Oil does not blend — water any more than iron
floats — it.

52 There is no need to boast — your deficiencies —
those subjects.

53 His genius borders — lunacy.

54 Don't bother — minor details; concentrate — the
general outline.

55 He is always bragging — us — his superior
education.

56 Who will broach the scheme — the director?

57 The old lady was brooding — the loss — her cat,
the only creature she had ever doted —.

58 You'll never guess who I bumped — last night —
the dark.

59 I don't want to burden you — my worries — the
future.

60 You can't hang — here, sir. Move —, please.

61 — speaking rudely — the judge, my sentence was
increased — fifteen days — contempt — court.

62 Why does everybody cavil — my excellent

suggestions — brightening the lessons — a little dance music?

63 If we press —, we'll get — Dover before the sun goes —.

64 The Indians were circling — the stockade, shooting — our sentries one — one.

65 The burglar clambered — the roof — the skylight.

66 Clap the thief — jail and deprive him — any further opportunity — stealing.

67 I refuse to be classed — the man — the street.

68 He was beaten — and knocked — but he didn't pass —.

69 A thin piece of ivy was clinging — the wall and trailing — the roof.

70 A thousand hysterical women clustered — the bronzed film star.

71 I am tired — depending — the tram service — getting — — town and back.

72 How good! Your birthday coincides — mine.

73 I am collaborating — Miss P. — writing a book.

74 Poor fellow, he collided — a tram — his way home — work.

75 She has gone — the country to commune — Nature.

76 Her beautiful voice compensates — her hideous face and lack — intelligence.

77 We compliment you — your good taste — literature.

78 Did the landlord comply — your request — a hot bath — night?

79 We will accept no compromise — the enemy — any terms.

80 You can't conceal your faults — your wife, so it is no use your thinking — excuses — yourself every time you've been — — something.

81 Does the other doctor concur — this opinion — your illness?

82 I've been looking forward — hearing — you — letter — ages.

83 The manager is conferring — the board — a matter — importance.

84   I confess — a secret love — tobacco.

85   I know I owe you £50.   I'll settle — — Friday.

86   Your story conflicted — that of other eye-
     witnesses, whose versions all tally — one another
     — — the minutest detail.

87   You must conform — the rules — the game, — all
     events.

88   We confronted the murderer — the body, — his
     utter dismay.

89   I must congratulate him — his success — the
     examination.

90   The police connived — her escape — her knowing
     — it.

91   Stop showing —. Everybody knows you're only
     standing — — the real boss.

92   The helicopter took — — the airport and put
     — — the school playing-field.

93   Content yourself — what you have and don't
     strive — the impossible.

94   He has not contributed much — the solution —
     our difficulties.

95   Her character contrasts strongly — his — all
     points.

96   — this point the railway converges — the river,
     only to strike — — a tangent a little further —.

97   He spends his nights conversing — his friends —
     all manner — topics, drawn — their joint
     reminiscences.

98   An ambulance was standing — — case — accidents.

99   I cannot convey — you the depth — my
     sympathy — your loss.

100 But I can convince you — the sincerity — my
     words.

101 Are you blind — what he is degenerating —?

102 The ships departing — the dock this morning were
     bound — the East Indies.

103 Can I depend — you not to be angry — me —
     being late?

104 I am afraid he has fallen — love — a girl who,
     although not exactly devoid — intelligence, or
     even deficient — common sense, is certainly a bit
     weak — the head.

105 I cut it — half, then — four pieces, and finally
     shared it out — any that weren't averse — having
     a piece.

106 I don't want you to be offended — me, or even
     offended — my encroaching — your rights —
     suggesting that you should give — your house —
     such circumstances.

107 He tried to hinder me — going out, but — spite —
     all his efforts he couldn't prevent me — doing so.

108 I suppose I must reconcile myself — the loss — my
     watch.

109 I am apt to be impatient — the efforts — people
     making an attempt — something they are not
     really capable — doing.

110 He may be slow — his work, but he is very quick
     — the uptake.

111 I'll enquire — this claim — the railway company
     and, if necessary, I'll see — it myself.

112 You cannot be happy if you live — your means;
     you must always live — them.

113 Since you have never had to reproach me —
     anything, perhaps you wouldn't be averse —
     sticking — — me now that I've run — debt, and
     convincing these people that it is — no way a
     reflection — my character.

114 I have a strong antipathy — people who are
     constantly irritated — small things, although I
     must confess — being liable — a similar tendency
     myself.

115 She is really quite indifferent — my regard — her
     feelings.

116 There's no need — you to be rude — me just
     because you're disgusted — my work.

117 He was ashamed — her low taste — amusements,
     and took — drink to forget — it all.

118 I value him — his reputation — honesty and his
     ability to be thoughtful — others.

119 He reckoned — prevailing — me to act — him, but
     I'm afraid I let him — badly; I think he is very
     disappointed — me — the whole affair.

120 I like listening — the radio, but I'm not always
     impressed — the quality — the programmes.

57 Accepted Phrases

It is impossible to give more than a random collection, graded (more according to value than difficulty) into elementary, intermediate or advanced. Any piece of modern reading will have several on every page; any conversation will produce dozens every five minutes. The idioms and sayings of the 'horse of another colour' variety may be useful passive knowledge for more advanced students, but far more useful practical work should first be done on the accepted phrases of everyday English.

The following three exercises are NOT intended to be done as a solid group; they should be split up and done piecemeal at odd times, the various phrases being added to and expanded at will.

Apart from the suggested sentence-making exercise, other work can be done, for example:

Write a continuous passage containing six of the following phrases.

Give an English phrase for [foreign equivalent]

Use the following phrase in your answer to my question [teacher asks question in the answer to which the required phrase can be logically introduced]. This exercise will need careful preparation on the part of the teacher.

Similarly, questions may be asked to ring the changes on a group of five or six idioms.

Here is a simple example worked out in detail for part of an elementary 'conversation' lesson.

The following elementary phrases are learnt:

(1) He's not back yet.
(2) Here you are! (for offering things informally),
(3) Never mind.
(4) What's he like?
(5) Have a good time.

Individual students are made to respond with one of these by such questions as the following:

Excuse me, can you lend me a pencil? (2)
I say, I'm going to a party tonight. (5)
I've come to see X, where is he? (1)

I have some news for you. You are having a new teacher next week. (4)

I'm going away for the weekend. (5)

I'm so sorry. I'm afraid I've broken your pencil. (3)

May I speak to your father for a few minutes? (1)

There's a strange man outside (the window). (4)

Have you got a match, please? (2)

Well, I'm afraid I can't think of a sentence for you. (3)

Many of these 'accepted phrases' can be worked into similar stimulated conversations.

57.1
Elementary

See introductory remarks.

* * *

● Make sentences containing each of the following phrases. Any tense or person may be used.

1 Take a fancy to, take a liking to; (not) to my liking.
2 Take place.
3 Go back for good (and all).
4 Do away with.
5 Leave her behind.
6 Get on well, get on well with a person.
7 Can't tell which is which, etc.
8 In nine cases out of ten.
9 The chances are that (=probably).
10 By the dozen, pound, etc.
11 In stock, out of stock.
12 It has nothing to do with you.
13 All day long, day after day.
14 I don't think much of —
15 Are you on the phone?
16 Don't mind me.
17 We haven't got room.
18 What's she like?
19 It will do them good.
20 We had better. We would rather.
21 I must be off. I'll be back in a minute.
22 What's the matter with her?
23 Come along.
24 You see, —. —, you know.
25 I've no idea.
26 He's not back yet. Hasn't come in yet.

27 Leave me alone.   Leave my things alone.
28 I shall miss you.
29 I'm pleased with.   I'm sorry for.
30 Here you are! (offering something)
31 Will you write and let them know?
32 Catch fire.   Set fire to.
33 Read between the lines.
34 Go in for (sport, etc.).
35 Out of order.
36 I can't help that.
37 Straight on for about a mile.
38 As far as the —.
39 Turn to the left.
40 Take the next turning to the right by the —
41 Put out the light, put the light out; also **on**.
42 Turn out the light, turn the light out; also **on**.
43 Switch off the light, radio; also **on**.
44 By return of post.
45 Out of place.
46 Let us in.   I let myself in (with this key).
47 Next door.   Next door but one.
48 Opens on to, out of.
49 Look forward to seeing you.
50 No small change.
51 Catch a train, bus, etc.
52 Spend the night.
53 Would you mind —.
54 See a joke, take a joke; a sense of humour.
55 Make a fool of; to fool someone (over something).
56 Not at all.
57 On the way.   By the way, —.
58 Come and fetch me; call for me; see me home.
59 Enough to live on.
60 Make fun of; poke fun at.
61 Not worth while.
62 Old-fashioned; up-to-date.
63 It's my turn; out of (his, etc.) turn.   Whose turn?
64 (I beg your) pardon!   (I'm) sorry!
65 (I beg your) pardon?   I didn't (quite) catch what
    you said.
66 And that reminds me, —.
67 It's very kind of you (to say so).

68   Pay you back; pay up.
69   Behave yourselves.
70   I don't care! I don't mind! I don't care for —.

57.2   See introductory remarks to Exercise 57.1.
Intermediate

＊   ＊   ＊

● Make sentences containing each of the following phrases.
   Use any person or tense.

1   The same holds good for —.   (The) same to you!
2   What are you hinting at? — getting at? Can't you
    take a hint?
3   Break the journey.
4   The ship put in at —; off Cape Town.
5   Take a chance on it.
6   Let yourself in for.
7   Not cut out for. Cut a person (in street).
8   Get over. (I can't get over his doing —.)
9   It didn't quite come off.
10   Have it your own way; to get one's own way in the
    end.
11   For good and all.
12   Are you pulling my leg?
13   For goodness' sake.
14   Lined the street. To crowd round; crowded out.
15   Highly probable; hardly likely.
16   That's all very well, but —.
17   To see somebody off, out, home etc.; to the door,
    across the street etc.
18   I saw her only the other day.
19   Is it worth while? Is it worth the candle?
20   Make up your minds.
21   If the worst comes to the worst.
22   That'll do; he'll do.
23   I've changed my mind.
24   How (what) about having some tea? Do you feel
    like a cup of tea?
25   You're wrong there. That's where you're wrong.
26   Doing her hair, nails, teeth, etc.
27   Don't lose your temper. Keep your temper. To
    be in a temper.
28   Not fit to be seen.

29   I've been looking forward to — ing —.
30   It won't work. It won't do.
31   Put in a good word for —.
32   A change for the worse (better).
33   Live beyond his means; within his means.
34   Getting on for fifty; in his thirties, teens.
35   Have no right to; every right to —.
36   Few and far between.
37   What's come over you? What's up (with you)?
38   I'll just have a word with — about —.
39   Hope for the best; fear the worst (has happened).
40   Let him off (lightly).
41   Keep doing something; keep it up.
42   It doesn't pay to —.
43   Burst into flames, tears. Burst out laughing.
44   Cope with (a situation or person).
45   From time to time; now and then; now and
       again; off and on.
46   He means well.
47   I don't know what he sees in her.
48   A trying time; she's very trying.
49   Somehow, (somewhere, someone, etc.) or other.
50   I'll see about rooms. I'll see about it, see to it.
51   She doesn't charge much; charge it up to me.
52   Have a good time!
53   Thanks to you —.
54   Without fail. For sure, certain.
55   Can't go into that now.
56   Do so by all means.
57   Flat on his face, back. Head over heels;
       headlong.
58   Do nothing of the sort, kind.
59   To see the sights; go sightseeing.
60   It is all fixed up.
61   At short notice. I'll need plenty of notice.
62   Think the matter over, talk the matter over.
63   No sooner said than done.
64   Up to something, up to some mischief.
65   Sooner or later.
66   By and by.
67   Come across, upon.
68   What do you take me for?

69   Worth waiting for.
70   Make one's way to; make a bee-line for.
71   Make sure, certain.
72   As good as ever, as good as new.
73   You've got a cold coming (on).
74   It doesn't go with —.
75   I hope you will keep it up; keep it to yourself.

57.3
Advanced   See introductory remarks to Exercise 57.1.

*   *   *

● Make sentences containing each of the following phrases.
    Use any person or tense.
1   She has a way with her.   Her charming ways.
2   It all boils down to this.
3   The lesser of two evils.
4   Part with something.
5   Cut down expenses, cut down smoking; cut it
    out altogether.
6   Let it out (the cat out of the bag).
7   Improve on acquaintance; take to someone (at
    first sight).
8   There's no telling; there's no knowing; there's no
    stopping him, etc.
9   Drag on, drag out.   Cut short.
10   Stand up on end, longways.   His hair stood on
    end.   For days on end.
11[1]   Pick his way, elbow his way, edge round.
12   We've got the decorators in; we're having the place
    done up.
13[1]   What about the — (=you haven't yet
    mentioned, brought, etc.).
14[1]   See about, see about getting —.   I'll see to it later.
15   To talk business, art, shop, scandal, etc.
16   Not that I know of, not that I'm aware of.   As far
    as I know, as far as I'm aware.
17   A lot of measles about.
18[1]   All to the good; all the better (for).   The worse for
    wear.
19   As good as his word.

[1] Examples of sentences containing these phrases will be found
after this exercise.

20 Idea has (not) caught on.
21 She was all ears (eyes).
22 Hand it over.   To hand out (round) books, etc.
23 On his own (initiative).
24[1] At stake.
25 Make up (for) lost time; make it up to you (for
   your loss); make-up box; kiss and make up;
   make up a parcel; make up a four.
26 Quick on the uptake.
27 Knows what he's about; mind what you're about.
28[1] To keep open house.
29[1] You have to take what's going.   To take pot luck.
30 Knit his brows; purse his lips; grind his teeth.
31 Hard to come by.
32 To hold good for.   That goes for you too!
33 Let's get off the beaten track; take a short cut.
34 Pander to his whims.   He'll have to put up with it.
35 Do it with (a) good grace.
36[1] Put her back up; rub her up the wrong way.
37 I don't feel up to it.
38[1] Lording it, footing it, pigging it, etc.
39 In the nick of time; by the skin of his teeth.
40[1] Eke out.
41 She does make a fuss of that child; fussy.
42 All over now, not nearly finished, all over bar the
   shouting.
43 Don't go (take) on like that; oh, you do go on so!
44 To make a mess (a good job) of something.
45 To run down (crack up) someone.

MODEL SENTENCES FOR SOME OF THE PHRASES FROM EXERCISE
57.3.
11   He picked his way carefully through a sea of suitcases,
elbowed his way through a queue waiting for the 6.10
express, and edged round the crowds of passengers pouring
through the station entrance.
13   I've made the tea. What about putting some cups out?
14   Will you please see about writing the invitations to
the party?
I'm rather busy now.   I'll see to it later.
18   The house will be all the better for this new coat of

[1] Examples of sentences containing these phrases will be
found after this exercise.

paint; it was really beginning to look the worse for wear.

24   So much was at stake that he didn't like to make the final decision without further advice.

28   It was their custom to keep open house on Sundays, and one could always be sure of meeting at least one or two interesting visitors.

29   (*a*) We're a bit late for lunch, so if the dishes we want are now off the menu, we'll just have to take what's going.
(*b*) Come home and join me for supper. I don't know what there'll be for us to eat so you'll have to take pot luck.

36   I should word your letter of complaint a little more mildly if I were you, or it'll only put his back up. There's no sense (in) rubbing him up the wrong way if you really want his help in the end.

38   (*a*) He likes to lord it over his workmates now that he's come into some money from the lottery.
(*b*) There's no bus at this hour, so we'll just have to foot it all the way back.
(*c*) If we go on this weekend hunt, we'll have to make do with scratch meals and sleep in a hut in the forest, so I hope you won't mind pigging it for a day or two.

40   There aren't many potatoes left. We'll have to eke them out with bread or macaroni till I can get some more tomorrow.

ANSWER to Exercise 19.4, No. 5: Australia, of course!

58   Appendix on Clauses

THIS book has dealt with only one type of clause (the conditional) in some detail, but exercises on other kinds of subordinate clauses are found under appropriate headings. A few types, notably CAUSE, PURPOSE, RESULT and CONCESSION, are not expressly treated. This appendix will give a practical outline of clauses and the conjunctions that introduce them. In keeping with the spirit of the rest of the book, exercises in this section will be constructive and not analytical.

GENERAL REMARKS

A clause takes its name from its function (i.e. a NOUN

CLAUSE behaves like a noun, an ADVERB CLAUSE like an adverb, etc.).

Students who have to analyse English sentences should note that many conjunctions can introduce clauses of more than one type; in fact any one clause is sometimes to be interpreted differently in different sentences. For example, the clause *when he left* looks like an adverb clause of time, as in the sentence 'The others came *when he left*.' But we could make it function quite differently:

Can you tell me when he left?	(NOUN: OBJECT)
When he left is still a mystery.	(NOUN: SUBJECT)
Do you remember the day when he left?	(ADJECTIVE)
How could he know the result when he left before the end?	(CAUSE)
They invited him again even when he left once without saying good-bye.	(CONCESSION)

NOUN CLAUSES

NOUN CLAUSE as OBJECT

The most usual form is the OBJECT-CLAUSE of reported speech. (See Section 51.)

The noun clause of a REPORTED QUESTION can be preceded by a preposition.

> It depends on what you want me for.
> I am anxious about where he has gone.
> It reminds me of when I first went to school.
> Don't let's worry about whether[1] we'll be in time.

See Exercise 51.7, etc., for clauses with *what, who, which,* etc.

REPORTED STATEMENTS are introduced by *that*, which is only rarely preceded by a preposition. The two principal ways of getting over this difficulty when a preposition is needed are:

(1)   Omit the preposition where possible.

proud of	*I am proud that you have won.*
surprised at	*He was surprised that I knew English.*
sorry for	*We're sorry that you can't come.*

This pattern is possible with most other such expressions of feeling, such as: *sure of, glad of, angry with, aware of,*

[1] *If* cannot be used here when the interrogative clause is introduced by a preposition; we can use *whether* only.

afraid of, *grateful* (*thankful*) *for*, *anxious for*. Many of them can be logically analysed as adverb clauses; e.g. the last two examples above could equally well be called clauses of reason, clauses answering the question *Why?*

A few prepositions may still be used before the conjunction *that*, the most usual being *except* and *in*.

> I forgot everything except that I wanted to go home.
> He takes after his father in that he is fond of music.
> (RATHER FORMAL)

In this last sentence *in that* might be considered as a conjunction introducing an adverb clause of manner, a clause answering the question *How?* (See under ADVERB CLAUSES, D.)

Note the expression *I don't care* (*for*), which has two meanings:

> I don't care for what she does.   (*I don't like*)
> I don't care what she does.   (*I'm indifferent*)

(2)   Use an introductory *it*, *this* or *the fact* before the conjunction *that*.

> You can depend on it that he won't be pleased.
> I'll see to it that you get home all right.
> It all amounts to this, that you have been cheated.
> We must allow for the fact that she doesn't hear well.

NOUN CLAUSE AS SUBJECT

> That he has gone for good is now quite certain.
> What you want is a cup of tea.
> (*A cup of tea is what you want.*)
> Whoever finishes first gets a prize.

The first type above is better expressed with an introductory *it*: *It is now quite certain that ...*

* * *

58.1   ● Say these sentences in a more natural way, using *it* as the first word.

1   That you are late is a pity.
2   How useful these sentences are is quite clear.
3   That you have come early is a good thing.
4   That you lost your way is unfortunate.
5   Whether he will come at all is doubtful.
6   Where he went or where he came from is still not known.

7   That we should leave without paying is quite out of the question.

8   How he knew my name is a mystery to me.

9   That we didn't get back before midnight is quite true.

10 How tea is made is important for everyone to know.

11 What you ought to say is difficult to suggest.

12 That we haven't met somewhere before seems strange.

13 That such a person ever existed must first be proved.

14 When he is coming back hasn't yet been decided.

15 What you look like is not important, but how you behave (is).

See also Section 50 on *it is* and *there is* (*are*), etc.

ADVERB CLAUSES

A   PLACE

Chief conjunctions: *where* (and its derivatives), *as.*

> Go where you like!
> Put it back where you found it.
> She shall have music wherever she goes.
> (CHILDREN'S RHYME)
> Wherever (it was) possible, they camped for the night.
> It's on your right as you face the station.

B   TIME

Chief conjunctions: *when* (and its derivatives), *as soon as* (*ever*), *as long as* (*ever*), *until* (*till*), *before, after, by the time, while* (*whilst*), *as, now* (*that*), *once, since*; and the compound forms *no sooner ... than; scarcely* (*hardly*) *... when* (*before*); *not long* (*an hour, a minute, far*, etc.) *... when* (*before*).

> Let me know when you've finished. (Can also be NOUN CLAUSE)
> Come back as soon as (ever) you can.
> You can stay as long as you want to.
> Wait till (until) the light changes to green.
> Look before you leap.
> After he had had supper he went to bed.
> I'll have finished by the time you get back.

Shoes repaired while you wait.

I met him as he was coming out of school.

Now you (come to) mention it, I suppose we *must* have met somewhere before.

You'll find the way all right once you get to the station.

She hasn't written since she went away. (Main verb always PERFECT TENSE)

[1]He had no sooner arrived than he demanded a meal.

[1]He had scarcely left the house before we missed the jewels.

They hadn't gone very far when they met an old man.

For FUTURE TIME sentences see Exercises 28.17 and 28.21.

* * *

58.2

● Join each of the clauses in (A) to the appropriate clause of time or place in (B):

A	*B*
1. Come again	as long as is necessary
2. Wait	by the time they got back
3. He went out again	just as he was ringing the bell
4. They must go home	
5. There was nothing left	as soon as you can
	after he had finished his dinner
6. He repaired our shoes for us	
	every time I meet her
7. I opened the door	since you went to live in London
8. I haven't heard from you	
	the moment he spoke
9. She asks after you	before they get too tired
10. I knew who it was	while we waited.

C   CONTRAST

Certain conjunctions of place and time are now used to introduce a contrasting clause, very like the clauses of concession (see section J below).

I wanted to go on, whereas my friend wanted to turn back.

Now there is nothing but desert, where there used to be a fertile plain.

[1] Also with inversion: *No sooner had he* . . . , etc.

At the same time that one side was disarming, the other was preparing for war.

While one half of the town was in ruins, the other half was almost intact.

D MANNER

Chief conjunctions: *as, how, in that*.

He did as I told him.

You may finish it how you like.

We were at a disadvantage in that they outnumbered us two to one. (RATHER FORMAL)

The list is as follows. (= as it follows)

The journey, as I recall it, was long and tedious.

Like.   Except in formal English, *like* is commonly used in place of the conjunction *as*. It is still frowned upon by purists, but has persisted in the popular language, as well as in the informal speech of those who would claim to know better, for centuries. The conjunction *as* serves many purposes, and is therefore a word of vague meaning; the earlier *like as* (= in the same way as) probably gave rise to the popular use of *like* by itself in clauses of that type. For this reason we feel that sentences like the following are quite good English, despite the die-hard theorists:

She swims like I do; badly.

You don't know Tom like I do.

We don't use that form in English, like they do in French.

They may beat us again, like they did in 1970.

The stones bounced harmlessly off him like water (does) off a duck's back.

Sink like a stone (does); drink like a fish; run like a hare, *etc.*

(These last may be considered as preposition phrases – in the manner of a stone, etc. – but it is logical to supply a verb, since it is the verb that is being compared.)

These sentences, though still not approved of in 'examination English', are certainly acceptable informal English. Notice that in each case there is an implied repetition of the verb: *X does something in the same way that Y does it.* Where this condition does not hold, we feel that *like* cannot be used, even colloquially. In the following examples we can only use *as*.

I'll do as you tell me.

It's only half a mile, as the crow flies.

Don't trouble to change; come just as you are.

You'd better write as I suggest.

(Compare this with: Write it like I do, in capital letters.)

Another kind of sentence we often meet is one of the type:

I want a new silk dress like my friend Mary has.

It looks like a clause introduced by *like*; but it can be shown to be a suppressed relative clause by adding *the one that* after *like*.

E   DEGREE (positive, also extent or amount)

Chief conjunctions: *as; as . . . as; not so (as) . . . as.*

The subordinate clause compares something to the main clause in equal degree. The recommended distinction '*as* good *as* he is' and '*not so* good *as* he is' is not in fact strictly kept, probably because of the similar origins of *so* and *as*. The form *not as good as he is* is quite acceptable English.

Life is as pleasant as you make it.

Nothing is so (as) bad as you think it is.

Nothing upset me so* much as that he had quite forgotten me.

(* Here *so* is stressed; *as* cannot take stress, and *so* is used when we want to emphasize the intensity of the degree by means of speech stress. It should not be confused with *so* introducing a RESULT clause, as in L below.)

This morning I'm as well as (I have) ever (been).

Mend it as best you can. (= *as well as possible*)

F   DEGREE (proportionate, or parallel)

Chief conjunctions: *according as (to), in proportion as, the . . . the.*

The quicker we walk, the sooner we shall get there.

We shall get there earlier or later according as we walk quicker or slower. Not used colloquially.

You'll get paid (more or less) according to how you work.

A person isn't always paid according as he works.

. . . according to how he works.

. . . in proportion as he works.

. . . in proportion to how he works.

The more (we are together), the merrier (we shall be).

G DEGREE (comparative)

Chief conjunction: *than*.

> She is much older than she looks.
> We arrived sooner than we thought.
> She was more intelligent than (she was) pretty.
> This morning I'm better than (I have) ever (been).

Because of the tendency mentioned in the notes to Exercises 6.3 and 6.4, one commonly hears:

> You're better than *me*; he's happier than *her*, etc.

As a predicate after a verb of the *be* type there is no real objection to using this disjunctive or separated pronoun form (like the French *lui*, *moi*), but students should note that it is still held to be a popular pattern not recommended for formal writing, and that it must NOT be used with TRANSITIVE verbs for fear of confusion:

> I like her better than (I like) him.
> I like her better than you (do).

H DEGREE (restriction)

Chief conjunctions: *as, so (as) long as, so (as) far as, in so far as, for all (anything)* [*that*], *(not) that*.

> You can stay here, so long as you are quiet.
> You can stay here, so (as) far as I'm concerned.
> You can stay here, for all I know (care).
> Has he stayed here before? – Not that I know of.
> Has he stayed here before? – Not so far as I know.

I CAUSE

Chief conjunctions: *because, since, as, when, seeing (that), for*.

> I can't go, because I have no ticket.
> Since we are early, let's have a drink first.
> As you have been here before, you'd better lead the way.
> We must finish now, for it's nearly bedtime. (See the note below.)
> You can't expect him to know the story when he hasn't read it.
> You can't expect him to know the story seeing (that) he hasn't read it.

For is really a co-ordinating conjunction, used to introduce a natural reason or obvious fact. It is included above because its meaning is approximately that of the subordinating conjunction *since*.   It is not very common in informal speech.

He is not allowed to smoke, for he is only a boy.

Since   also implies that the reason is obvious or natural. A *since*-clause usually precedes the main clause; there is more interest in the main clause for the speaker or hearer than in the reason introduced by *since*.

Since he is only a boy, he is not allowed to smoke.

As   also usually comes first in the sentence, and (like *since*) also throws the speaker's emphasis on to the main clause. The reason introduced by *as* is not necessarily obvious or natural.

As I'm very busy these days, I shan't be able to take my usual holiday.

Because   seldom comes first in a sentence. There is more interest in the reason introduced by *because* than in the main clause.

I can't come just now, because I'm busy writing a book.

A common meaning of a clause beginning *or else* is 'because otherwise'.

Come early, or else you won't find a seat.

= Come early, because you won't find a seat if you don't.

J   CONCESSION (and contrast)

Chief conjunctions: *although*, (*even*) *though*, (*even*) *if*, *as*, *whoever*, etc., *no matter who* (*when*, etc.).

(Al)though it is late, we'll stay a little longer.

Late though it is, we'll stay a little longer.

Bad as things are, we mustn't give up hope.

Even if (though) things *are* bad, we ...

However bad things are, we ...

No matter how bad things are, we ...

I shouldn't worry if he *has* forgotten you. (= *even though*)

I'll buy one whatever it costs (*may cost*).

K   PURPOSE

Chief conjunctions: *that*, *in order that*, *so* (*that*), *lest*, *for fear* (*that*), *in case*.

The words *may*, *might*, *shall*, *should* commonly occur with the verb after these conjunctions. *Might* and *should* must be used when the verb of the main clause is in a past tense. *That* can be omitted wherever it occurs between brackets in this section.

They rented the top floor that they might have a good view.
(But the simple *that*-clause is not much used to express purpose in modern English.)
They have arrived early so that (in order that) they may (shall) not miss the overture. (Literary style.)
They've come early so (that) they won't miss the overture. (Good spoken English style.)
They arrived early so that (in order that) they might (should) not miss the overture. (Literary style.)
They came early so (that) they wouldn't miss the overture. (Good spoken English style.)
Make a note of it so (that) you don't (shan't) forget.
Make a note of it lest you (may, might, should) forget. (Literary.)
Make a note of it in case you forget. (Good colloquial.)
We didn't move lest we should (might) wake him up. (Literary.)
We didn't move for fear (that) we should (might) wake him up. (Literary – *for fear* (*that*) is mainly used with a negative main clause.)
We didn't move in case we woke him up. (Good colloquial.)

L   RESULT

Chief conjunctions: *that, so* (*that*), *so* (*such*) ... *that; but that* (negative).

RESULT clauses are like an inversion of clauses of CAUSE. The *so that* introducing a clause of PURPOSE can always be replaced by *in order that*; we cannot do this with *so that* introducing a clause of RESULT. We can, however, reverse the clauses in such a sentence, changing the main clause into one of CAUSE (introduced by *as, since* or *because*).

She bought a book so (that) she might learn English. (PURPOSE)
She bought a book in order that she might learn English.
She bought a good book, so (that) she learnt English well. (RESULT)
She bought so good a book that she learnt English well. (Literary)

She bought such a good book that she learnt English well.

Notice that we sometimes find sentences that can be interpreted either way. In the spoken language the RESULT sentence would be heard with two phrases of FALLING INTONATION, the PURPOSE sentence with RISING INTONATION ON THE MAIN CLAUSE.

PURPOSE: I wrote clearly so (that) anyone could read it. (*in order*
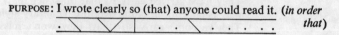
that)

RESULT: I wrote clearly, so (that) anyone could read it. (*because*
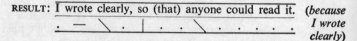
I wrote clearly)

Examples of clauses of RESULT:

Are you deaf that you didn't hear me?
= Did you fail to hear me because you are deaf?
It was quite windy, so (that) we had to button our coats up.
We were so hungry (that) we couldn't wait for knives and forks.
It's such a good story (that) I'll never forget it.
It's so good a story (that) I'll never forget it. (Literary)
I shall never be so tired but that (but what) I shall be able to write to you. (Literary style only)
I shall never be so tired that I shan't be able to write to you.
It never rains but it pours. (Old proverb)
= Once it starts to rain, it rains hard: troubles multiply.

* * *

58.3   ● Complete the following sentences of purpose or result:

1   He was so kind (that) . . .
2   Come a little nearer so that . . .
3   I'll give you some money in case . . .
4   He ran so quickly (that) . . .
5   They live such a long way away (that) . . .
6   We mustn't make a noise for fear . . .
7   He hurried back in order that . . .
8   He didn't shout lest . . .
9   She was so lazy (that) . . .
10   I'm so tired (that) . . .

11 (You'd) better buy one now in case . . .
12 I've ordered a deep-freeze so (that) . . .
13 It was such a dull party (that) . . .
14 He hid behind the door in order that . . .
15 I didn't come any earlier for fear . . .

58.4   Here are seven short sentences or clauses:

> *a* Just sit where you like.
> *b* No, keep it as long as you wish.
> *c* Just do as I tell you.
> *d* Well, it's not so bad as I thought.
> *e* The earlier, the better.
> *f* In case it gets broken.
> *g* Well, fasten them like I do. (See note in D above.)

● Use one of the above as a response to each of the remarks below. The teacher should make the remark, and the student choose one of the above seven phrases as a suitable response to it.

1 Which is my place?
2 I expect you found a lot of mistakes in my homework.
3 Why are you wrapping the vase in a cloth?
4 Let's see if we can start before breakfast, shall we?
5 You don't mind my borrowing this, I hope?
6 That's a dull grammar you're reading, isn't it?
7 My skis are slipping.
8 Why do you keep your pen in your inside pocket?
9 My entrance ticket hasn't (got) a number on it.
10 Would you like me to bring the book back next week?
11 My papers won't stay in the folder.
12 What are you putting the microscope away for?
13 I hope I don't do anything to displease the visitors.
14 I hear you've hurt your finger badly.
15 What about leaving this dull party before the end?

M CONDITION
(See Section 31.)

Infinitive phrases, often a shorter way of expressing a clause, can be practised in Section 38.

Index *Numbers refer to exercises and their notes.* In a few cases section numbers (marked §) are given.